AMERICAN APOCALYPSE

How to Stop the Destruction of Liberty

ISBN 978-1-61434-437-7

Printed in the United States of America.

Julio M. Lara c/o
SASO Cultural Foundation, LLC
P.O. Box 8327
Sebring, FL 33872

www.saso2016.com

Published 2011

Cover Design by
Cecil G. Rice

AMERICAN APOCALYPSE

How to Stop the Destruction of Liberty

Julio M. Lara

ACKNOWLEDGEMENTS

It has taken more than a decade to record the nightmarish events in my life under communist rule. Although my English and grammar may not be perfect, my story is true and accurate. I want to acknowledge my family, friends, fellow writers, and researchers for helping me to bring *American Apocalypse* to my readers.

Special thanks go to R.T. Byrum and Paul Levey for their invaluable contributions throughout this project; their great assistance, good judgment and wise counsel.

Very special thanks to my wife Melissa, and my children Julio Jr., Jorge, Aracely, Peter, Melissa Lynn and Jessica for their love, encouragement, support and forbearance.

I am grateful for the love my father and mother gave to me and the Christian family foundation and perseverance they impressed on me during their lifetime. Without their longsuffering commitment to me, I could never have overcome my struggles, which at times were even between life and death.

Last but never least; I thank America and her people for welcoming and embracing me as one of their own, and for allowing me to become a free and prosperous man. *God Bless America.*

TABLE OF CONTENTS

INTRODUCTION

Author, Julio (2nd from left front), as an 18-year-old Captain

My name is Julio M. Lara, born in 1942, the son of a Cuban cattle rancher. I spent the early years of my life on our ranch, where I developed a love and caring for animals that has lasted even until this day. Then at the age of eight, we moved to the city where my brothers, sister and I were able to go to school to learn about God, as my mother put it.

Mother died when I was thirteen and her death left me wondering if life had any meaning. My emptiness made me an easy target for the Communists, who saw in me a means of transportation with my Jeep, a gift from my father. I was a potential candidate who was connected to the young elites of the area. Soon I made it into the ranks of Fidel

Castro's communist agenda known as the "26th of July movement." In a very short period of time, they made out of this God-fearing, animal-loving, Christian child, an efficient killing machine.

We were made to think we were socialists, not communists—a name associated with the cruelty of Lenin, Marx and Stalin. As socialists, we nevertheless started reading a lot of communist material, and had to attend several indoctrination discussions every week. I recall spending hours in those classes, which, said our instructors, were preparing us to be future leaders.

A year later, only 15 years old and consumed by their doctrine, I joined Castro's army, where I continued to be indoctrinated and sent on secret missions. Most of my duties were to collect arms for our troops, in most cases, taking them from the owners at gunpoint. That also disarmed the people, making them helpless. *Gun control* is an early tactic of any communist takeover.

Assigned as a clandestine soldier, I spent a lot of my time around the camp, but much of my work was also driving my Jeep; so I was able to visit my house frequently. I was disguised as a civilian to protect my father and neighbors. During my visits, I talked with my Uncle Raul Lara, who tried to help me understand the truth about communism. I listened, and although he did a good job of warning me about the ideology, I didn't take it seriously.

After so many missions, we at last fell into a trap, where we had to fight so furiously that left my Jeep behind to save our lives. My Jeep had identified me; so from that day on, I had to stay in the mountains as a full-time soldier.

My indoctrination continued as a part of my duties. Because of my convictions and my knowledge of the area, I was finally selected to guide Che Guevara when he came through our area on his advance to Fomento, Caibarien, and then Santa Clara, the last city before the fall of Batista.

The killing, after the triumph of the revolution, was indescribably horrible. Even though I had been involved, I found it dishonorable and cruel. Still, my programmer had me believing that the country had to "clean out" the bourgeois (middle class and business owners). I was told they were the ones responsible for all the bad things that happened to my country.

Later, when the Castro regime turned on my own family, took our lands, our wealth, and arrested my father, I realized that my family and I were part of the bourgeois class. It was as if I had awakened from a horrible dream. One again, I had to fight to defend my homeland. I fled into the hills—a hunted fugitive.

Castro sent nearly 100,000 of his soldiers after less than 3,000 men in our insurrectionists' army. He removed the peasants from our area, destroyed our sources of food, and surrounded us with a large military force.

That year, we spent three months fighting vicious battles inside that circle and running every day for our lives. During a one month period I was able to eat only three meals. My companions and I stayed alive by drinking fetid green water from ponds and eating whatever we could find. Only 41 of us miraculously survived out of those 3,000 men. The rest were killed or imprisoned. For whatever reason, I was spared—perhaps to write this book of warning.

My family helped me to get diplomatic protection and I was able to escape to Venezuela, where I spent four turbulent years before coming to America. Shortly after arriving here, I formed my first corporation based on the communist mentality that the end result justifies the means.

I became an unscrupulous businessman. My wealth grew rapidly, and fifteen years later I was a millionaire with established businesses in the States and Venezuela. However, I was full of hate with an inexplicable inner struggle for something I couldn't explain. I ran around like a mad man with an uncontrollable ambition, believing that having wealth would solve all my problems. Sadly money never did, for I always wanted more, which drew me down to my own destruction.

My behavior landed me in jail for more than a year, a blessing, for that was the way God reached down and saved me. Today, I know His purpose behind the trials and temptations that I endured throughout my life. Without that struggle and suffering, I would not have had the experience and the knowledge that I gained and needed to be able help and guide others. That struggle for my freedom, took me to the place where I discovered God.

My time in prison provided a fountain of knowledge for me where I really had the chance to know our Savior. I read three and four books a week to learn what I could. In prison I started writing *God, Satan, and Me*, my autobiography. Then I began writing *American Apocalypse – How to Stop the Destruction of Liberty, a book* which compares socialistic changes taking place in America with those that I had experienced in Cuba and Venezuela leading up to communist takeovers.

Once my three youngest children began attending school, I started to see the transformation of American society, and to learn that the indoctrination the children were receiving in the American educational system was frighteningly similar to what I had received as a youth in Cuba. I saw the same socially corroding tactics taking place with my children only under different players and circumstances.

That's when I really began paying careful attention to everything that the communists were and are doing in the United States. I have uncovered countless examples of how our American society is being cleverly brainwashed by the same poisonous ideology that ravaged my life and my family as I was growing up.

The first decade of the twenty-first century has been agony for me. First, watching how communist infiltrators in our government are spreading their socialistic venom across the United States, and doing so with little resistance from a country I have learned to love more that my own.

We have been living through a decade of recession where I have witnessed nearly all of my savings being drained away. Once again, my wife and I wonder if we will have to seek refugee in another foreign land. If so, where would that be if America falls under the boot of communism?

My hope is that "American Apocalypse" will sound an awakening alarm to warn the American people about the very real threat of communism.

My soon-to-be-released autobiography will reveal the detailed step-by-step events of my life growing up as a native-born Cuban, and the nightmare of becoming a communist killing machine for Fidel Castro. It is a story about a lifestyle under tyranny that neither you nor your children or children's children will ever want to experience, but that has been my purpose for my writing it.

Julio M. Lara

FOREWORD

During an interview with fellow conservative radio personality, Laura Ingraham, TV talk show host, Bill O'Reilly, quoted a recent poll, which found that 62% of the American people have a *favorable* opinion of socialism. That fact left me shocked and dismayed, and if you are an American conservative who believes in our constitution and our capitalist system, you should be shocked as well.

How could it be possible that citizens of this country that I had assumed was the safe haven of anti-communism have such an astonishing and outrageous opinion? From that moment on, I knew that as a naturalized American I had a duty to reveal the truth about communism, and the enormous threat that this poisonous ideology represents.

American Apocalypse—How to Stop the Destruction of Liberty is the product of ten years of research, combined with my own experiences growing up in Cuba, and my years in Venezuela. Born and raised in Cuba during the Fidel Castro revolution, I knew firsthand the insidious nature of *socialism*—that less intimidating alias of *communism*. As a young soldier for Fidel, I was indoctrinated (brainwashed) as a teenager, and became part of the creeping destruction of my country's freedom: the cause of death and devastation to thousands of innocents. Taught that the means justifies the end, I was turned into a deadly killing machine.

My past is not completely hidden from those who knew me during and after the revolution. At best, I could be incarcerated and stripped of my new business and bank accounts once again. My wife and children would be left on their own. But I would not be alone, for many Americans who refused to listen and learn from my life's experiences, would be along side of me in concentration camps being established even now by FEMA.

America has become my home: a country that has treated me better than had my own native land. Loving the U.S. with such a passion and dedication, I simply could not turn my back and allow such a horrible misjudgment of the intent of socialism to continue.

I know that I needed to tell the American people the full documented truth about communism, the menace that this system represents, its future repercussions to our capitalist system, and, most importantly, how to combat it. The best way was to write a book: a record of the real experiences of one who had been active in communist activities, suffered under communist oppression and punishment, and then had awakened to the major threat that communism represents to the people of every class in America.

The most powerful destructive tool the communists have today is the "New World Order," a plan to subjugate nations around the entire world. The 1992's UNICED meeting in Rio de Janeiro, they developed the Sustainable Program of Action, or "Agenda 21." It called for the sustainable control of water, forests, markets, agriculture, and society. The eventual outcome would be the International Community, World Religion, World Bank, World President, World Alliance, World Principles, World Laws, and World Union.

It is true that those who ignore history are doomed to relive it. This book is the history of communism's tyranny, cruelty, greed, and murder. America must understand and heed the warnings ignored by other nations before the Erosion of Liberty leads to the total destruction of our God-given way of life.

CHAPTER 1

The History Of Communism

Let me begin by saying, this is book is not intended to entertain. What you are about to read compares the insidious spread of communism's poison within other nations with what is happening day by day in America. It is a book based on my living nightmare of seeing my Cuban homeland and its people destroyed and murdered. Worse than that, as a youngster I was indoctrinated into the very ideology that was responsible for all that horror, and became a part of Fidel Castro's weapon of massive destruction by joining his revolution.

The cruelty of communism with its lies, its greed, its immorality, and its power hungry leadership eventually drove me back into my Christian upbringing. Once again, I became a soldier, armed not with a rifle, but with words of warning. I plead with you; if you love America as it was intended to be, then learn from my experiences and from my research conducted over ten soul-searching years.

Throughout these pages, you will see numbered references such as "C1-6" that are hyperlinked to videos on the Internet if you are reading this as an Ebook. If you are reading a hardcopy then you will be directed to the Video References at the end of the book. There you will find the URLs that you may enter into your address bar.

Those videos expand the content of the book, and, in many cases, allow you to see and hear quotes directly from the people who made them. Other videos, taken from the Russian archives after the fall of the communist government, show scenes that are often hard to watch, but which will burn a warning into the most jaded mind. America needs desperately to understand that Communism is not just another form of government; it is an ideology based on a dictatorship ruling over a nation by tyrants who conquer through indoctrination rather than with bullets.

As Editor Stéphane Courtois put it in the introduction of *The Black Book of Communism,* "...Communist regimes...turned mass crime into a full-blown system of government."

What is Communism?

Marxist communists have always attempted to create and maintain a false and more acceptable face to the world by making everybody believe that they are *only socialists*, rather than *communists*. They are lying...there is no difference between the two.

Socialism, communism, feudalism, and fascism all spring from the same basic precepts: take power over the masses through hunger, control of the economy, education, transportation, communication, military, and the courts. All those ideologies have been interchangeable since their inception: all using the same Marxist doctrines. Even if each tries to look like something other than communism, their modus operandi and actions result in the same repression.

The Communist Manifesto

Karl Marx (1818–1883), was a German philosopher and communist revolutionary, whose thinking played a dramatic role in developing of communism and socialism.

Marx thoroughly outlined his approach in the very first line of his co-authoring with Friedrich Engels (1820–1895), *The Communist Manifesto*, published in 1848: "The history of all hitherto existing society is the history of class struggles," according to his demented ideas. He theorized that capitalism, like previous socioeconomic systems, would inevitably produce internal tensions, which would eventually lead to its demise. He said that just as capitalism replaced feudalism in society, socialism would replace capitalism, and lead to a stateless, classless society called *communism*.

Friedrich Engels was a German social scientist, author, philosopher, and co-father of communist theory, along with Karl Marx. In addition to his contributions to *The Communist Manifesto,*

Engels also edited and published the second and third volumes of Marx's *Das Kapital* after Marx's death.

The work is an extensive discussion about political economies written by Karl Marx with his radical ideas, with portions edited by Friedrich Engels. A critical analysis and criticism of capitalism, its first volume was published in 1867.

While the communists often try to use sophisticated phases to confuse people, only those who have lived under the iron boot can expose the truth about communism. It is vital to understand the ways in which they use underhanded tactics and criminal activities to accomplish their goals. I am one who is able to call upon my own experiences and beliefs to show precisely what is really taking place.

Socialism was born when there was a valid need for true social reform. It came about during the period of monarchies and inquisitions. A very small percentage of the population was wealthy and enjoyed all the benefits of an elite status. Meanwhile, the working class toiled up to 15 hours out of each day. The workers were isolated, abandoned, suffering from a variety of diseases, extremely hungry, and afflicted with all the slings and arrows of their low social status.

Along came the communist doctrine with a benevolent facade: a fallacy maintained to this day. Their reign of cruelty and totalitarianism is a matter of record in every country in which they have been in power. Tragically, men of goodwill have bought into communism's false promises of equality and fairness, and have believed the lies that communists actually care about society. The evidence of sheep-like belief within the United States is proven by the poll revealing that 62% of the population has a *favorable* opinion about socialism.

I believe that this is mainly because Americans have forgotten to teach their younger generations what being an American really means, and about the enormous threat that communism represents. As a result, the new generation knows nothing about how socialism, a.k.a. communism, works in governing the conquered. Much of this hiding of the truth has been accomplished because of the massive power socialists have obtained via the liberal news media.

A simple comparison of Christianity and communism shows that Christianity has been a beacon for goodwill and family structured society throughout the world. Conversely, communism has brought forth massive atrocities wherever it has been a dominant doctrine. Instead of bringing relief from oppression of the underclass majorities, as it promised, communism has been shown to be a dismal failure.

Even Fidel Castro, after 51 years in power, recently declared that his communist revolution was a failure for Cuba. But that admission came only after his close brush with death from illness, and only after the destruction and death sown by him and his followers across Cuba, too late to undo the devastation in my birth country.

Examining history, we discover that communism was born from pure materialism, an older and adverse ideology of Greek philosopher Democritus, who proclaimed, "…nothing comes out of conflicts and problems." Atheists of the first millennium after Christ readily accepted this doctrine as the only reasonable philosophy to combat religion.

Another ancient ideology known as *Dialecticism* proclaims that conflict is the basis of all natural laws. Also known as *Dialectic materialism*, this doctrine proclaims that human beings are nothing more than an animal species that evolved through conflicts and problems.

The most outrageous aspect of these ideologies is that they deny the Creation. In my opinion, that false doctrine, which teaches that the human being is nothing more than an evolved species of animal, is one of the basic tenets of the misleading and dangerous communistic ideology. After Karl Marx and Friedrich Engels published their *Communist Manifesto*, their words became the engine and propeller of Marxism until the current day.

Even with its broad acceptance in many quarters, the Manifesto created a substantial amount of controversy among some educated communists. As a result, they have spent decades discussing the various aspects of the Marxist theories.

Most notably, the majority of these theorists have refused to accept the totalitarian ideas and procedures exposed by Marx. Author, economist and philosopher, Friedrich Hayek (1899–1992), wrote of those discussions. He detailed the danger of eliminating the free market system and the centralization of all production, distribution, and transportation. Without free markets, the economy would simply collapse.

Thinking Americans will note how many of Hayek's warnings apply to changes being made even now within our own country by those in power in Washington today.

Unfortunately, Hayek and his believers weren't able to change enough people's minds to keep these theories from coming to fruition. As a result, Marxism-Leninism revolutionized the blue-collar proletariat, and in 1917, the Russian Bolshevik revolution took place with the result that communism was established for the first time on a large scale.

The Darwin Influence

In 1859, Charles Robert Darwin (1809–1882) published *The Origin of Species* in which he theorized that all living things evolve through a series of consequences brought about by conflict. It's the same thinking that the materialist philosophers used in *Dialecticism*. In short, Darwin accepted the Dialectic materialism premise.

Due to the lack of scientific foundations, all the prominent scientific minds of that era refused to accept Darwin's theories. But Darwin's thoughts were exactly what Marx and Engels were waiting for to consolidate their atheist system of rule. The relationship between Marxism and Darwinism grew into a bond of concrete strength. Marxists immediately adopted Darwin's *Theory of Evolution* as their own scientific foundation.

As a combined force, Darwinism and Marxism grew together. Communist posters showing the books of Marx and Darwin together seemed to be displayed everywhere.

The 1871 Paris Commune was the first true communist revolution to take power, even though it was only active for a few weeks. It clearly demonstrated the destructive and criminal behavior patterns that were to follow in every communist revolution that has taken power since that time.

History and the sad statistics show that more than 18,000 people died and the Paris communists caused millions of dollars of destruction. Unfortunately, most of the destruction was done to churches since the leadership was made up of atheists and other barbarians who were the forerunners of those who continue to lead communism to this day.

Since those dark days in Paris, historians have been collecting solid information on how Marxist communism really works. It has been a sad history. [C1-2]

The comparison between Communism and Christianity shows that human destruction, genocide, and hunger have been the prevalent conditions in every country where communism has been dominant, while Christianity has brought goodness, strong family structure, love, and justice wherever it has flourished. In strong Christian families within our society today, we rarely see someone lost in the depravity of immorality or in substance abuse.

My own life qualifies me to take readers through the history to write and speak of well-documented facts about how truly evil communism is, has been, and always will be. I can reveal in first person how destructive communism has been to society, not just with my words but also with inescapable facts taken from reports by highly reputable organizations.

Learn what communists have promised, and how they adapted and changed from one decade to the next with positive proof of their lies and outright cruelty to fellow human beings. Absolute domination is the only goal that matters to these unscrupulous leaders

This book, along with those videos and other sources, are proof of the iron-fisted tactics and uncontrolled brutality used in every country where communists have been in power. They brainwash people to do whatever their leaders demand. They are tyrants so destructive and power hungry that it is nearly impossible for God-fearing Americans to comprehend how communism could exist and flourish in today's world.

The Iron Fist of Communism

The first thing the Bolshevik Revolution did in the Soviet Union was to expel, execute, or imprison anyone who disagreed with their ideology. They exterminated the bourgeois society. It wasn't just an attempt to quiet opposing voices; it was to totally silence any dissenting elements. That is how communism works its devastation in every country it conquers.

Communism is one of the greatest evils in governance that mankind has ever known. It has been responsible for more than 94 million deaths – more than every war in history *combined.* That statistic by itself is inconceivable, but there's more.

- Communism has created millions upon millions of destitute refugees and has conquered and put into slavery over 2 billion people just since World War II.
- Communist regimes always follow a predictable, similar pattern. First, they must orchestrate a revolution. They dissolve private property, nationalize the media (so it only has the communist voice and point of view), and begin a brutal and merciless purge of those in politics and the bourgeois class. They make slaves of them, pure and simple.

To conduct its class warfare and maintain control of the revolting people, the leaders will militarize on a grand scale, establish a large secret police, and create horrific forced-labor camps.

Then, as predicted, the economy collapses, failed farm policies cause widespread starvation, refugees flee, and then the government begins to export communist revolution to other countries. How far the communists are willing to push their philosophy will be directly related to the severity and sequence of events, and the inevitable and planned suffering of their people.

This precise pattern has come to pass in Soviet Union, Laos, China, North Korea, Iraq, Iran, Vietnam, Cambodia, Hungary, Romania, Yugoslavia, Angola, Nicaragua, several African countries, Cuba, and is now happening in Venezuela.

The two main sources for the above statistics are found in *The Twentieth Century Atlas*; *The Black Book of Communism* by Rudolph J. Rummel, Professor Emeritus of Political Science at the University of Hawaii and one of the world's foremost experts on conflicts and communism, and *The Bloody History of Communism* by sociologist Fatih Kocaman, a treasure chest of collected data in an outstanding film.

Lenin's Bloody Rule

Let history expose the Vladimir Lenin (1870–1924) regime that held sway in the Soviet Union from 1917 to 1922. The *Twentieth Century Atlas* records that under the dictatorship of Comrade Lenin, 9 million men, women and children died. Only the most or cold-hearted programmed person could read that fact without feeling a sense of revulsion and horror. Kocaman's film about the bloody history of communism contains much more collaborating evidence. Links to that and other hard-to-watch videos are listed in the Internet Video Reference pages in the appendix section. [C-1, C1-2, C1-3, C1-4]

In October of 1917, Lenin's armed militants attacked the Winter Palace in Petrograd, then the center of the government. They simply killed any of the guards who resisted and carried out one of the easiest coups in recorded history. Soviet propaganda films made years later would portray the coup as a huge popular uprising started by Lenin's fiery speeches. The truth was that there were less than 100 people who attacked the Winter Palace and only five people actually died.

Among other atrocities, Tsar Nicholas II, his wife, his son, his four daughters, the family's medical doctor, the Tsar's valet, the Empress' lady-in-waiting, and the family's cook were all executed in the same room by the Bolsheviks in July 1918 at the order of Lenin.

Cities, which refused to support the Bolshevik regime, were summarily ruined. In telegrams to his militant leaders, Lenin ordered all those who opposed the communist regime should be shot. The Bolsheviks arrested tens of thousands of people for the crime of "opposing the regime." Most of them were tortured before being executed en masse.

The famous Russian writer, Maxim Gorky (1886–1936), described this example of Bolshevik savagery:

> "In Tambov province Communists were nailed with railway spikes by their left hand and left foot to trees a meter above the soil, and they watched the torments of these deliberately oddly-crucified people. They would open a prisoner's belly, take out the small intestine and nailing it to a tree or telegraph pole, they drove the man around the tree with blows, watching the intestine unwind through the wound. Stripping a captured officer naked, they tore strips of skin from his shoulders in the form of shoulder straps…"

A terrible fear gripped Russia, but the communist savagery had only just begun. A famine hit the country as a direct result of Lenin's actions and directions. With the enthusiastic assistance Felix Dzerzhinsky (1877–1926), a man who headed up the Cheka, and was well known for his ruthlessness. Lenin had Cheka officers descend on villages all over Russia and to steal peasants' crops and livestock at gunpoint. Then a quota was given to every peasant to supply the Bolsheviks. The result was that the peasants had to give up whatever they possessed. Those who protested were silenced by the most savage means. On February 14, 1922 one inspector, who visited the Omsk region, wrote:

> "Abuses of position by the requisitioning detachments, frankly speaking, have now reached unbelievable levels. Systematically, the peasants who are arrested are all locked up in big unheated barns; they are then whipped and threatened with execution. Those who have not filled the whole of their quota are bound and forced to run naked all along the main street of the village and then locked up in another unheated hangar…"

Lenin was enraged when he realized that the quotas set for the villages would not be met. In 1920, he inflicted a fearful punishment on some regions that had resisted the requisitions. Not only would the peasants' crops be seized, but also all the seeds they possessed.

Confiscating the seeds meant that the peasants would be unable to produce any new crops. In short, they would have nothing to eat.

In 1921 and 1922, some 29 million people in Russia battled with starvation and 5 million agonizingly starved to death. Reportedly, Lenin watched what was happening with enormous pleasure. In his view, the famine was most useful: he calculated that it would help to destroy people's belief in God and religion and force them to bow down to communism.

According to *the Black Book of Communism*, his hard-hearted response sent shock waves around the world. One of Lenin's friends later recalled his appalling thoughts on the starvation of the Russians: "Vladimir Ilyich Ulyanov had the courage to come out and say openly that famine would have numerous positive results. 'Famine,' he explained, 'would bring about the next stage more rapidly, and usher in socialism, the stage that necessarily followed capitalism. Famine would also destroy faith not only in the tsar, but in God, too.' "

Lenin wrote to the members of the Politburo on March 19, 1922: "The present moment favors us... With the help of all those starving people who are starting to eat each other, who are dying by the millions, and whose bodies litter the roadside all over the country, it is now and only now that we can—and therefore must—confiscate all church property with all the ruthless energy we can still muster. ...Our only hope is the despair engendered in the masses by the famine, which will cause them to look at us in a favorable light or, at the very least, with indifference."

These communications in the Soviet archives have revealed that Lenin deliberately brought about that dreadful famine which cost five million lives. That is the same conclusion arrived at by the historian Richard Pipes, who spent years researching the archives, for his book, "*The Unknown Lenin.*" He wrote, "For humankind at large, Lenin had nothing but scorn: ... individual human beings held for Lenin almost no interest and ... he treated the working class much as a metalworker treated iron ore."

The reason why Lenin and the other Bolsheviks were so utterly ruthless was the dialectical materialist philosophy they so believed in. This philosophy regarded human beings as a species of animal and maintained that violence and conflict were necessary for the development of mankind.

Not only did Lenin regard human beings as animals, he also employed animal methods to train them. On October 1919, he paid a personal visit to the Russian scientist Ivan Pavlov (1849–1936), famous for his conditioned reflex experiments on animals. Lenin wanted to impose these conditioned reflex methods on the whole of Russian society.

Fatih Kocaman, a collector of videos on communism, was astounded by Lenin's ideas. "The truth is that human beings are not a species of animal, but are honorable beings created by God, in possession of a soul. The reason for their existence on earth is not, as communists and Darwinists would assert, conflict, war, and bloodshed, but for them to display a morality that is pleasing to God. Only when man has understood this concept, in other words only when he lives by the true religion, will he find peace and happiness."

The end of Lenin, who denied that fact, is a terrible warning to any despot who desires to follow his lead. From 1922 on, an increasingly serious illness slowly began to paralyze him. He spent most of 1923 in a wheelchair, suffering from terrible headaches. In March 1923, he had a stroke, and was left unable to speak normally.

In the final months of his life, those who saw Lenin were terrified at his appearance: His face had taken on a very peculiar expression, and he was half mad. Lenin died on January 21, 1924.

My Indoctrination Into Communism

All these historical facts considered so far have an important moral for mankind. False ideas lead to disaster for people and societies. Communism is one such false idea, which has inflicted dreadful suffering on billions of people around the world.

I write as one of those who suffered the injustice and cruelty of communism. I was born in Cuba, and, by the age of 14, was indoctrinated (read as brainwashed) with Fidel Castro's communist agenda. Back then it was known as the "26th of July Movement." We were never to admit being communists, and indeed thought we were only socialists.

Luckily, my uncle Raul Lara, a loyal communist in the 1940's, saw what was happening to me. He had had earlier opportunities to visit several communist countries, which for him was a great eye opener. The result was a complete turnaround in his thinking.

When I told him that I was starting to like socialism, and began sharing with him a recollection of my experiences, he tried to make me aware of the reality about communism. Although I listened to his words, they did not, at the time, fully sink into my head.

Instead, I listened attentively as my communist instructors taught me how to destroy an imperialist's society.

- They declared that the family really does not exist; that the family is overburdening our purpose in life.
- They said that we have to corrupt the masses without being corrupted ourselves, and that socialism cannot be established with a family structure, with moral principles, or with God.
- They said that God is a myth, which capitalists have used for millennium to pacify the masses.
- They said 50 percent of those people seek guidance and it had to be us, the socialists, who would be their guide.
- They taught that we have to be their divine being—the ones that the masses must follow.
- We were to corrupt the young generation until 50 percent of them took their socialist guidance from us. Once youth were corrupted, their parents would no longer be their guides.
- As future Communist leaders we were not trained to serve the masses, but rather to govern and control them.
- We were made to understand that the bourgeois were the oppressors, exploiters and dictators, which used God to subjugate the masses.
- Our task to "liberate" the proletariat could not happen as long as the bourgeois class remained. Their elimination had to take place.

That was the reason given for eliminating God, the churches, and the bourgeois class. We were told that all of those were an impediment to our cause. Instead, we had to love our leaders, because they were *our* guides, *our* future, and *our* protectors. They said our comrades were our real family, that they would never betray us and we should never betray our comrades.

These are but small examples of the deluge of propaganda poured into our heads. Yes, I remembered my uncle's teachings on the reality of communism, but for the next few years, his words were not a priority. I still followed the communist theology.

At age 15, I joined Castro's army in the Cuban mountains where I continued to receive further indoctrination along with military training, clandestine missions, and war duties.

But before I was totally brainwashed, and even after the triumph of the revolution, I saw so much cruelty, lack of justice, physical and mental abuse, and the deaths of thousands of Cubans killed by firing squads, many for no reason at all.

From Soldier to Fugitive

Then Fidel Castro's men confiscated all of my father's properties. He had been a hard working Christian man who never had a problem with the law. His only crime was to have wealth. His only dream was to reach old age without being broke. He never reached his goal; twenty-eight years later he died without a penny.

From that time on, I started to fight *against* communism. A month later, I found myself hidden up in the mountains fighting *against* Fidel Castro and his cronies. It was the worst year of my life, as described in the following account taken from my soon to be released autobiography, *God, Satan and Me.*

> "The next day, we fell into an ambush, shots coming from all directions. The situation was very serious; we were completely surrounded with few options and little time to make decisions. I ordered the digging of trenches placed where we could get protection from the shooting. I assigned

three men to each pit, but with no tools for digging, and with the half stony-half sandy soil, we were only partly successful.

"The difficulty of digging between fighting for our lives over the next six hours was horrible and unforgettable. The shooting, the noise of explosions, the hiss of incoming shells landing around and among us, the lack of supplies, no reinforcements, and not much ammunition, made those long hours a terrible nightmare.

"So terrible, in fact, that my future, or lack of one, was replayed over and over in my mind. Every minute the situation got worse, and for the first time in that war, I felt the dread of an intolerable defeat, but surrender was not an option; I resisted accepting reality by deceiving myself with illusions of escape.

"Then a shot killed one of my men. He was a young boy, no more than nineteen years old, very willing, brave, agile and having great courage. Because of these qualities I had him by my side. A bullet pierced his head as he was attempting to observe what was happening outside of the trench.

"One of my men and I moved his body to one side and continued fighting I had to ignore death inside my trench as if nothing had happened. With our many other fallen comrades, he was but one more. Besides, we were convinced that death would be the only way out for us all, as it was almost impossible to keep up the hope of victory. At other times in the past we had been in close contact with death, but this time death felt closer than ever before.

"Throughout that terrifying day, the falling of mortars and bazooka shells didn't stop: they fell everywhere, even into our trench. That afternoon, a black cloud covered the sun, and heavy rain poured down with thunderclaps so intense that it seemed the sky shuddered as if announcing the last day of our lives.

"Finally, around five p.m., the rain had stopped as a shell fell into one of the pits adjacent to mine, killing two men and

> wounding another. Pieces of human flesh sprayed into the air by the explosion fell on top of us. How can a human mind describe such a sickening experience? Death flying through the air in thousands of pieces is beyond horror."

That war and my four years of communist programming left me mentally damaged as a human being for another 24 years. I was a brainwashed mad man without scruples or principles until I rejoined Christianity in the 1980's.

Indoctrination creeps up on victims and transforms them in a way that I only became aware of after becoming a born again Christian. Until then I was doing business under the communist mentality that the end justifies the means.

Working under that programmed state of mind, I eventually wound up in jail. It was a blessing, for that was when God reached down and saved me. Today, I know His purpose behind all of the trials and calamities that I suffered throughout my life. Without those struggles, those trials, those sufferings, I would not have the knowledge and experience that makes it not only possible, but also necessary to warn and guide others in these fading days of America's glory.

Knowing communism as I do up close and personal has shown me how that evil doctrine is responsible for millions of the world's atrocities. Not only does it change people's minds and behavior, but that doctrine combined with Darwinism, as it was with Hitler, Lenin, Stalin and Mao, creates a new life form: making monsters of those who are robbed of morals and compassion.

That terrible year, Castro sent almost 100,000 of his soldiers after us where we had fled into the hills. He removed the peasants from our area, destroyed the sources of food, and encircled us with a large military force. Inside that circle, we spent three months fighting vicious battles and running every day. Out of the almost 3,000 men in our insurrectionist army, only 41 miraculously survived. All the rest were killed or imprisoned.

While fighting against Castro in the hills, during the entire month of February 1961, I only ate three times, and one of those meals was raw goat. I was fortunate, with my family's help and diplomatic protection; I was able to escape from Cuba.

Déjà vu All Over Again

Living in the United States, 30 years later, my 12-year-old daughter came home one day to tell me that her teacher told her that homosexuality is a way of life and not a sickness. Two years later, the same people told me that my daughter, now only 14, was old enough to go out of the house alone, wherever she wanted to go. They also informed me that if I punished or hit her, I would be arrested and charged.

I know exactly where those ideas come from. Marxism ideology is designed to corrupt family structure and values. I went through my childhood under that same socially corroding tactic only with different players.

It is also the same teaching that I received from "The Second International," the alias that communism was hid behind in those days to separate us from the stigma of evil that the ideology had earned. In Cuba, at first, we wanted the Cuban people to accept homosexuality, but after the revolution took power the homosexuals were incarcerated, persecuted, and put in concentration camps. This is no different from what is happening here: different names, but the same dark evil.

Our leaders taught us that we were going into a socialist future, a classless society where we would be free of struggles, suffering, and exploitation of man over man. As newly indoctrinated members, it was our duty to corrupt and disorient the young generation until they looked to us for direction and guidance, rather than to their bourgeois parents and priests. Then we had a clean slate to teach them socialism.

After becoming an American citizen, I began paying special attention to everything the communists are doing in the United States. One glaring example is the Association of Community Organizations for Reform Now (ACORN). ACORN worked through the judicial, legislative and financial institutions to introduce socialism to all parts of American culture. Yes, believe me, they are here and are very actively at work. I read articles and watch the news, and observe how this American society is being brainwashed by this poisonous ideology.

What is happening here is nothing different from the same programming received in my teenage years. I see it being repeated again and again on almost every social, environmental, educational, political, and moral level of American society.

The communists want all Americans to believe that the problem is between the right wing and left wing; it is not. The problem is with communistic thinking, influence, and action.

When our founders organized the United States, we had both left and right wing thinking in our society. That caused few problems, and, in fact, helped to maintain balance. Then the communists began stealthily conditioning many of our people, making them believe that socialist ways were the true balance. I believe extremes on either side cause problems, not stability.

When I had joined Castro's communist agenda, I was seeking a balance for my country: wanting better social laws where everyone could equally share in the richness of life. I still want a better standard of living for everybody, but I want to avoid having what Lenin did to Russia to happen in America. There is a huge difference between offering equal opportunities to succeed and the communist version of taking from those who work to give to those who do not.

Understand this, Communism never was, is not, and never will be about balance; it is about murder, totalitarianism, and power. It is clear what communists are planning for the world. It is equally clear that we must stop them.

CHAPTER 2

Hitler Was Also a Communist

Now, let's take a look at one of the most despised leaders of the twentieth century, Adolf Hitler (1889-1945). While he has been categorized as a fascist by the Stalin propaganda machine and others, Hitler's atrocities cannot be separated from their communist underpinnings. That's what has been tried purely because of the bad reputation that the Paris Commune left across Europe about communism. The results that Hitler produced for the Germans and other subjugated people were genuine communism.

Actually, Hitler was born in Austria, not Germany, and did not become a German citizen until 1932. As a youngster, he was thrown out of school for his disruptive behavior. Supported by his deceased father's orphan pension, he assumed a bohemian lifestyle and as a teenager, moved to Vienna to continue his socialist studies, where he was inspired by the mayor of the city, Karl Lueger (1844–1910), a virulent hater of anything Jewish.

Following his father's death in 1903, Hitler began reading texts on communism and anti-Semitism. In 1913, the 24-year-old socialist anti-Semite moved to Germany and enlisted in the infantry, where he served in Belgium and France as a regimental runner. After the end of World War I, he blamed the Jews for Germany's defeat.

Returning to Germany, he joined the National Socialist German Workers' Party. His oratorical skills soon took him to higher positions within the socialist party and by 1921 he became the party leader at the age of 32.

Hitler organized a failed coup against the government and was sentenced to five years in Landsberg Prison. During his trial, he was allowed almost unlimited time to speak, and his popularity soared as he voiced nationalistic sentiments and became a nationally known personality. He continued his socialist studies and his anti-Semitism in jail. The young Adolf was already revealing his megalomaniac tendencies.

The confinement converted him to the perfect anti-Semite and socialist. His environment was his inspiration for working on his book, *Mein Kampf* (My Struggle), an assortment of extreme racial, political, and socialist reflections that captured the imagination of a generation.

In his book, he portrays the Jews as evil, unscrupulous people who are capable of destroying the world. He says they are hungry for power and capable of using communism to accomplish their ambition of domination. Of course, that was exactly what he himself was doing.

Adolf proclaimed that the salvation of humanity rested on the shoulders of Germany. Regrettably, many people believed him. Helped by the World Communist Media Pressure, he was released from prison, like many other world leaders: Fidel Castro, Stalin, Mandela and Hugo Chavez.

His book was his first attempt at publicly trying to separate himself from communism because of the Paris Commune's legacy. His doctrine of good against evil, us against the Jews, and his party slogan *Rotfront und Reaktion* (Reds and Reactionaries) made him a leader, using all the standard communist tactics. Hiding his real colors, using the money and support of the capitalists, and helped by his oratorical skills, in January of 1933 he became Germany's Chancellor.

Hitler's plan was to establish a majority of the elected Nazis in the Reichstag who would then become a rubber stamp for him, passing whatever laws he desired while making it all appear perfectly legal. Hermann Göring (1893–1946), who was Hitler's new Minister of the Interior for Prussia, took control of the police. Göring immediately replaced hundreds of police officials who were loyal to the republic with Nazis officials loyal to Hitler.

He also ordered the police not to interfere with the Sturm Abteilung (*Storm Section*) also known as the SA. The SA's storm troopers or brown shirts were instructed to disrupt the meetings of political opponents and to protect Hitler from revenge attacks. The police were also told to ignore the actions of the Schutzstaffel (*Protection Squadron*), usually abbreviated SS, a major paramilitary organization. Under Heinrich Himmler's (1900–1945) command, the SS was responsible for many of the crimes against humanity during the period of 1939-1945.

Göring also ordered police to show no mercy for everyone who opposed the government. This meant that anyone who was harassed, beaten, or even murdered by the Nazis was on their own having no one to turn to for assistance. This helped to finalize the extermination of the German bourgeois class.

In yet another tyrannical move, Göring set up an auxiliary police force of 50,000 rowdy men, composed mostly of members of the SA and SS. The vulgar, brawling, murderous Nazi storm troopers now had police powers.

Then Göring falsely claimed he had discovered plans for a Communist uprising. When the Reichstag was torched (undoubtedly at Göring's instructions), he blamed the destruction on the communists. Meanwhile Hitler left the fire scene and went straight to the newspaper offices to oversee and direct its coverage of the fire. He stayed up all night with Joseph Goebbels (1897–1945), the Reich Minister of Propaganda, putting together a paper replete with many stories of a communist plot to violently seize power in Germany.

Hitler continued to use his anticommunist histrionics, accusing all his opponents of being communists and then began to fill up the concentration camps with victims. Then, with a carefully executed plan of economic destabilization, he took over the country.[C1-5, C1-6]

The majority of the Nazi party were communists, like Gregor Strasser (1892–1934) and Hermann Goebbels: notorious criminals who used their evil doctrines to destroy the country's economy and to subjugate the lower classes through poor conditions and military oppression.

Two Dictatorships

A major English newspaper published an article entitled "*Two Dictatorships*" that said there were significant similarities between Russian Bolshevism and German National Socialism. The author stated that the two ideologies which are today opposed to one another stand for regimes which "in essential structure are similar and in many of their laws—their buttresses—are identical. The similarity is moreover increasing."

The article went on to say, "In both countries are the same censorships on art, literature, and of course, the press, the same war on the intelligentsia, the attack on religion, and the massed display of arms, whether in the Red Square or Tempelhof Field." Surprisingly the author was none other than Joseph Goebbels. He continued, "The strange and terrible thing is that two nations, once so widely different, should have been schooled and driven into patterns so drably similar."

Another Goebbels quote says, "Bolsheviks carry on a campaign, directed by the Jews, with the international underworld, against culture as such. Bolshevism is not merely anti-bourgeois; it is against human civilization itself."

Stalin's communist propaganda machine used its power and the media to fool the world into believing Hitler was not a communist; because his reported atrocities would have been damaging to the communist party's image. Years later however, when the Soviet Union opened its archives, it was easy to see that the Soviet atrocities were far worse than Hitler's.

Hitler once again demonstrated that communists can and will disguise themselves as whatever is necessary to accomplish their goals. Everything that happened in Germany after Hitler's takeover was identical to what happens under other communist regimes. His hatred toward the Jewish people and his bitter rivalry with Lenin and Stalin for world leadership forced him to create a form of communism known as Nazism. He had the idea that he would take Nazism to another high, without changing anything of the doctrine and procedures of communism except the name.

We can readily see from Hitler's own words how his beliefs were in line with standard communist ideologies:

> "Those who want to live, let them fight, and those who do not want to fight in this world of eternal struggle, do not deserve to live.
>
> "Struggle is the father of all things. It is not by the principles of humanity that man lives or is able to preserve himself above the animal world, but solely by means of the most brutal struggle. If you do not fight, life will never be won."

Those two statements are right in line with Darwinism as well. Hitler had more to say.

> "In actual fact, the pacifistic-humane idea is perfectly all right, perhaps, when the highest type of man has previously conquered and subjected the world to an extent that makes him the sole ruler of this earth…Therefore, first struggle and then perhaps pacifism.
>
> "The [Nazi party] should not become a constable of public opinion, but must dominate it. It must not become a servant of the masses, but their master.
>
> "It must be thoroughly understood that the lost land will never be won back by solemn appeals to God, or by hopes in any League of Nations, but only by the force of arms."

Those quotations from Hitler are plain and simple, old communism at its best…or worst. Both Hitler's record and quotes clearly provide a solid foundation to include Nazism among the world's communist atrocities.

Looking back at the Holocaust and devastating statistics for the number of people who died at the hands of Adolph Hitler, it is clear there are wide differences in what some people are telling us.

In his book, *The Final Solution*, published in 1953, Gerald Reitlinger (1900–1978), a scholar of the Holocaust, says between 4,194,200 and 4,851,200 died in Europe at the hands of the Nazis.

Renowned history author, Daniel Chirot said the number should be more like 5,100,000: 3,000,000 died in death camps, 1,300,000 were massacred, and 800,000 died from disease and/or malnutrition in the ghettos of Europe.

How sad that millions of lives were reduced to numbers. How tragic that between the highest and lowest estimates, human lives were considered production quotas for the death squads that tortured, shot, hung, gassed and starved men, women and children. Could it happen here? Ask the victims in Russia, China, Vietnam, Korea, and, sadly, in my native Cuba.

We can compare estimates to estimates—imprecise or "ballpark" statistics with other imprecise or "guesstimate" statistics—to get a reasonable feel for the *magnitude* of the numbers. It is thought that the Nazis were responsible for perhaps 6 million deaths. Hitler's barbarianism, serving as proof to those who believe that these atrocities can't be real shows the inhuman capacities of a leader indoctrinated with Marxism and Darwinism. General Dwight D. Eisenhower ordered the photographing of the familiar gruesome and historic scenes of death camp atrocities when the Nazis surrendered. C1-6

Joseph Stalin, Master of Murder

After the death of Vladimir Lenin in 1924, Soviet leader Josef V. Stalin (1878–1953) rose to become the leader of the Soviet Union, where he ruled as a dictator from 1924 to 1953. His death toll statistics show that Hitler was a "small-fry" by comparison. Stalin's regime was responsible for the death or imprisonment of 21,000,000 people. This is truly a staggering number – more than *three* times as large as the Holocaust. Since the press was so completely subjugated in the Soviet Union, these atrocities were never reported until 1991 when the Soviet Union opened their archives.[C1-7, C1-8]

However, we do know as fact that ordinary citizens were executed or imprisoned in labor camps that were actually *death* camps. Political orientation was the key in these mass atrocities. In many respects, the Purge Years in Soviet history can easily be considered the worst genocide of the twentieth century.

The source of most of the following comes from *The Bloody History of Communism* videos produced by Fatih Kocaman, who utilized archival films from Russia after the dismantling of the communist regime.

Stalin ruled the Soviet Union through a comprehensive system of fear, intimidation, and torture for nearly 30 years. During that time, he was responsible for some 40 million deaths, of which over 21 million are fully documented as communist atrocities. The rest, even though they were related to Stalin, are reported as war deaths.

Stalin spent his first years in power consolidating his position and working on eliminating Leon Trotsky, whom he rightly perceived as his major rival.

In 1929, Stalin implemented a brutal scheme known as "collectivization." Lenin's experiment in nationalizing the land was only half finished. Stalin set out to finish Lenin's initiative to take away all the peasants' lands and produce in the name of the state.

Collectivization began with a series of propaganda films. Stalin was prominently featured on top of a tractor playing the role of a benevolent leader who would guide Soviet agriculture towards a new dawn. Russian peasants were shown enthusiastically celebrating communism in front of posters of Karl Marx; some were even shown dancing with happiness.

Sadly, the truth was quite different. In 1930, the peasants' produce was collected as the Red Army systematically seized all of the production from every single field. Of course, some peasants were clever enough to hide their goods rather than give them up. But communist party officials searching high and low eventually discovered all the hiding places.

Then, on orders, the communist officials also confiscated the peasants' agricultural equipment. They were left with nothing to eat and nothing with which to work the soil to produce anything more to eat. It was a truly desperate time for most people.

Famine and Cannibalism

Eventually, that planned catastrophe that Lenin had triumphantly described as "the most useful for communism" raised its ugly head again under Stalin through widespread famine. [C1-9]

In the Ukraine, the normal breadbasket of Soviet farm production, some six million people starved over the next few years. Another two million died in Kazakhstan and one million more in the northern Caucasus region.

Innocent children were reduced to skin and bones and literally died in agony. There was yet another ghastly result of the famine inspired by Stalin: cannibalism. Peasants, maddened by overwhelming hunger, actually began to eat corpses. But, even that wasn't the worst of the problems.

Even more horrible, some desperate peasants kidnapped children and actually ate them. Reports indicate that two Russian peasants caught eating human flesh, still had the remains of the young children they had snatched and killed.

Stalin's regime had successfully turned ordinary human beings into savage beasts…just as communism had intended.

Anyone and everyone who opposed Stalin's collectivization policy paid with their lives. The primary targets were the landowners known as "kulaks." Mean-spirited posters denigrating the kulaks were posted everywhere. Tens of thousands of landowners were detained and then summarily shot.

In actuality, the scheming communist regime branded everyone it saw as opposing their ideology as kulaks, whether they owned land or not. Large numbers of priests and members of their congregations who attended church regularly were arrested and imprisoned under the guise that they were kulaks. Some were just executed while others were sent to the regime's forced labor camps, where a lingering and horrible death slowly and deliberately overtook them.

I experienced almost the same in Cuba, right after the triumph of the Castro's revolution. Of the thousands that Castro killed publicly by firing squads, many were charged with being anti-revolutionary and killed without a trial, just because they had been accused.

The labor camps that were built all over the country were nothing more or less than another of Stalin's murdering techniques. Millions of people branded as "enemies of the state" were literally worked to death in labor camps under some of the most intolerable conditions imaginable.

Some were made to do brutal work on canals in the heat of the blazing summer. Others were whisked off to break up rocks in bitterly cold, sparsely populated Siberia. Forced to do grueling labor under the most severe conditions, many were turned into barely living breathing skeletons. The vast majority never left the inhumane camps alive.

Of course, Comrade Josef Stalin was absolutely delighted by all of these events. In a speech to the Communist Party Congress in 1934, he triumphantly pronounced collectivization as an overwhelming success, and received an enthusiastic ovation from the assembled delegates. One by one, Stalin's closest supporters took the floor at the Congress and warmly praised him as a *genius*.

However, a secret vote at the end of the Congress produced a totally unexpected result: out of the 1,900 voting delegates, 300 independent thinkers voted against Stalin. The dictator was stunned.

Immediately ballots were collected and unceremoniously burned, the vote was declared invalid, and it was announced that Stalin had been unanimously elected Secretary General of the Communist Party. However, Stalin could not allow that to be the end of the matter; the alleged treachery could not go unpunished.

Within just a few short months approximately 1,000 of the 1,900 delegates were killed by Stalin's secret police, the NKVD. In addition, Stalin is reported to have ordered Sergei M. Kirov (1886–1934) assassinated. Kirov had been a prominent early Bolshevik leader, an organizer of the opposition to the more outrageous of Stalin's policies, and a popular figure who had the audacity to get a larger ovation than Stalin at the Congress.

Then Stalin staged a huge funeral ceremony in Kirov's memory where he had the insolence to walk behind the coffin of the man he himself had had murdered. The NKVD eliminated dozens of people linked to Kirov over the next several weeks. Fidel did the same when he killed one of his right hand men, Camilo Cienfuegos. That is a very common practice among communist leaders.

During the 1930s, many of the most senior officials of the state were summarily killed by order of Stalin. Some were forced to submit to show trials, duly found guilty of trumped-up charges, and quickly executed. To survive by Stalin's side, it was essential to be a loyal yes-man.

Out of fear they might ultimately become rivals, Stalin had many very able leaders killed, including a number of prominent army generals. In 1938 and 1939, the most skilled of the Soviet generals were either killed by the secret police or condemned to death at specially rigged trials. This implausible policy of slaughter meant the country was nearly defenseless against the Nazi invasion, which took place on June 22, 1941. Mechanized German units pressed hundreds of kilometers into Russia in just a few short weeks, burning and destroying everything in their path.

Meanwhile, the headstrong Stalin had totally ignored numerous intelligence reports warning of a German invasion, and the commanders who sent such reports to him were labeled as cowards. Stalin dismissed the Nazis as inconsequential even as they pushed Russia into the deadliest war in recorded history where some 25 million Soviet citizens were killed.

It still remained that the number of Russian citizens slaughtered by Stalin was even greater than the 25 million Soviet citizens killed in the war between 1941 and 1945. In 1937 and 1938 alone, 7 million people were accused of political offenses and 1 million of them were put to death. The staggering annihilation of Russians during Stalin's regime eventually reached an astonishing 40 million people.

Under his merciless leadership, Stalin forced millions of people from their homes with orders for internal exile executed in the middle of a single night. Crammed into trains, they were carted off to the isolated and freezing climate of distant Siberia.

Stalin was especially ruthless to the Muslims living in the Caucasus and the Crimea regions of the country. On the night of May 18, 1944, some 400,000 Muslim Tartars in the Crimea were unceremoniously herded from their homes and transported to forced labor camps in the most distant corners of the Soviet Union. Not surprisingly, over half of them died before they reached their destinations.

Mounted NKVD units thundered into Muslim communities, murdered tens of thousands of women, children, and the elderly, and left in their wake thousands of deserted villages. Traces of Stalin's barbarism are just now being revealed.

A mass grave of 30,000 bodies has been found close to the city of Minsk. Many bones bore the unmistakable evidence of brutal torture and most of the skulls had bullet holes. This is just one small example of the unbelievable atrocities that communism has brought to an unsuspecting world.

While communists were slaughtering millions of citizens, they also terrorized millions more they did not kill. Communism has literally brought about a "reign of terror" since it has always regarded society as a collection of animals that needed to be herded and managed. The communist belief is that the only way to subjugate people is through fear and terror—pure Marxist ideology.

A ludicrous example of how far the charade of support would be carried was how Stalin would be applauded for minutes on end at communist party congresses. The reason was quite simple: no one wanted to be the first to stop applauding. Stalin had already demonstrated his brutality by killing a number of delegates who failed to demonstrate the necessary enthusiasm.

The communist party organized rallies to protest against so-called traitors and agents: anyone could be a target of that campaign. For example, people regarded as exemplary communists one day could subsequently appear in the columns of the newspaper, *Pravda,* depicted as dangerous savage dogs. Everyone was terrified lest the same fate might befall them.

Mass executions were some of the favored tools to subjugate people; thousands were publicly exterminated during Stalin's reign. Communism was also deadly for the arts. Pre-communist Russian society had enjoyed a very rich culture with superior creative writers, painters, and composers working throughout the land. But with the communist state, ugliness and crudeness dominated Russian art and culture. The new style was known as "Socialist realism" and locked all of the country within narrow, dark, and lifeless limits.

The frozen, sterile nature of communist art, music, and writing is a result of a philosophy that regards human beings as simply a collection of matter; it's a painfully simplistic belief that reduces everything and everyone to a standardized sameness.

Applying this dull, lifeless outlook to art resulted in a complete failure, as it did in all other avenues. True art is free aesthetic expression and a delight given to man by God. For art to develop and flourish there has to be a necessary prerequisite of freedom and yearning in the soul that comes from being able to create with a lack of stifling restraints. Under communism, that atmosphere of freedom was purged and artistic expression died a miserable death as people suffered under the withering pressure to conform to the rigid norms.

In its bumbling management of society, communism dealt yet another critical blow to the field of science. At Stalin's insistence, every scientist was required to sign an oath of loyalty to *dialectical materialism.* All scientific research was perverted to agree with materialist doctrine. The theory of evolution enjoyed an exalted position among those dogmas so fiercely defended by Stalin.

The Soviet dictator's devotion to the theory went straight back to his youthful beliefs. Stalin had been brought up in a strict religious household, and had been sent to be educated at a church school. Yet, as he was preparing to become a priest—as unbelievable as that seems—he read a summary of Darwin's *Origin of Species,* and all aspects of his life suddenly changed.

Stalin was easily deceived by the unproven, superficial claims of Darwinism, and he ignored his religious upbringing to become an atheist. In his "heightened state of ignorance," he joined the ranks of the Bolsheviks.

When he came to power many years later, Stalin's own theory of evolution became his most important source of inspiration. He made extraordinary efforts to insure that the theory should be taught in Soviet schools, and boldly declared, "There are three things that we do to disabuse the minds of our seminary students. We had to teach them the age of the earth, the geologic origin, and Darwin's teachings."

Based on his education and associations, perhaps President Obama is also a Darwinist. If so, that is reason for exercising caution in our actions. The risk is great when the leaders have little regard for other human beings.

Americans, for the sake of our country, take note that when your children speak of Darwin, evolution, and survival of the fittest, they are being taught that God is dead!

Stalin, who carried out all this vicious savagery in the name of materialist philosophy and communist ideology, died in 1953. His cold, arrogant, and merciless conduct was nothing if not a clear reflection of the dark world of communism itself.

While communism surrounded itself with high-sounding slogans of justice and equality, it really brought humanity nothing but bloodbaths, deaths, and destruction. Communist ideologues and dictators who followed these tenets such as Marx, Engels, Lenin, and Stalin have been responsible for the deaths of millions. Rather than bringing justice and equality, communism literally turned their part of the world into a cruel slaughterhouse.

But be fully aware that such evil is not laid on the shoulders of communist leaders alone. No, another ideologue who must share a major part of that responsibility is Charles Darwin, the man who built "...the basis in natural history for the communist view," as Karl Marx put it.

What Can Americans Do?

It is definitely time for the American people to wake up and look at history because what is taking place today in our own country, took place in Germany several decades ago. One day, as happened to the German and Russian people, we could wake up in a totalitarian communist country with all of our freedoms and liberties taken away. The rhetoric will sound right, but the actuality will be totally wrong, and the results will be catastrophic.

To prevent a progressive slide into communism, we have to correct mistakes that we seem to keep repeating.

- What we will not tolerate in our homes must not be allowed to happen around us in our communities.
- When we see something obviously wrong, we cannot just look the other way and allow it to take place without taking action.
- We must speak up for what is right, not being timid or afraid of creating waves or hurting feelings.
- We have to safeguard our freedom and liberty won by fighting for them so long and hard.
- We must face up to the challenges of bad government and fight for changes.
- We have to start calling communists what they really are. They are not leftists, socialists, statists, progressives, liberals, or the dozens of other names that people in the media, writers, show hosts, leaders, etc., use to hide the true nature of that evil ideology.

CHAPTER 3

The Real Che Guevara

It is widely rumored that Fidel ordered one of his right hand men, Camilo Cienfuegos (1932–1959), to be eliminated. Then Castro sent his second-in-command, Dr. Ernesto Che Guevara (1928–1967), the Argentine-born Marxist revolutionary, physician, and military theorist, out of the country, because he considered Cuba too small for two leaders of his and Che's strength and stature.

Subsequently, Guevara was captured and killed as a revolutionary guerilla leader in Bolivia. Now he is revered as a communist hero, one to be idolized by communist sympathizers around the world. However, most people do not know the real Che Guevara.

The truth is that when people wear his image they are wearing the image of a sociopath serial killer not a revolutionary. After the revolution's success, the 26th of July Movement was joined with other bodies to form the United Party of the Cuban Socialist Revolution, which in turn became the Communist Party of Cuba in 1965. Che's legal name was Ernesto Rafael Guevara de la Serna, a man of Spanish-Irish descent.

In 1928, he was born into an aristocratic and politically Marxist family in Rosario, Argentina. As a boy he played rugby and was nicknamed, "The Raging" because he was extremely aggressive.

Later in 1959 he decided to marry a Cuban, Aleida Marsh. They had four children. In 1964 this *loyal* father had an extramarital affair with Lilia Rosa López, and they had a son named Omar Perez.

His closest friends described Che as a father of his own beliefs and the son of the revolution. In reality he was, like every communist, obsessed with his cause and personal pleasure instead of the well being of his family. Che Guevara was the Killing Machine. His instruction to his underlings concerning a prisoner, "If in doubt, kill him."

In 1960, Che set up the first forced labor camp, Guanahacabibes, in the province of Camagüey. By 1965, the camp was the precursor to the eventual systematic confinement, of dissidents, homosexuals, AIDS victims, Catholics, Afro-Cuban priests, and others judged as scum by the communists. The camps operated under the banner of Unidades Militares de Ayuda a la Producción, or Military Units to Help Production.

Herded into buses and trucks, the "unfit" would be transported at gunpoint to these camps organized on the Guanahacabibes mold. The majority never returned. [C1-29, C1-30]

José Vilasuso, was a lawyer as well as a professor at Universidad Interamericana de Bayamon in Puerto Rico, and once belonged to the group in charge of the summary judicial process at La Cabaña. That was the infamous prison where Castro had put Che in charge of the extermination of the bourgeois class.

Mr. Vilasuso spoke from his home in Puerto Rico. "Che was in charge of the Comisión Depuradora. The process followed the law of the Sharia there was a military court and Che's guidelines to us were that we should act with conviction, meaning that they (the prisoners) were all murderers, and the revolutionary way to proceed was to be implacable.

"My direct superior was Miguel Duque Estrada. My duty was to legalize the files before they were sent on to the Ministry. Executions took place from Monday to Friday, in the middle of the night, just after the sentence was given and automatically confirmed by the appellate body. On the most gruesome night I remember, seven men were executed."

Javier Arzuaga was the Basque chaplain who gave comfort to those sentenced to die and personally witnessed dozens of executions. A former Catholic priest, now seventy-five, he recalled that, "There were about eight hundred prisoners in a space fit for no more than three hundred: former Batista military and police personnel, some journalists, the majority businessmen and merchants. The revolutionary tribunal was made of militiamen.

"Che Guevara presided over the appellate court. He never overturned a sentence. I would visit those on death row at the Galera de la Muerte. A rumor went around that I hypnotized prisoners because many remained calm, so Che ordered that I be present at the executions. After I left in May, they executed many more, but I personally witnessed fifty-five executions."

Arzuaga continued, "There was an American, Herman Marks, apparently a former convict. We called him 'the butcher' because he enjoyed giving the order to shoot. I pleaded many times with Che on behalf of prisoners.

"I remember especially the case of Ariel Lima, a young boy. Che did not budge, nor did Fidel, whom I visited. I became so traumatized that at the end of May 1959 I was ordered to leave the parish of Casa Blanca, where La Cabaña was located and where I had held Mass for three years.

"I went to Mexico for treatment. The day I left, Che told me we had both tried to bring one another to each other's side and failed. His last words were: 'When we take our masks off, we will be enemies.' "

Fidel Castro, like Stalin and every other communist tyrant, killed his competition, in this case Che Guevara, and then made a martyr out of him. Today, Che is a symbol of resistance and struggle around the world, primary because the leftist media refuses to broadcast the unbiased truth.

Communism's Deadly Statistics

Let me be perfectly and honestly clear here: communism has an absolutely appalling record in governing people and countries. In the introduction to *The Black Book of Communism,* Editor Stéphane Courtois writes, "…Communist regimes…turned mass crime into a full-blown system of government." He states that the direct death toll from communist carnage is nothing short of 94 million people, not counting what he calls the "excess deaths," meaning the decrease of the population due to lower than expected birth rates.

Courtois reveals the breakdown on those horrific death statistics:

- 65 million in the People's Republic of China,
- 20 million in the Soviet Union,
- 2 million in Cambodia,
- 2 million in North Korea,
- 1.7 million in Africa,
- 1.5 million in Afghanistan,
- 1 million in the communist states of Eastern Europe,
- 1 million in Vietnam,
- 150,000 in Latin America, and
- 10,000 from actions of the international communist movement and communist parties not in power.

Courtois said that communist regimes have been responsible for more deaths than any other political ideal or movement. That is truly startling information. Those unbelievable death statistics include executions, intentional destruction of populations by starvation, and deaths resulting from deportations, physical confinement, and forced labor.

The foreword of the Black Book anthology states, "Ten years ago, the authors of *The Black Book* would have refused to believe what they now write…exploration of the Soviet archives – and eventually those of East Asia – will continue to redress the balance."

The writers said they felt a "duty of remembrance" to the 100 million victims disposed of under Marxist regimes declaring, "Surely, then, the Party of humanity can spare a little compassion for the victims of the inhumanity so long meted out by so many of its own partisans."

The various contributors say their initial intention was a book that would serve as both a historical reference document and as a memorial to those victims whose very memory has been wiped out. Incredibly, the very crimes of communism have yet to receive a fair and just assessment from both historical and moral viewpoints.

American Apocalypse may well be one of the first genuine attempts by a first person authored book to study communism with a focus on its immoral and criminal dimensions.

Pure communism has perpetrated a wide variety of merciless and outrageous crimes not just against individuals but also against the world's civilizations and national cultures. Look at the record:

- Stalin destroyed church after church, first in Moscow and then across the Soviet Union
- Nicolae Ceausescu demolished the historical heart of Bucharest just to give free reign to his megalomania
- Pol Pot dismantled the beautiful Phnom Penh cathedral stone by stone, those remarkable temples of Angkor Wat
- During Mao's Cultural Revolution, priceless treasures were smashed or burned by the Red Guards.

Tools of Mass Murder

However atrocious this senseless destruction of property may ultimately prove for the nations in question and for humanity in general, those acts could never compare with the mass murder of millions upon millions of defenseless human beings—men, women, and, yes, even little children.

Communist crimes tend to fit a clearly recognizable pattern, one that includes execution by firing squad, hanging, drowning, beatings, and in certain cases, poisoning, or arranged car accidents.

Then, there is the destruction of entire populations by starvation, through purposely-produced famines, by deportation (with intended deaths in transit, either through physical exhaustion or through confinement in an enclosed space), and by forced labor (which produces exhaustion, illness, hunger, and hypothermia leading to death).

The Red Terror in Russia, published in Berlin in 1924, cites Russian, Sergei Petrovich Melgunov (1879–1956), the historian who wrote about Latvian-born Soviet politician and leading state security officer (one of the first leaders of the Cheka, the Soviet political police) Martin Ivanovich Latsis (1888–1938).

He quoted Latsis as giving the following instructions in November 1918 to his henchmen, “We don’t make war against any people in particular. We are exterminating the bourgeoisie as a class. In your investigations, don’t look for documents and pieces of evidence about what the defendant has done, whether in deed or in speaking or acting against Soviet authority. The first question you should ask him is what class he comes from, what are his roots, his education, his training, and his occupation.”

The mindset of socialist, communist, Nazi leaders like Guevara, Castro, Stalin, Lenin, Pol Pot, Hitler, et al, transfers from one age to another and from on evil tyrant to another. As Americans, we do not dare to imagine that we are immune from the horrors of falling prey to an evil empire.

Do not fail to notice as you read on, how the seeds of the destruction of liberty in other nations are being planted in our own soil, and, as is usually the case, by people who live among us, passing themselves off as loyal patriots.

CHAPTER 4

I Am a Survivor

I have always been very strong physically and mentally, I was one of only 41 survivors out of 3000 men fighting in the Cuban revolution. The rest of my fellow rebels were captured or killed because they could not stand the pressure any longer.

Still, I struggled against my inner feelings of destruction. Hate and ambition drove me like a crazy man for decades after my brainwashing. I loathed the government, the rich and powerful, people with education, and the establishment. I felt betrayed by society, by the government, and even by my fellow countrymen.

I never tried to resolve any problem in a Christian manner, but always through the medium of violence, a behavior that created hundreds of enemies for me. Then, unbelievably, only four years after my knowing God and accepting Christ, the judge who sentenced me received 49 letters of recommendation from my friends.

Only after becoming a Christian was I able to see who I really was. My soon to be released autobiography, *God, Satan and Me*, explains in detail the struggles and the transformations I went through…

Although no one can condone their actions, I can almost understand why young people like Kimveer Gill, Jared Lee Loughner, Robert Butlers Jr., Charles Carl Roberts and Stephen P. Kazmierczak became killers. Like me, they had allegedly been under too much pressure from communist indoctrination until they reached the point that they erupted. All these young killers were discovered to have communist literature.

More than once, I saw myself in a situation where the destruction and killing of those I believed were my enemies was unstoppable. Blowing up a truck's gas tank, dynamiting bridges, or ambushing men in military jeeps, was a pressure release for me. But, what happens when you have no wartime escape from that pressure?

While the media was eager to falsely paint Jared Loughner, the Arizona gunman, as the face of conservative talk radio and associate him with Republicans, they completely ignored dozens of allegations, such one by *RIGHT-NETWORK*: "AZ SHOOTER: Left-Winger, Jared Loughner—He Likes Watching US Flags Burn & Favorite Book is Communist Manifesto." Posted by Jim Hoft on Saturday, January 8, 2011 at 2:58 PM.

Take a look at Prince George County in Maryland, which borders on Washington, DC. Democrats dominate the county, and 89% of the residents voted for Obama. Hidden in the back pages of newspapers was the story of 13 shootings in the first 13 days of 2011 year in PG County.

Why didn't the press report that this overwhelmingly *Democrat* area was the face of today's liberals—violent and out of control?

What would the mainstream media say if this occurred in a county that was overwhelmingly Republican? They would claim that the mayhem and murder was fueled by Republican hate. The communist playbook calls for ignoring such actions bordering our national Capital if it reflects on their ideology and behavior.

I fight communism because this poison factory destroys human beings. As an example, take the teaching of one of the founders of communism in this country, Saul Alinsky. In his book *Rules of Radicals*, he wrote on the first page, "*The Prince* was written by Machiavelli for the Haves on how to hold power. *Rules for Radicals* is written for the Have-Nots on how to take it away."

Communism is not based on the American mentality of producing; it is based on taking away from the ones who are producers. It is not based on liberty for all; it is based on the subjugation of the masses. It is not based on peace and understanding;

it is based on struggle, murder and war; it is not based on exposing the truth: it is based on twisting the truth through biased news.

Listen to me, "Christians are givers—communists are takers." Communists know and admit that they are radicals. In my days as one of them, we used to brag about doing crazy things, and were encouraged to do so. Communist indoctrination is a constant drumbeat of struggling to meet goals of achieving their agenda or eliminating obstacles.

I call the indoctrination process the dehumanization of the mind in that God, your father and mother, and your family no longer exist, but are only a myth. You, as a leader, become your own god. What could be more insane than that?

In his book *Underdogma*, Michael Prell asks this question, "But we can look at the broad and sustained assault on America's post-9/11 underdog status, and at the equally broad campaigns to systematically ascribe nobility and virtue to the 9/11 hijackers, and ask: what force could have brought these millions of disconnected people together in undirected campaigns to realign the world along Underdogma's lines of power and virtue?"

I congratulate Mr. Prell for recognizing the problem the world is facing with the dilemma that 90% of the American people don't understand. At the same time I must point out to Mr. Prell, whom I admire, that the "unknown" force is Communism. That is why I say we must call this evil by its real name, or the Americans are never going to identify it.

These same "unknown force" people are the ones who have transformed 62% of the American people's minds to have favorable opinion about socialism.

These are the same people behind the brainwashing of students aged 13 to 15, which resulted in a 2004 survey showing that 70% had a bad opinion about the American system.

These are the same people who have prevented America from drilling its own oil, and making us dependent on foreign oil.

These are the same people, who over the last 40 years have removed Christianity from our children's schools, our Federal buildings, courts, and from much of American's minds.

These are the same people who want Americans to believe that communism doesn't exist anymore, and that only the ignorant think otherwise.

These are the same people plotting to take over America today.

Time to Stand and Be Counted

Most hardworking and loyal Americans understand the dangers of communism, but they also need to know what has to be done to stop communists. It is time to stand up, to be counted, and to make waves—no, to make tsunamis. If we don't get involved in seeing that we remain a free republic under our Constitution, then positive change will never happen and our slide into the abyss will inevitably take place.

We must learn to strenuously resist communistic thinking and actions wherever and whenever we see it. We have to act as boldly and decisively as did the people of ACORN, but we must do so on the side of justice. The old mindset of caution, apologies, political correctness, and apathy, simply don't work anymore because bullies only understand "an eye for an eye, a tooth for a tooth." Our choice is to confront them or face destruction. This is the land of the *free* and the *brave*. How else would we have been victorious in World War I and II?

The big difference now, is that if we don't fight with ballots, the next battle will be with bullets...or worse. U.S. General George Patton (1885–1945), and U.S. President Ronald Reagan (1911-2004), knew very well that the only language communism understands is brute force.

The biggest mistake too many Americans make is believing the subtle lies from smooth talking people, or accepting at face value what they hear, see or read in the newspapers, on radio, or TV, or on the Internet. Believing without examining the background of a source and verifying the content can be a very costly mistake.

The media and the Internet are important foundations of information, but today's news is too often biased, and filled with socialist propaganda and misinformation. A true saying is: "A big lie often repeated, becomes a truth." The Bible even praised Christians who checked out what the Apostle Paul had to say before accepting his teaching. Acts 17:11 says, "Now the Bereans were of more noble character than the Thessalonians, for they received the message with great eagerness and examined the Scriptures every day to see if what Paul said was true."

Is that not a greater warning to us when the message comes from a possible socialist/communist source? Consider what befell the citizens of countries who ignored the signs of impending disaster.

- Twentieth Century Atlas records what happened in Romania during the period from 1948 to 1989. Over 435,000 people were killed during and following the Soviet invasion of the country: [C1-10, C1-11]
- The Hungarian bid for independence from Moscow began in 1956 but was soon crushed in a savage fashion by Red Army tanks. The streets of Budapest were literally full of bloody corpses.
- In Yugoslavia, according to *Twentieth Century Atlas*, from 1944 to 1980, forces under the command of Marshal Josip Broz Tito (1892–1980) killed over 200,000 citizens during his first three years in power.
- Meanwhile, a merciless Red Army put down another resistance movement in Czechoslovakia during the spring of 1968. The Czech communist regime lasted from 1948 to 1989. [C1-12, C1-13]
- The communist invasion of Afghanistan took place during the period from 1979 through 1988. According to *Twentieth Century Atlas* from 1979 to 2001, some 1,800,000 people were killed. As recorded in *The Black Book of Communism*, the Red Army invaded Afghanistan in 1979. With Soviet support prior to the invasion, Afghan communists staged a revolution and massacred religious figures. Then, the Red Army entered the country to help increase the scale of the slaughter. Through 1989, Soviet units rained death and destruction upon the Muslim Afghan people. Soviet planes and helicopters ruthlessly bombed Afghan villages. There are many other sources that support such grim statistics, but

> they all tell the same dismal story: communism brings death, destruction, poverty, and hunger. [C1-14]

The Red Army units reportedly inflicted the most barbaric tortures on Muslims. Here's a first person account from a young child saw his family murdered by Soviet troops in a frenzy of communist savagery:

> "They shot my father three times in his chest, his shoulder, and the back of his neck; he fell down dead. My brother and his commander got very angry and decided to fight back. My brother jumped up and grabbed one of their weapons. Then the Russians came and cut my brother's fingers off with a bayonet; so of course, he was helpless. After his fingers had been cut off, they beat him. Then, they shot him in one ear and the bullet came out of his other ear."

Five million Afghan civilians fled the barbarism and instantly became refugees. They ran to seek refuge in neighboring countries such as Pakistan and spent years living in makeshift tents in dreadful conditions.

At last, despite its overwhelming military strength, the Soviets failed to overcome the Afghan resistance and the Red Army was forced to leave the country in 1988. But those Russian tanks and troops left hundreds of thousands of devastated Afghan people behind them. More proof-positive of the suffering inflicted on humanity by the flawed and evil ideology, communism.

In the Far East lay the monster known as the People's Republic of China under the reign of Chairman Mao Tse Tung (1893–1976) also known as Mao Zedong, a Han Chinese revolutionary, political theorist, and the communist leader of Red China from 1949 until his death.

According to the *Twentieth Century Atlas*, over 40 million people were systematically exterminated in very similar patterns to the other communist leaders: by execution, starvation, and forced labor in concentration camps. The bloody and tragic record of Mao's reign of terror is recorded in the "*The Bloody History of Communism*" as referenced here. [C1-15, C1-16, C1-17]

Thirty-six years after its initial publication in 1895, Darwin's *The Origin of Species* was translated and published in Chinese. In a short time, it became very popular among the country's intellectuals. Books by other evolutionary theorists who supported Darwin's viewpoints also began to circulate throughout the country. These included Thomas H. Huxley (1825–1895), an English biologist known as "Darwin's Bulldog" for his advocacy of Darwin's theory of evolution.

The common thread among these theorists was their belief that man and all living things are in a constant state of conflict, which leads to the survival of the fittest and allows for evolution. They totally denied creation theory, saying that mankind emerged by pure chance and portraying man as merely a species of animal with no divine responsibility.

Just as it did in a host of other countries, the spread of Darwinian thought through society led to social turmoil, unrest, and conflict in China. Darwinism had an enormous impact in China in the 20th century, so much so that renowned Harvard University historian James Reeve Pusey wrote a book on that very subject entitled, *China and Charles Darwin*.

According to Pusey's book, Darwinism had a profound effect on Chinese intellectuals, encouraged them to adopt a revolutionary worldview, and provided major ideological support for the development of communism in the country.

The leader who directed the Chinese change that began with Darwinism was Chairman Mao Tse Tung whose political ideas took shape during his student years in the early 1920s. His greatest influence came from the general secretary of the Communist Party, Chen Duxiu (1879–1942), whom he met in Shanghai, devoted to Darwinism, Duxiu taught Mao both Marxism and Darwinism. Written in his later years, Mao's memoirs said, "Nobody influenced me as much as Chen Duxiu."

The young Mao very quickly came to prominence within the Communist Party, rising to the leadership position in the second half of the 1920s. Led by Mao, communist guerrilla fighters began a long, bloody war against the central government led by Chiang Kai-shek

(1887–1975), who, by the way, had also been heavily influenced by Darwinism. The prime difference between the two dictators was that Mao was a communist and Chiang Kai-shek was labeled a fascist.

During World War II, Mao Tse Tung's and Chiang Kai-shek's troops formed a temporary alliance so they could jointly fight against the Japanese occupation forces. But as soon as the war against Japan was over, they promptly began fighting each other again. During the fight between the two Darwinist ideological armies, hundreds of thousands of innocent people were slaughtered.

Then when the Communist Party flag was hoisted over the walls of Beijing, it ushered in an even darker period for the people of China, a land that was already in total chaos. Mao's rule began with an enormous show with crowds applauding communism by gathering in a huge display of red flags in Tiananmen Square.

Soon after, Mao announced the wonderful-sounding promises of communism in his startling, high-pitched voice. Soon, most of those who so cheerfully applauded Mao's taking control of China became victims of his savagery.

That is the same thing that occurs in almost every communist revolution. *The Communist Manifesto* teaches that "The friend of today will be the enemy of tomorrow, and you have to kill him." *This should serve as a chilling warning for anyone who would be a communist follower.*

In the early years of China's communist regime, the government's most ardent supporter was, of course, the other communist government in the Soviet Union. The bloody tyrant in Moscow, Josef Stalin, saw Mao as both an ally and a personal friend. Mao took his place beside Stalin at the latter's extravagantly showy rallies.

The first blood-spilling cooperative effort between the two communist dictators came in Korea in 1950. Acting with both Chinese and Soviet support, communist North Korean forces suddenly attacked and occupied South Korea.

United Nations forces were sent in to try to balance the situation. That "police action," as it was called by then President Harry S.

Truman (1884–1972), lasted for three years and cost the lives of more than three million people.

When U.N. troops seemed to be overcoming the North Korean forces, the Red Chinese army entered the war supporting North Korea while the Soviets provided arms and equipment. Although denied, it is said that many of the aerial dogfights in the skies over Korea were not between U.S. and Koreans, but rather between U.S. and Soviet pilots.

The Korean War turned out to be one of the bloodiest conflicts in history. After that struggle, Mao Tse Tung shifted his attention to internal Chinese affairs. He frequently addressed the Chinese people and millions were forced to listen to his lengthy speeches over loudspeakers. Again and again he would promise industrialization and regeneration saying, "Marxism-Leninism is our only guide." [C1-18]

Like his Russian comrade, Stalin, Mao wanted to implement a ruthless collectivization program across the enormous breadth of the land. His first action in that program was to confiscate private property. In support, propaganda films repeatedly showed the staged but alleged enthusiasm and happiness this heartless measure would bring to the Chinese people.

Businessmen, whose assets had been confiscated, were forced to put on false displays of joy. Everyone who appeared in the slanted films had to show the same bogus images of joy. In reality, however, the communist regime spread fear among the people, not happiness.

As is standard operating procedure in communist takeovers, hundreds of thousands of people were tried in the so-called people's courts set up in Mao's first years in power. The sham trials were always the same: the defendants were found guilty and condemned to death often for minor offenses.

When the communists took over, the majority of the Chinese population was living in rural poverty, working under harsh conditions in rice fields, and barely producing enough food to feed themselves; but at least they had enough to eat. However, the real tragedy for the Chinese people began with Mao Tse Tung's "Great Leap Forward" plan, an economic program begun in 1958, which led China into utter and total disaster.

The program started with the objective of doubling China's industrial and agricultural production. A flood of propaganda posters were put up all over the country explaining how jealous Western countries would be of Chinese productivity. Mao was portrayed as a magnificent and brilliant leader who would solve all problems by implementing communist ideological solutions.

At the outset of the program, agriculture was collectivized. Individual farm production was banned, and villagers were placed in enormous communes consisting of thousands of people who were forced to participate in collective production under strict military discipline. Mao often visited the fields inspecting the work and the villagers.

At the same time, the communist party instituted a program designed to rid the country of "harmful" animals; common sparrows topped the list because they were thought to eat and damage produce. Hundreds of thousands of ordinary Chinese set about exterminating sparrows with any implements they had at hand including slingshots, rocks, sticks, and guns. Those bringing in largest numbers of dead sparrows were praised as model communists.

Yet this bizarre and ill-thought-out program resulted in a calamity that the "all-knowing" communist leaders had failed to foresee. Reducing the sparrow population to near zero simply led to an enormous rise in the insect populations, which the sparrows had formerly fed upon. The insects then caused far more harm to the country's produce than sparrows ever would have.

In 1958 there were competitions conducted between communes to determine which ones were the most productive; the best ones were honored and exalted as exemplary. Every commune wanted to be the best so they all promised to produce higher quotas for the following year. According to the announced results, they all improved dramatically; however the production figures were all falsely inflated. Some communes even reported that they had filled their quotas by replanting their harvested crops in the inspected fields.

The forced communal system simply led to widespread reporting of totally false statistics, which in turn gave rise to an even greater catastrophe. In their enthusiasm, the communist leaders announced that China had an overstock of rice and grain, and that in the future the system would be forced to give priority to other tasks.

As a result of this gross misinformation, tens of millions of peasants were removed from working in the fields and were put to work on the construction of a giant canal. Of course, the triumphantly productive villagers were portrayed in propaganda films as happy and highly motivated, although they were about to suffer a debilitating moral and physical collapse.

In the dangerously hazardous conditions in which they were made to work, tens of thousands of people died in industrial accidents for which they were totally unprepared and untrained. Meanwhile, the "omnipotent" communist leaders came up with a very inaccurate and crude calculation that "Every worker will build one meter of canal, and the project will end in three months." In fact, the terrible canal project took more than ten full years to complete.

In yet another example of cruel ineptitude during the Great Leap Forward years, factory workers' hours were doubled and machinery was made to work nonstop. Nothing could interfere with production, including needed maintenance and repairs. As a result, the machinery simply began to fall apart; factories all over the country were ruined.

In these artificially euphoric times, Mao declared that yet another target for the Great Leap Forward was that steel production for the country was to be doubled within one year. Such production was to come not only from heavy industrial complexes, but also from small village furnaces all over the country. Mao and his followers believed that workers' power was almost a magical force.

As a result of this total miscalculation, or just wishful thinking, tens of millions of ordinary Chinese set out to produce steel by amateur methods. Anything and everything made of iron, from doorknobs to saucepans, was melted down in primitive furnaces in an effort to produce the required quota of steel.

Women dutifully cut off their hair and mixed it with clay in the furnaces. Forests were decimated to provide enough wood for these primitive village furnaces. People of every walk of life, whether living in the cities or in the countryside, worked to produce steel. Reportedly outside their normal working hours even physicians joined in the steel production effort since it was regarded as a national obligation.

The Great Leap Forward campaign was totally irrational; the Chinese people were busily producing more steel, but not making anything useful out of it. What is even more irrational, the steel that was produced was such poor quality that it could serve absolutely no purpose.

The true dimension of the catastrophic program slowly emerged in 1959. While villagers were busy working on making steel or building canals, their fields were left empty, non-productive. Falsified figures throughout the country showed huge production, although in reality there was an enormous production gap.

As a result, a massive famine took hold and the disastrous situation was made even worse by a severe drought. By 1960, the worst famine in recorded history took place in China; some forty million people starved to death in just two short years. Mao's Great Leap Forward was a total disaster.

It should be emphasized that the thinking and behavior of the communist regimes are unrealistic and flawed. The reconstruction program that Mao called his *Great Leap Forwar*d was nothing short of a monumental jump totally backwards. The clichés of communist ideology bear absolutely no relationship to the real world; the great ideas of communist theoreticians such as Marx, Lenin, and Mao, supposedly so scientific and clever, are in fact nothing more than empty-headed and nonsensical pie-in-the-sky promises that cannot and will not work.

Communists believed in a mistaken ideology and in trying to impose that false ideology on society, they repeatedly inflicted terrible suffering on mankind.

The reason Chinese communists found it so easy to be so ruthless to their fellow man was because of the way they regarded humanity; just like Lenin and Stalin, Mao considered human beings as a species of animal, with no important value. That was a natural consequence of his faithfulness to the Darwinism he had swallowed "hook, line, and sinker" in his youth. That same pattern of dehumanizing people happened in Cuba and in every other communist country.

When he said, "The basis of Chinese socialism rests on Darwin and his theory of evolution," Mao Tse Tung was actually justifying the savagery he put into action on his own people. Harvard University historian James Reeve Pusey described Mao's Darwinist philosophy as, "The thought of Mao Tse Tung was, and remains, a powerful mixture of Darwinian ironies and contradictions."

In an angry comment in 1964, Mao swore, "All demons shall be annihilated." He simply dehumanized his enemies, partly in traditional hyperbole, partly in Social Darwinian "realism." Like anarchists, he saw reactionaries as evolutionary throwbacks, which deserved extinction. The people's enemies were non-human and did not deserve to be treated in a civilized manner as people.

According to the heartless communist leaders in China, the people to be treated most harshly are the Muslim Uighur Turks of East Turkestan. With a long-term policy of ruthless genocide, millions of innocent people have been slaughtered. As an example of their reprehensible indifference to the fate of the Uighur Turks in East Turkestan, the Chinese government carried out a series of nuclear tests in the region, which left tens of thousands of children handicapped. This information is substantiated by the reports of various international organizations, which point out the brutality that is still going on to this very day.

Between 1949 and 1975 a total of 26 million Uighur Turks were murdered by a wide variety of inhuman techniques. Some 46 nuclear tests have been carried out in East Turkestan since 1964; alone these have led to the deaths of 210,000 Muslim people. In 1949, Muslims made up 75% of the population of East Turkestan; as a result of the China's cruel policy of genocide, the Muslims now constitute just 35% of the population.

Following the dismal failure of the Great Leap Forward, Mao withdrew from the major leadership role and went into seclusion. The country was run by a group of more moderate civil servants. The battered Chinese population was partially able to return to normal life and breathe a collective sigh of relief.

But Mao Tse Tung was not done; he was still planning new murders. He determined that communist ideology had not spread sufficiently in society, and attributed the failure of the Great Leap Forward to that major deficiency.

Mao's faithful supporters printed millions and millions of copies of his *Little Red Book*, consisting of a variety of his speeches. Known as "The Great Helmsman," Mao re-emerged onto the Chinese and world stage in the latter half of the 1960s.

A display of his powerful swimming in the Yangtze River demonstrated both his energy and his resilience. As the first order of business, Mao was critical of the classic Chinese arts and promoted the ideological program he dreamed of. He was adamant about grafting the ideas of violence and conflict, the mainstreams of communism, onto society in general and began by attacking and transforming Chinese opera.

The face of communist insanity could clearly be seen in the expressions of the operatic performers, who had been force fed Maoist doctrines. A simple visit by Mao to the opera was the greatest honor imaginable for such fanatical supporters.

The Maoist doctrine was pushed so hard and was so pervasive that all across China it became the only way for the masses to think. People were forced to idolize their omnipotent leader and master to the point that the great majority actually believed that Mao was a super human being. Of course, they were making the worst mistake imaginable because they never knew the truth and blindly followed their leader.

Mao's second attempted leap forward got started in 1966; it was called the "Great Proletarian Cultural Revolution." Once again, the propaganda machine went into overdrive portraying Mao as a divine figure and posters were put up all over China. Schoolchildren were made to rattle off his Little Red Book from memory, his slogans were put up on walls all over the country, and the posters portrayed him as a superhuman being.

The vanguard of the Cultural Revolution was the millions of young students known as Red Guards. On August 18, 1966, a million Red Guards, totally indoctrinated with Mao's ideas, gathered in Tiananmen Square. It was utter chaos as they trampled each other in an effort to catch just a glimpse of Chairman Mao.

Reportedly one young female student was brought to Mao's side and shook his hand. Of course, there was little significance to Mao himself, but it was a matter of the greatest consequence to the girl and all her friends, who fell all over themselves just to touch the hand that had been shaken by Mao.

The Red Guards were so perverted and cruel in their activities that many were even capable of humiliating and beating their own parents for supposed infractions of dedication to the Cultural Revolution. These fanatical young people would stop passersby and ask them about passages from Mao's Little Red Book, beating those who failed to answer their questions correctly.

Unbelievably, the marauding Red Guards killed more than a million people. Here is a first-person account of the inhuman treatment meted out to university professors detained during the Cultural Revolution:

> "Before a new four-story classroom building, I saw rows of teachers, about 40 or 50 in all, with black ink poured over their heads and faces... They all wore dunce caps and carried dirty brooms, shoes, and dusters on their backs. Hanging from their necks were pails filled with rocks... Finally, they all knelt down, burned incense, and begged Mao Zedong to 'pardon their crimes.'
>
> "Beating and torture followed. I had never seen such tortures before: eating night soil [human excrement] and insects, being subjected to electric shocks, being forced to kneel on broken glass, being hanged 'like an airplane' by the arms and legs."

But even those indignities were not the end; the Red Guards also attacked Western diplomats. Chaos and violence were rampant throughout the country. Museums were ransacked and ruined, books were burned, and fighting even broke out between rival Red Guard factions. Schools, hospitals, factories and other vital services stopped functioning.

The mix of communism with Darwinism has led to a horrendous effect on human beings. History records animal-like barbarianism in almost every country under the rule of communism.

Mao's utter insanity had led his entire country into a state of anarchy and turmoil. The only way to restore order was have the army intervene. The disorderly Red Guards were defused and rapidly sent off to labor in the fields.

Even so, the madness of Mao's Cultural Revolution only ceased at his death in 1976. Yet, the Communist Party's loyalty to him and to the strict communist code of obedience was continued until his funeral; there was a lengthy, sorrowful lament written and read and the bloody dictator was portrayed as a superior being. Chairman Mao's body was even mummified and preserved. But his brutal ideology survived and directly led to even more blood being spilled.

The further tragedy about Mao's communism is that the death and destruction was not just reserved for China, but was heaped upon other countries influenced by China. When Sino-Soviet relations deteriorated in the 1960s, Maoism found new life in a variety of other countries, as an alternate model of communism. Misguided regimes based on Maoist principles were set up in Albania, Cambodia, and North Korea. And of course, those terrible regimes inflicted almost unimaginable suffering on their people.

The Cambodian killing fields in particular brought us tales of a savagery unequalled in recorded world history. According to the *Twentieth Century Atlas*, the Khmer Rouge in Cambodia ruled from 1975 to 1978 and was responsible for the majority of the country's population.

When the Khmer Rouge took Cambodia, they forced the people to leave the cities and live in the countryside. Cities totaling a population of about 2.5 million people were soon nearly empty. The roads were clogged with evacuees. Similar evacuations occurred throughout the nation, and 1,650,000 people died from starvation, overwork, and executions.

The leader of the Khmer Rouge was the ruthless communist dictator, Pol Pot (1928–1998), who was born as Saloth Sar in a farming family in central Cambodia, then part of French Indochina. In

1949 at the age of 20, he went to Paris on a scholarship to study radio electronics. But Pot became involved in the communist movement and neglected his studies; as a result, he lost his scholarship and had to return to Cambodia in 1953. He joined the underground Communist movement in his country.

In 1954, Cambodia was granted full independence from France and was ruled by a royal monarchy. By 1962, Pol Pot had become the leader of the Cambodian Communist Party and was forced to escape into the jungle to avoid the wrath of Prince Norodom Sihanouk, the recognized leader of the country.

In his jungle camp, Pol Pot formed an armed resistance movement that became known as the Khmer Rouge (Red Cambodians) and waged a guerrilla war against Sihanouk's government. After taking over the government, among other atrocities, the Khmer Rouge arrested, tortured, and eventually executed anyone suspected of belonging to an undefined element known as "enemies." Of course, it was, again, the extermination of the bourgeois class.

The precise number of people killed as a result of the Khmer Rouge's policies is unknown as is the exact causes of death for those who were slaughtered. Access to Cambodia during the Khmer Rouge's rule and during subsequent Vietnamese rule was extremely limited. In the early 1980s, the Vietnamese-installed government following the Khmer Rouge did a national household survey, which concluded that over 4.8 million people had died. However, most knowledgeable, modern historians do not consider that number to be very accurate.

Modern searches have found thousands of mass graves all over Cambodia from the Khmer Rouge era; they contain an estimated 1.39 million bodies. A number of other studies have estimated the death toll at between 1.4 million and 2.2 million, with perhaps 50% of those deaths being due to executions, and the other 50% from starvation and disease. . [C1-19, C1-20, C1-21, C1-22]

Whatever the accurate figure, we must never forget that the numbers refer to once living, breathing human beings.

As previously mentioned, in North Korea, it was more of the same. The Korean War, which lasted from 1950 to 1953, resulted in 2.8 million deaths. But, according to R.J. Rummel, more than 1.66 million ordinary citizens were exterminated by genocide, starvation, and concentration camps by the communist government of North Korea.

To this day, North Korea has the largest concentration labor camps in the world. Reportedly, the North Korean government is the greatest killer of innocent people on earth today. Estimates range from 2 to 2.5 million people died just in a recent famine. That would make it the worst state killing anywhere since the atrocities in Cambodia in the 1970s. The North Korean bloodbath is yet another of the pictorial records in *The Bloody History of Communism.* [C1-23]

Let me tell you the story of Cuba, the country that I know about firsthand. Despite what I would wish to relate about the land of my birth and childhood, I cannot tell a different tale than that of communism's annihilation of all that was good. It was more of the same, as it always is and will be.

Reports of the exact number of my fellow citizens of Cuba, a country slightly smaller than the state of Florida, who had their lives snuffed out by Cuban communism, range up to over 45,000. That includes 13,000 drowned trying to escape Cuba. The point is indisputably clear that communism and communists kill in dramatically large numbers and with merciless precision.

To compare what Cuba was like in the 1930's, I was able to locate a video that I've referenced below. Viewers can see how people dressed, shopped, and socialized, how the buildings looked, and how refined was the Cuban society.

At that time, Cuba was the youngest republic in our hemisphere; it was an incredibly vibrant nation. Everywhere there were signs of progress, stability, wealth, and national pride; people enjoyed a healthy, affluent lifestyle. They dined in upscale, fine restaurants and their dress was that of a sophisticated and successful society; they were relaxed, friendly, and confident. Cuba was a vacation spot for many foreign visitors, including those from America.

Havana was a grand blend of the best of the old and new worlds. The impressive homes, ornate monuments, and remarkable fortresses told part of the story of Cuba's rich and vibrant history and the splendor of the Spanish aristocracy. The newest areas of the city were ultra-modern, with splendid wide avenues and lush broad promenades. Arcades were built over sidewalks to protect pedestrians from the sun.

Millions of Cuban pesos were spent to create verdant parks, a modern university, striking statues, and prosperous businesses. Success, wealth, and well-being radiated everywhere. [C1-24]

Photos taken in Cuba in 1954 before Castro came to power compared with today are startling in their contrast. But, there are other measurements that show how depressed Cuba has become. For example, back in 1954, there was one automobile for every 10 Cuban citizens; today less than 1% of the population has a car, and most of them are the same continually rebuilt and repaired 50's models. [C1-25]

The 1956 Cuban Carnival celebrations were filled with the enthusiasm and vibrancy of the happy and free Cuban people. [C1-26]

Then there is the Cuba of 1958. Castro, like other communist/socialist leaders, including Hitler, Mao, and Lenin promised big changes. They kept that promise, but in each case those changes were for the worse not better. Significantly, President Obama campaigned with that same drumbeat of change with a side offering of hope. [C1-27]

Just over seventy years later, today's Cuba makes the 1930's Cuba nearly impossible to even imagine. Cuban society has been turned upside down. Now, repression, poverty, and hunger choke and suffocate the once-vibrant population. Today, survival preoccupies the people and there is no time or opportunity for the leisure, or stability that once was so omnipresent. The basic necessities of life and, indeed, human dignity are available only to the communist elite class of the country.

Viewing photos and videos of what Cuba looks like after suffering for 50 years under communist Fidel Castro, you can see how the dress has changed, how the beauty that once was there is gone, how old structures have been abandoned. What you may not be able to see so readily is the loss of refinement, social etiquette, and the good life that once was Cuban society.

Compare stores once filled with the goods of a pre-Castro era to the almost empty stores of today. In the days before communism, Cubans ate more meat per capita than Americans. Consider the living conditions of the Cuban population today after the communists "rescued" the proletariat from capitalism. Everything is rationed, including food. Go to http://www.therealcuba.com/ and see the heartbreaking changes.

Cuba's economy is centrally planned and tightly controlled by the government. Although the government claims full employment, this is another socialist lie. For those who are able to find work, the average wage is about $10 per month. The majority of Cubans live in poverty, barely able to make ends meet from day to day. The people are issued rations cards that can only be used in government-run stores.

Tourism still brings in much needed foreign money. Remarkably, Cuba has the largest, most extravagant resort in the Caribbean. However, the majority of the people do not benefit at all from the tourist trade. At the time of this broadcast, Fidel Castro was ill and showing his age. His absence from public view left many Cubans wondering what change, if any, would follow. Their decline is heart wrenching to me and to others who had to leave their homes to survive. [C1-28]

Even though the media seems to paint Fidel Castro as a kinder and more benevolent leader than the other monstrous communist leaders, I can personally tell you that he was actually a criminal of the worst kind. At the very least, he subjugated a vibrant culture for more than 50 years. We Cubans paid the price of ignorance then, and now I see western nations beginning to pay the price for indifference and shortsightedness.

Fidel appears to have been the fruit of the communism from the very beginning. When he was in prison, communists around the world put pressure on the Cuban government for his release, just as they had done for Mandela in South Africa, Hitler in Germany, and Chavez in Venezuela. And so Castro was set free. But then, like Hitler and

Chavez, Castro became a communist dictator and remains so to this very day. Think about these facts about my now conquered country:

- In 1958 Cuba had a higher per-capita income than Austria and Japan.
- Cuban industrial workers had the 8th highest wages in the world.
- In the 1950's Cuban stevedores earned more per hour than their counterparts in New Orleans and San Francisco.
- Cuba had established an 8-hour workday in 1933—five years before FDR's New Dealers got around to it.
- Added to this: one month's paid vacation.
- Cuba, a country 71% white in 1957, was completely desegregated 30 years before the U.S.
- In 1958 Cuba had more female college graduates per capita than the U.S.
- Cuba was the first Spanish speaking country to have electricity in 1889.
- Cuba also was the first Spanish speaking country to have the first car.
- Cuba was the first country in the world to have a direct dial phone system in 1906.

CHAPTER 5

The Truth About Communism

Communism governs through the elimination of private sectors, the installation of a centralized totalitarian style government, and the creation of a classless society.

The collapse of the American economic system would automatically create a sustainable economic or self-sufficient system; based not on production, but rather on the masses using available resources.

This type of economic structure, used by the Marxist communist for almost a century, forces three generations of families to live in the same house. The idea is for the older generation to take care of the youngest generation, while the productive generation (parents) works. The struggle is designed to make families more united and to save on food, gas, transportation, etc., and by limiting the number of households.

The result is understandably a painful culture transformation and results in the development of a new economy characterized by slavery, rationing and tyranny. This *sustainable society* has been established in over 20 countries and stands as living proof of the system's failure.

The collapse of the capitalistic system would force people to invent ways to survive. In transportation, as shown in familiar scenes of other lands, sailboats are used to transport cargo, bicycles to transport people, and beasts of burden to take produce to market.

This represents the socialistic principle of a *Sustainable* economic system: i.e., produce something without using non-renewable resources. Of course, the communists always use different words to disguise the reality of their catastrophic ideology to hide the impact upon public opinion. Are we willing to take this great leap backward?

Communist regimes utilize the same tactics after taking control of a country. They install a totalitarian government to: destroy or control the transportation and production systems, confiscate private properties, centralize distribution and production centers directed by government planning, and eliminate the bourgeois class. Of course, everyone is told that this enormous change is "all in the name of the people."

They embellish their big lie with the promise that in twenty years, every worker will have a house, car, and a much better standard of living. Then they allow the workers to take over the factories and businesses that have been taken from the bourgeois class.

Not having the training, drive or resources that the eliminated industry leaders had to first create the economy, the workers end up destroying the free market, which in turn, causes the complete collapse of the economy. It would be like handing over the auto industry to the unions, which has already occurred under Obama's White House.

From that point on, the people of the proletariat class, that the communists claim to protect, are subjugated without transportation, communication, or food supplies. This is part of the well-orchestrated communist plan, to overpower the people and bring them completely under the strict control of the new communist government, with all the degradation and problems already pointed out.

Travel outside of the local area becomes impossible. There are no more visits to friends and families in other towns. The proletariat can only travel as far as a bicycle can take them. Then they have very little to sustain their lives and everything is rationed "for the good of the people." The totalitarian government is the only one with transportation, money, arms, and a small amount of food and supplies to distribute. Accordingly, when citizens reach that state of existence, the omnipotent government is in complete control of their lives.

That is the simple reason why the plan of conquest calls for the government to own and control everything. Below the top leadership there is only one class, the poor. The government establishes a rationing system and distributes half of what is needed for survival to the poor class their system has created.

Simultaneously, the communist leaders establish a defense committee that places one person (a block captain) in charge of each block to watch over the rest of their neighbors. The defense committee person's real job is to inform the leaders of everything the others in that block do, where they go, what they are eating, in short, to monitor and report all their movements and activities.

By the time those controls are in place, all aspects of society have been changed. Education, for example, has been replaced by a system of indoctrination and communist instruction. The legal system becomes a farce because then there is only one governing law, meaning whatever the highest ranking communist declares *is* the law.

Religion is put under attack until it is eliminated, or reduced to insignificance and irrelevance. The political system is diminished to whatever the communist leader says or orders. That leader becomes the one voice of the people, one that cannot be challenged. Everyone, without exception, must obey or face the very unpleasant consequences.

The promises of improvements and innovations to enhance society never take place. Instead, there is a radical departure from the past, just as the Marxist theory dictates. When everything is in chaos, communist leaders find ways to profit from the circumstances.

Unsurprising, the working classes are blamed for having destroyed the economy, and predictably, the dictators issue hollow promises that with a lot of sacrifices, the proletariat class will have utopia in another 20 years or so. In truth, the leaders of this subterfuge know very well that having a home, a car, and a higher standard of living for the lower classes will never come to pass.

They change the national constitution to suit themselves and adopt socialist policies and laws in their cruel, totalitarian government to make the world believe that everything they do is legal. Soon the bourgeois or middle class is totally eliminated. During the elimination process, the communist leaders desensitize and dehumanize their selected ruling class, the communist elite, to the point that they become cruel tyrants without conscience.

These two remaining classes have very conflicting interests. The poor class becomes desperate to find survival methods while the communist elite takes steps to hoard all the good things that the old bourgeois class left behind or had taken from them.

The communist elite class is very different from the disappearing middle class. The old bourgeois class was paid good salaries, but this new communist elite, is rewarded with higher-ranking positions and a higher status in the socialist society. All at the expense of the working class, which is suffering from the injustices of communism.

The new elites have been trained on how to oppress the rest of the population with total immunity. They become nothing more than a gang of liars, swindlers, and cheats.

Even though they do not receive large salaries, they take all the best goods of the country, and have the power to impose burdensome problems on the poorer class. The elites become the only ones with transportation, good houses, and all the better things of life.

Those in the higher social class are usually capable of being merciless killers, a quality that they must possess to achieve their status as an example of a good communist. In communism, a member of the elite can kill any citizen, whether there is a good reason or not, without being judged for such a crime.

The elite can only keep their positions by following strict communist teachings of obedience, compliance, and fidelity to the party. In short, the communist elite can do whatever they want and take whatever they like (including people), as long as they are good communists and loyal to the party and its leaders.

A terrible example of what happens when one does not follow the rules to the letter is that of Roberto Robaina, Cuba's Foreign Minister from 1993 to 1999. He represented the Castro government's policies and political positions around the globe.

He reportedly gave a small amount of money to his mistress in Spain. His comrades assumed that he was leaving the country. Robaina was promptly fired from his position, stripped of all of his elitist perks, and relegated to a job of cleaning up a park in a small rural town for about $25.00 per month. He had no car and all the trappings of his previous high-level position were gone. It was only due to his submissiveness and reverence of the party that he was barely able to save his life and those of his family.

The governing position is that as a member of the communist elite class, the mere appearance of impropriety is sufficient to deflate one's status so a person has to be constantly vigilant never letting their guard down. Loyalty and subordination to the party trumps everything and everyone. Records prove that Stalin killed thousands of his elites, just for being the first to stop applauding after his speeches.

In short, under communist oppression, the average citizen has only half of what he needs to survive from one day to the next. This guarantees that citizens will concentrate every waking effort to acquire their other half of food and other immediate needs to survive. It also guarantees that they will not have enough time or means to challenge anything that the ruling class does.

If someone does confront the government, he is instantly accused of treason, judged, and executed in public by a firing squad. This serves to prolong the panic and chaos among the population that is already frightened into submission. It also keeps people in constant fear of being caught doing or even being thought of doing something wrong in the eyes of the governing.

Communists call this *equality* in a uniform economic and classless society. What a dramatic difference from the equality our forefathers envisioned and built where it is the natural right of every individual to live freely under a system of self-government, to be free to acquire property earned through their own labors, and to be treated fairly and impartially under a just and reasonable system of laws.

Under a communist system that is so repressive, theft becomes a way for the average common citizen to survive. Keeping in mind that the communist elite accounts for only 3% of the population, the other 97% has to find techniques for survival, like theft. As a result, the elite routinely look the other way when things are stolen whether in production or distribution centers. It might even be said that the elite authorizes a black market.

Turning Citizens Into Drones

The communist goal seems to be to keep the working class occupied for as many hours as is possible. When the working class oversteps its bounds, as in thievery, the laws are enforced harshly. That quite naturally results in a continuation of the feeling of helplessness for the common people. These are the same people who were "rescued" from capitalism a short time before with false promises and fake visions of prosperity; now they are forced to live lives of desperation with a loss of identity, no power, no rights, and all potential for bettering their situation.

As might be expected, the working class citizens who make themselves submissive to the communist elite are often treated somewhat better and sometimes the elite even trick them into believing that they have been accepted into the party. But to truly belong, they must surrender their lives to the cause. While a very small minority may actually rise in rank, for the vast majority, it is the equivalent of humbling yourself for pennies.

It is among the working classes where the reactionaries exist. They are rebels, the ones who talk and do things to try to undermine the repressive government. And, when they are caught and identified as a contra, they are the ones who pay dearly for everybody's mistakes. They land in jail when the government needs scapegoats; they are the most rationed in society; they are the lowest of the low. For them, there are no opportunities of any kind and the vast majority end up dying in jail or being killed by one of the elite.

Under communism, it is almost worse than dying to be identified as a rebel or contra or whatever label fits for someone who is against the overwhelmingly heartless government. These are the wretched who work in the most dangerous jobs. For example, in China last year, more than 6,000 miners were killed in fires, floods, cave-ins, and explosions. Those statistics make China's mines the world's most deadly. Lax safety rules and poor equipment are among the factors most often blamed for the so-called "accidents."

A recent news report tells of a methane explosion in a coalmine in a Siberian region notorious for mine accidents. A reported 38 miners were killed in a community only two months after another 100 had died.

The list of death and destruction for workers like these goes on and on. For these "insignificant people," life has little meaning. There is no compassion or caring for them; only the party is important: the people live in poverty, misery, and cruelty.

A culture of conformity and dependency develops where the ideal qualities for a citizen are a zeal for serving the state. Family, community, and faith, all of which have the potential of threatening the government, are eliminated. Individualism is frowned upon; uniqueness and self-worth are to be destroyed.

Under a Marxist and Leninist system, everyone and everything belongs to and is for service to the government, including the people. At the tender age of 12, children are sent away from their parents to the place that government officials deem based on tests of intelligence, attitude, or estimates of how the child will best serve society. The children know only what they are told and the propaganda is rampant.

Children in communist countries know next to nothing about the reality of the world or of human conditions. They hear a constant drumbeat of propaganda in school with more misinformation circulated by radio and TV, which, of course, is under the total control of the communist government.

By the time the children have reached 20 years of age they actually believe that life in Cuba gives them more freedom, more food, and more advances in technology than anywhere else on earth. Then, they also learn that in the U.S., people are dying in the streets of hunger, murders by gangs are everyday events all over the country, the streets are totally unsafe, and all Americans live in a constant state of fear.

Those same continuing doses of misinformation are being fed to young people in the Soviet Union, China, Vietnam, Cambodia, Laos, Hungary, Romania, Yugoslavia, Iraq, Iran, North Korea, Angola, Nicaragua, several African countries, Cuba, and now Venezuela. The rest of the world has ignored the conditions in all those countries; one day they will pay the consequences.

Of course, to insure their programs of propaganda and outright lies are not challenged by the truth, they do not allow their people access to the Internet because it will open their eyes.

After communism has been in place for at least 40 years, the leader may slightly soften the laws, but by then no one knows or remembers capitalism, and any rebellions against the communist rulers are almost nil. Nevertheless, loss of freedom, rationing of necessities, and horrible production records are endemic: a way of everyday life.

Evolving Communism in Venezuela

In the past decade, Marxist and Leninist communism has changed little, although some countries like Venezuela had adopted evolutionary techniques rather than revolutionary policies. Hugo Rafael Chavez, president of Venezuela, seemed to promise a hope for the future of communism in South America. His evolution had the appearance of becoming victorious.

But an increasing number of frustrated people have been watching Chavez. After ten years in power, he began nationalizing and confiscating many big companies and radio and television stations. Observers know that he is also establishing government-run centralized production and distribution centers for all products. That has a familiar ring here in America.

Chavez is a Marxist Leninist, and in the near future, he will turn Venezuela into a totalitarian country just like Cuba, North Korea, and other communist-run nations. The only difference may be the way he is completing the transition from capitalism to communism. Instead of making radical changes as was done by Castro in my Cuba, he is using a subtle evolutionary technique to remake the country over time.

I am quite certain that this evolutionary technique is going to grow in status in communist takeovers. Meanwhile, avowed socialists Rafael Vicente Correa Delgado of Ecuador, and Juan Evo Morales

Ayma of Bolivia, are attempting to imitate the Chavez evolution right now.

The communists entrenched in America have worked diligently over the years to take over our government using the evolutionary techniques. In the last 40 years they have been responsible for a host of major changes that have resulted in more and more citizens being totally dependent on the government as the economy is crippled.

My biggest concern is that in these poor economic times that we are suffering through now may trigger the evolutionary process into a full-scale crisis—bringing about a complete breakdown of our republic. The slower evolving process would then be accelerated for a quick take over: exactly what the communists want.

Fortunately for the communists in Venezuela, Ecuador, Bolivia, and in the United States, time is in their favor as long as they can continue indoctrinating our youth through the state-run schools.

For many years, the world has watched communism evolve in Western Europe. The style of takeover appears to also be less confrontational, somewhat more benevolent, and is driven by election results, rather than revolutions. No one knows how it will work out if and when socialism wins the majority rule. What is currently a minor annoyance to some could suddenly be a horrifying way of life.

The danger exists that they could continue changing laws in various countries so that the people will become more dependent on the government. At that point, communism could step up the pressure, and people would finally learn of that ideology's true intentions. Or they could be just waiting for their New World Order to shift the entire balance of power around the globe.

At the moment, a substantial part of Europe is unhappy with its communists. For example, France and Germany have moved their governments further to the right, away from communist ideals. But no matter what anyone says or thinks, the reality is that Western European communism is a threat even when it appears to be a much softer menace than that of Marxism or Leninism.

Communism "Made in China"

Most recently, China has opened sections of their economy to free market activities. Prosperity is taking over where only a decade ago that would have been unthinkable. Industrious people exercising their ingenuity and productivity have once more demonstrated that they are the best medicine, in fact the only remedy, for reviving the economy. But is that good news?

Consider: if China continues following this trend, it will soon become a world super power. Despite their current prosperity that occurred when they provided a narrow opening for capitalism to work, there is no proof that it will continue, especially in a society that has had decades of oppressive communism.

Some knowledgeable economic analysts have predicted turbulent times ahead for China. Others have even suggested that there will be dreadful times ahead for the world's most populous country.

The Ten Planks

I am now asking readers to carefully study the following ten steps that Karl Marx laid out to destroy a free enterprise system of government. Then compare them to capitalism before replacing it with a system of omnipotent socialist communist government. Outlined in *The Communist Manifesto,* these are known as *The Ten Planks*.

1. "Abolition of private property and the application of rent on all land for public purposes."

This plank is clear evidence that under Marxism there will be no personal property; only the government will own property, insuring that all citizens will be poor and under the control of the government.

2. "A heavy progressive or graduated income tax."

The progressive income tax is a tool that Marxists used to force the middle classes to yield and give in to the communist approach, or to move outside the communist sphere. It had another bonus for the communists: to help raise money for the fledgling government.

3. **"Abolition of all rights of inheritance."**
   The Manifesto called for the elimination of all who were against them, so abolishing inheritances prevented any conflicts with heirs of those who had been killed or forced to flee.
4. **"Confiscation of the property of all emigrants and rebels."**
   Since all citizens are losing their property, it is only necessary to take over the property of the emigrants and "rebels" first. It teaches seizure by levels, so that the process doesn't affect everyone at once.
5. **"Centralization of credit in the hands of the state, by means of a national bank with state capital and an exclusive monopoly."**
   It is obvious if all property will be confiscated, the banks have to be included. But this is more far reaching: with the power of the banks, all other institutions or persons in the country can be watched and controlled.
6. **"Centralization of the means of communications and transportation in the hands of the state."**
   This is one of the prime techniques for controlling the masses. Without transportation and communications systems, people are forced to live in a very small world, one that is limited to where you can go via bicycle. Further, subjugated people and the world only knows what the communist government reports.
7. **"Extension of factories and instruments of production owned by the state, the bringing into cultivation of waste lands, and the improvement of the soil generally in accordance with a common plan."**
   This plank teaches comrade leaders to expect all the industries to fail, so that agricultural production will be the main work, which will also keep a limited supply of food flowing within the country. That also prepares for the new era of Sustainable agriculture or self-sufficiency.
8. **"Equal liability for all to labor and the establishment of industrial armies, especially for agriculture."**
   Here communism is teaching everyone that agricultural work is most important to provide the food everyone needs. The plank

also teaches how to create armies of workers from students, housewives, and other groups.

I know how this worked in Cuba. After Castro took over, thousands of students, housewives, and others were forced to work in the sugar cane fields to increase sugar output.

9. **"Combination of agriculture with manufacturing industries, gradual abolition of the distinction between town and country, by a more equitable distribution of population over the country."**

   For the communist system this plank teaches reducing the big populations in cities, and to spread people to the agricultural zone, and also teaches how to convert a capitalist society to a self-sustaining communist society. In a free society culture like we have in America, it would be impossible to make this to work.

10. **"Free education for all children in public schools and abolition of child factory labor in its present form. Combine education and industrial production."**

    This plank requires that every child be indoctrinated with the communist ideology—pure propaganda. Communists teach that sending an army of school children to pick tomatoes is different than child labor doing other tasks. They explain that the child's tomato picking is patriotism rather than labor; it's clearly a way to camouflage slavery to all ages.

Sadly, there are literally thousands of people throughout both North and South America who are willing to do whatever is necessary to enhance and expand communism. We could easily dismiss them as people who have been *brainwashed,* but many believe that the end justifies the means, no matter how harsh is the process.

Meanwhile, there are those in the middle and upper social classes totally unwilling to sacrifice in any way because they need time to earn, spend and enjoy their money.

Conquering these upper classes in a more informed era is why communism stealthily creates changes, which seem good and compassionate. These include passing laws and resolutions that redistribute wealth, regulate medicine and industry, cite unsupported environmental studies to control production, and rewrite school curriculum for children. Do you recognize the technique? This isn't happening in some far off land; it's occurring daily right here in the heartland of the United States of America. [C2-1]

The methods exposed here are the same that communist leaders employ to make themselves super human beings in the minds of vulnerable and impressionable citizens, especially youngsters—the same indoctrination tactic used in every communist country in the world. Children are programmed to idolize the leaders, no matter how corrupt the government may be. And, while the younger generations are getting indoctrinated, the leaders are continually developing complex plans to lead the country into catastrophe.

Meanwhile, the majority of Americans are doing nothing but sitting like a flock of pigeon waiting for the death and destruction that is to follow an American Communist Apocalypse.

WWW.SASO2016.COM (Save America Save Ourselves

Our SASO2016 organization's effort to combat this inactivity and lack of attention, includes our website to investigate where America is heading, and how likely we are to get there. Common sense messages without hysteria and down-to-earth solutions will be used to tell the truth about communism and its threat to our American way of life. We will use any and all techniques and tools available to fight this evil.

Without using fancy words, or empty rhetoric, or histrionics, www.saso2016.com uses clear English understandable in every classroom in the country. Visitors will learn how communism operates, expands, attacks, and indoctrinates. We will expose how people under communism are forced to behave and live, and how the communist doctrine is continually spread.

SASO2016.com uses attention-getting videos, reports, and documentation to expose, trace, and report the history and accomplishments of communism. We are developing state-of-the-art virtual classrooms that will appeal to both children and adults. We will supply a new avenue for information that up to this point has been denied to the American people by the education department.

In fact, while it is still under construction, we already have the domain name: *www.saso2016.com*. Please make a note of it.

On this dynamic Internet site, we will show visitors how evil and downright destructive communism can be, not with a bunch of words, but with facts extracted from materials produced by organizations with the highest reputations for honesty and ethical behavior.

Frankly, no one else is telling the stories and providing the background information that we intend to present. You will learn about things that happen every day in our country that never get reported and yet have important implications for our future and the future of our children and grandchildren.

These are both exciting and scary times for all of us. Events, which take place in far off lands, can have an impact on us, to say nothing of the events in our own country. But, if we know nothing about these incidents and their implications, how do we know what is likely to come? How do we know how to act, react, or protect ourselves?

We are working to expose hundreds of laws that intentionally have been enacted to impact the economy, make us dependant on foreign oil, disable our industries, indoctrinate our kids, demoralize our younger generations, and confuse the general public. We are going to reveal how much money communist organizations are getting, how they are spending that money, and what we can do to stop them.

When things are going well and there are no problems, we'll let you know that. But, if things are dark and likely to be difficult, we'll report that as well and offer action guidelines for you to consider. At this time, we are very concerned that if some major changes are not made soon, we could be in for a very dark period ahead in America.

America was established of the people, by the people, and for the people, and it is up to us to make sure our leaders enact laws that are constitutional, and then to enforce them. We will be teaching how to have a strong voice through referendums, and how to organize them and put them into practice.

Saso2016.com will assist citizens in understanding what we need to do as concerned and informed individuals. Through up-to-the-minute information, experienced reporting, and testimonial forums, we will invite readers to report and document what they have seen and heard to help everyone better understand what is happening from a person-to-person perspective.

If you discover that anything on our site has somehow disappeared or been corrupted, please let us know and we will take steps to correct and restore whatever is missing or changed.

I am comfortable doing what I am committed to do because I am a totally free man. I am not the fruit of any university or college; college, but yet I am a successful American businessman. I am not heavily influenced by any culture since by age 18 I was already living in a different country from my parents, and during my lifetime, I have lived in four different countries.

I am not stuck in the mold of any particular religion although I consider myself a born-again Christian. I began life as a Catholic, but in the 1980's I joined and was very active in the Southern Baptist Church. So I believe that I am therefore able to learn, judge and teach without external influences.

In over 49 years of experience and studies battling this poison factory known as communism, I am at the point where I can assess things from a truly neutral point of view. When you can separate yourself from prejudice, hate, mind conditioning, doctrines, and religions, you can judge without bias; you can guide without hatred; you can teach without brainwashing; and you can preach without dogma. In this circumstance, I believe that I can understand life and many of its complexities.

I accept the idea of being a bridge for Americans, and an avenue of information about communism and communist threats throughout the world. I'll do this through the SASO2016 Cultural Foundation, which will hopefully guide good citizens to lives of prosperity, love, and understanding of all others.

We must each seek to keep our nation the way our founding fathers wanted: retaining the original ideas of freedom and progress for Americans. Each of us must work to eradicate communism from our land. Communists are tyrannical, irresponsible, dishonest, and dissatisfied with how our system operates, and they are out to destroy American society piece by piece.

Their goal for America is to take it apart, to conquer it, to enslave it, and to ruin it. Our goal must be to stop them from succeeding. Whoever wants it the most and is not afraid to do what is necessary to fight will be the victor.

I vividly remember when I arrived in this great country. I soon learned how great living here could be, and how wonderful the American people of every race, religion, and ethnicity really are. The very thought of losing this paradise is inconceivable to me, and should be to you.

CHAPTER 6

Communism In America

Americans have to be some of the most benevolent and naive people on the face of the earth. They will quickly mobilize to help anyone anywhere that has problems; yet, at the same time, they will ignore some of the most obvious anti-American activities.

The majority believes that communism died after the fall of the Berlin Wall and the Iron Curtain was removed. The ironic truth is that communists have just switched tactics because they have a planned agenda to communize the *entire world*, including the United States of America.

Sadly, Washington D.C. is becoming just another of the New World Order of atheist governments. With the last remnants of Christian law being removed from our public way of life over the past two decades, we are no longer a threat or force against communism. Too many of our American citizens believe the lies and half truths, and have helped to elect leaders who publicly applaud the "fall of communism," while quietly selling out our country to anti-Christian, anti-American, and solidly communist agendas.

Nikita Khrushchev—"We Will Bury You"

In the 1960's, many will remember former Soviet Premier, Nikita Khrushchev (1894–1971), as he pounded his shoe on his desk in the United Nations General Assembly and shouted to the West, "We will bury you." Fearing an invasion from the Reds, the U.S. built the most awesome military machine in recorded history.

Unfortunately, we forgot to protect our home front from being taken over internally by socialist-communist-liberal activists. While we were concentrating on the Soviets, homegrown communists were busy gaining political offices and working to destroy America's freedoms and ideals by the slow but sure process of gradually installing the communist programs within our legal system and all branches of government.

Khrushchev clearly spelled out his sinister communist plans. Read and digest what the former Russian leader said about you. *"We can't expect the American people to jump from capitalism to communism, but we can assist their elected leaders in giving them small doses of socialism, until they awaken one day to find that they have communism."* You are already getting those doses now, but they *will* get larger as the days go by.

Since the Bolshevik revolution of 1917 imposed communism in the Soviet Union, the United States became the refuge for anyone forced to flee from any communist country around the world. This brought the U.S. a new bourgeois class that has been assimilated and provided another source of ingenuity and growth that has helped bring about more of an American growth boom and an era of greater prosperity.

But this American progress also created a sense of envy and hatred in the entire communist population around the world. They despise our high standard of living and absolute freedom because it is the complete opposite of communist barbarism. Since there really isn't much negative information that they can cite about the U.S., they revert to criticism based on misinformation in slanted articles and biased news to defame and denigrate the United States.

With a constant drumbeat of big lies told over the years, they have succeeded in creating a dislike of anything American, including the people. Anti-capitalists have promoted such an atmosphere of aversion to us that it may be considered anti-social to even speak in positive terms about America.

Propaganda Pressure

The propaganda pressure has been so intense through the World Communist Media that many nations have forgotten how the United States has always been a global leader in contributing to mankind's well being. Those contributions include tens of thousands of inventions and innovations in electricity, aviation, communication, transportation, computers, industry, technology, medicine, and finance.

But the most important contribution to mankind has been the nearly 633,000 American lives that have been lost in a variety of wars since the Civil War. Mostly, they were defending nations around the world from communism and Nazism. Brave American heroes are buried all over the globe.

Julia Gillard, the Australian Prime Minister, gave a speech to Congress on March 10, 2011, which demonstrated how grateful Australia was, is, and will always be with America. Every country in the world should feel the same:

> "There is a reason the world always looks to America. Your great dream – life, liberty and the pursuit of happiness – inspires us all. Australia's darkest days in the last century followed the fall of Singapore in 1942. And you were with us. Under attack in the Pacific, we fought together. Side by side, step by bloody step. And while it was Australian soldiers at Milne Bay who gave the Allies our first victory on land in the Pacific War, it was American sailors at the Battle of the Coral Sea who destroyed the fear of an invasion of Australia."

In all the countries we have saved, we have only requested enough land to bury our fatalities. This is in complete contrast to what communists do when they take over a country; they ruin the country's economy, kill millions of citizens, and enslave billions of people in their quest to dominate the world with their totalitarian system.

In the 1970's, the poison factory developed a comprehensive plan to occupy and destroy our country. The scheme called for a massive invasion of our society disguised as socialists, leftists, progressives, liberals, and anything other than the title of communists. They had been studying the American society for decades. They formulated an idea of what made Americans so strong and united.

Their idea was built on Stalin's statement, "America is like a healthy body and its resistance is three-fold: its patriotism, its morality and its spiritual life. If we can undermine these three areas, America will collapse from within." Knowing how to combat Americans, all they needed was a well-designed plan to accomplish their goal of conquest.

They translated into English the 3,000 pages of notes of the Marxist Antonio Gramsci (1891–1937) an Italian writer, politician, political theorist, linguist and philosopher, who wrote the concept of cultural hegemony (dominance of one state over another.)

He came to his conclusion through his studies that Christian's societies are hard to penetrate, especially the Christian working class, a class that is vulnerable in other religions. He developed a systematic cultural transformation through the education (brainwashing and programming) of the young generation. Gramsci's formula for informal education lies in three realms.

First, his exposition of the notion of hegemony provided a way of understanding the context in which informal educators function, and thus offered the possibility of critique and transformation.

Second, the role of organic intellectuals deepened the understanding of the role of informal educators.

Third, his interest in schooling and more traditional forms of education stressed the need of not dismissing the more traditional forms.

Gramsci's analysis went much further than any previous Marxist theory to provide an understanding of why the working class had on the whole failed to develop revolutionary consciousness, but instead moved towards reformism i.e. tinkering with the system rather than working towards overthrowing it.

Christianity: Communism's Major Roadblock

They learned that they have to break down the Christian ideological bond, and then build up counter hegemony to that of Christian ruling class. They had to see structural change and ideological change as part of the same struggle. The labor process was at the core of the class struggle but it was the ideological struggle that had to be addressed if the mass of the people were to come to a consciousness that allowed them to question their political and religious masters' right to rule.

It was popular consensus in civil society that had to be challenged and in this we can see a role for informal social education. The communist saw the role of the intellectual as a crucial one in the context of creating counter hegemony.

We know it happened in our universities, where they had created hundreds of thousands of new intellectuals, and their effect in the media, unions, school systems, movies, television, radio, and political system. The task was to demoralize our society through informal education filled with lies to control the public mind by directing our parameters of thought.

They had the power to make the people believe that homosexuality, pornography, abortion and lawlessness is okay, while Christianity and God are myths that the bourgeois class use to exploit the masses.

Since the late seventies, the poison factory made extensive use of media pressure throughout the world. With editorial criticism, attacks, riots, strongly biased articles, and slanted TV and radio news stories, they succeeded in stopping the Vietnam War. Of course, we lost the fight but, more importantly, we also lost the will and power to battle against communism. The communist movement had already deeply influenced our youth with their ideology and began separating them from their Christian roots.

Communism's new class of intellectuals learned to manipulate the American system, the people, our political system, and even the government to further their agenda and to intimidate our leaders. All of it was part of the same extensive and well-thought-out master plan from that malevolent force: what President Ronald Reagan called, "The Evil Empire."

At the end of World War II, many of the western world's people wanted the U.S. to become a world leader by establishing an American system in their countries; we were admired in those days.

Unfortunately, the U.S. fell short in taking advantage of the occasion and as a result, lost a golden opportunity to change the world for the better.

A survey conducted in 2004 among students between 13 and 15 years old found that fully 70% have negative opinions about the American political and financial systems. In another survey last year, we learned that even in a close, friendly country like Canada to our north, more than half of the citizens dislike us.

It's a result of that same *extensive and well-thought-out master plan* that uses the incessant flood of communist propaganda against our American system. At the end of World War II, America had the best global opinion, but since the late 1960's this new communist technique has had tremendous negative results for us.

"Turning the Other Cheek?"

Too often, Christians face attacks by "turning the other cheek," forgetting that God's people were sometimes sent out to defend themselves and to punish evildoers. For example, in I Samuel 15 beginning in verse 1, the prophet Samuel spoke to King Saul saying, *"I am the one the LORD sent to anoint you king over his people Israel; so listen now to the message from the LORD. This is what the LORD Almighty says: 'I will punish the Amalekites for what they did to Israel when they waylaid them as they came up from Egypt. Now go, attack the Amalekites and totally destroy everything that belongs to them. Do not spare them; put to death men and women, children and infants, cattle and sheep, camels and donkeys.' "*

God was not ordering the destruction of unbelievers as Muslims claim their god, Allah, commands. Rather, the God of our fathers took revenge on those who came *against His chosen people.* Blinded enemies of modern Israel have still not learned that lesson yet. Nations who disrespect Israel have suffered swift defeat and terrible natural disasters. Today, America's leadership is putting our country in the same danger.

God-fearing leaders founded America, and this country has been the major source of sending the gospel to all nations. Would our God abandon the people who are doing His work in this critical period before the return of Christ? Would He deny our people the right to defend our lives and property against the evil of the godless? I think not.

At the end of World War II, many of the western world's people wanted the U.S. to become a world leader by establishing an American system in their countries; we were admired in those days. Unfortunately, the U.S. fell short in taking advantage of the occasion and as a result, lost a golden opportunity to change the world for the better.

In fact, we must learn to measure and respond to our enemies with God as our strength and hope, even as they measure and respond to us. We must reverse the adverse opinions and the negative results created outside our borders, but not by spreading money around, but with good foreign policies that bring about world stability and prosperity.

Empty Promises, Broken Treaties

Leaders of the three superpowers, President Franklin D. Roosevelt (1882–1945) for the USA, Winston Churchill (1874–1965) for England, and Josef Stalin for the U.S.S.R., signed a peace pact that included provisions those countries that had been invaded by the Red Army would be allowed to have elections. Then the Red Army would restore power to the elected officials and withdraw. Of course, this never happened, as with so many of its other treaties and agreements, the communists never complied with their promises.

Unfortunately, U.S. leaders sat back, closed their eyes to world events, and allowed the evil poison factory to continue on its course. Our leaders totally ignored the warnings of hero General George S. Patton, Jr. (1885–1945), who said it would be a huge mistake to allow the *real* enemy (the Soviet Union) to continue on its path of world domination. Patton correctly predicted that after the common threat of Nazi Germany was defeated, the Soviets would cease to be an American ally.

He was alarmed that some 25,000 American POWs had been freed from Nazi prison camps by the Soviets, yet were never repatriated to the U.S. He strongly urged his superiors to evict the

Soviets from central and Eastern Europe while the Red Army was weak, under-supplied, and vulnerable. He said the U.S. should take advantage of those weaknesses before the Soviets could get reorganized.

He told Undersecretary of War, Robert P. Patterson (1891–1952), the "three point system" used to demobilize the Third Army was destroying it: creating a vacuum that the Soviets would quickly exploit.

General Patton is quoted as saying, "Mr. Secretary, for God's sake, when you go home, stop this point system; stop breaking up these armies. Let's keep our boots polished, bayonets sharpened, and present a picture of force and strength to these people, the Soviets. This is the only language they understand."

Patterson, who became Secretary of War a few months later, asked Patton what he would do. Patton's response was quick and sharp: "I would have you tell the Red Army where their border is, and give them a limited time to get back across. Warn them that if they fail to do so, we will push them back across it."

In 1945 when Patton died, the United States lost its only leader who correctly saw the world reality of the times. The Soviets not only failed to withdraw from the occupied countries, but they also continued enslaving millions of citizens, building their evil empire, unscrupulously destroying national economies, and killing anyone who got in their way.

At the same time that they were becoming the world's second superpower to rival the United States, their own people were suffering from persecution, oppression, humiliation, famine, and poverty. Nearly 60 million people died while the Soviets were showing the world that they were a victorious, noble, and prosperous country.

After World War II, the USA tried many times to stop this immoral ideology, but communism continued to spread through countries by force. A few successes were accomplished in the reuniting of Germany, and in the liberating of the Chinese island of Formosa, the Dominican Republic and Granada. In Korea, the USA was halfway successful, but the Vietnam War was the first frustrated attempt by USA forces to stop this evil ideology from expanding further.

The Enemy Within

For the first time after the World War II, communist militants inside America were able to manipulate American citizens and successfully intimidate our leaders. They learned that they have to fight this war from inside their worst enemy, the USA. Demoralizing our society, corrupting our political leaders, brain washing our young people, weakening our economy, and making United States dependent on foreign oil became their goals. Looking back, it's unbelievable how much progress they have made.

Within our borders today they have over 2,100 non-profit organizations with millions of communist followers 100% devoted to their cause; shockingly, and the vast majority of them are being paid by taxpayers' money. They have thousands of our teachers and college professors corrupting our young people, creating a leftist way of thinking, and producing a culture of conformity and dependency where the ideal citizenship qualities are to serve the State.

Meanwhile, other teachers and professors are simply confused. Thousands of news reporters and television anchor people are twisting the news and fabricating rumors further confusing Americans. All this discord and upheaval is discouraging and intimidating our political leaders and supporting their communist comrades.

Tens of thousands of other communists are at work in unions, universities, and in the government. They write books, draft laws, and organize protests that are meant to further confuse the general population. There are thousands that are being paid to work for the United States interests, but are, instead, striving to convert capitalism to communism.

Along with the efforts of their Communist World Media Pressure they are attacking our very way of life in order to accomplish their agenda. Among them are even sitting members of the U.S. House of Representatives and the Senate.

The Fall of the Soviet Union.

Still the dangers persist. In the 1980's when the Soviet socialist system was defeated, its indoctrinated people didn't disappear; they spread out, reformed, and started to multiply again. Moving to different positions, they made corrections to their mistakes, began to recruit new people, and further developed their master plan for a world government—the New World Order.

One of their major accomplishments was to convince unsuspecting people throughout the world that the threat of communism had been eradicated and the Iron Curtain torn asunder. Nothing could be further from the truth.

Their tactics worked very efficiently. By the year 2000 communism was again spreading and thriving throughout the world. People, who at the end of World War II viewed the United States as a shining example of humility, honesty, and humbleness, now saw us as an evil, dominating, and dishonest power manipulating and corrupting the rest of the world.

Here in America the communists have grown stronger and are intimidating those who have the courage to do or say anything against their malevolence. They are steadily corrupting our moral values and are influencing the way we raise and teach our children.

They are strategically positioned in schools, universities, and government agencies such as OSHA, the Environmental Protection Agency, and other important locations where they easily can plan, attack, and confuse our good intentions. They are able to flood the American public with distrust, demoralization, and dishonesty, all produced by Communist World Media Pressure.

Americans In Name Only?

When people like the junior U.S. Senator from Minnesota, Democrat Alan "Al" Franken, and the 45th Vice President of the United States, Democrat Albert "Al" Gore, protest against drilling oil wells to preserve our environment, what they really are doing is keeping America dependant on foreign oil which is weakening our economy.

Remember, communists don't need our economic system; they are after our country, our army, and the overall control of the

American people. For that, everyone has to be broken spiritually, mentally and financially. Only after the population has been rendered poor and penniless, and without transportation or communication, can they oppress a nation. When that happens, it is too late to stop them.

When a person like the retired bishop of the Episcopal Diocese of Newark, NJ, liberal theologian, John Shelby Spong, criticizes the bible and calls for a fundamental rethinking of Christian beliefs, the goal appears to be to try and confuse believers and followers by creating doubt.

When liberals attack Wal-Mart, the most successful retailer in the country today, they are attempting to create economic instability while at the same time generating hatred against capitalism and our free enterprise system.

When people like liberal Hollywood actor, Warren Beatty or any other well-known personality protests to protect illegal immigrants, they are looking to increase our population with people easy to manipulated and indoctrinate.

When people like filmmaker Michael Moore or film director and screenwriter Oliver Stone make movies mocking our conservative presidents or patriots like General Patton, they are teaching disrespect. They have the right to air their pet peeves, living in a free country, but they are using their bully pulpit to destroy that very right for others.

Communists want Americans to view themselves through the lenses of those who hate them. They want Americans to be far less confident, leading to an inevitable culture of conformity and dependency. They want a country in which ideal citizenship qualities are to serve the state; where the individual has no uniqueness or feeling of self-worth. At the same time, they project a false display of human compassion, which is a far cry from what they really are.

I see them being as successful at doing in the United States what they did in the Soviet Union, China, Vietnam, Cambodia, Laos, Hungary, Romania, Yugoslavia, Iraq, Iran, North Korea, Angola, Nicaragua, some African countries, Cuba, and Venezuela. They always portray such an air of caring for the purported downtrodden, and, sadly, many believe they are truly sincere.

Don't doubt me when I say from personal experience, that these are the very same people that, once they gain power, will oppress you, step on you, and kill you. Communism says, "Ignore what is behind the curtain," else you see the bodies of the 94 million human beings that they killed after taking over country after country.

In each of these "workers' paradises," the common man has no voice, no rights, and no freedom at all. It's where independent thinking is non-existent for people who then become dependent on the government. The conquered nation becomes a land where the citizens are hungry and miserable, and where the *pursuit of happiness* is but a faded memory.

Where is the love of country we used to have? Unfortunately, it has been destroyed by the communist mass propaganda and indoctrination techniques. Even President Barack Obama has demonstrated that he has a bad opinion about America.

When movies and computer games are made in which the bad guys are the heroes and succeed in doing evil, then the wrong impression is conveyed to our younger generation and it helps to further damage society for the future. Communism needs a corrupted society to control with their godless ideology.

Whenever false and biased stories are spread through the media that portray a communist nation or a communist leader in a positive light, then the uninformed are being programmed to disbelieve in the American system. This is especially true in the mind of a younger generation that only knows reality through a state controlled media. Socialism is seen as balanced, and capitalism is pictured as unfair.

A recent example was when Michael Moore did his phony report about how good health care is in Cuba. In truth, he reported on the one and only hospital in the whole country that is up to U.S. standards. He tried to show how good communism is while insinuating that other reports about the reality of Cuban health care were lies. He was referring to reports from our own government and unbiased TV stations that had dared to tell what Cuba is really like since Castro took power.

We can no longer allow our society to swallow this poison. It is going to take brave Christian people to return to the teaching about the strength and goodness of the American way as founded by our forefathers and established under our constitution.

In recent years, the U.S. has fought a number of conflicts. The most critical of them were Vietnam and Iraq because both countries were essentially communist regimes. What happened in those two wars?

The World Communist Media stopped the Vietnam War, and, through criticism of the Iraq War, crippled the White House and its decision-making abilities. The pressure of so much criticism from the left-leaning media was designed to sicken Americans with daily reports about killing, bombing, and alleged mistakes made by the Bush administration. That style of biased news is rarely heard when liberals are in control of the government.

In Chicago, before becoming President, Barack Obama received $49 million in grants to help improve neighborhoods. Incredibly, there were more people killed in Chicago street shootings and gang related activities than died in the Iraq War during the same time period. Why was it that none in the media reported on all the Chicago deaths, not even most conservative reporters?

Isn't it becoming more and more obvious how strong this poison factory and the World Communist Media Pressure really are? Their propaganda and persuasive abilities are so strong that they even dictate what our own conservatives can say and do.

In November of 2010, the Obama administration imposed a very restrictive process for checking people through security at airports in the U.S. This relatively minor irritation conveniently appeared in time to divert public attention away from the unparalleled momentum that the Republicans had gained in the election.

If the present administrations really cared about our security, why do they still leave the Mexican border wide open at many places where there are no security checkpoints? Why are they taking Arizona to court for trying to close off the flow of illegals into America? The majority of U.S. citizens are aware that radical Islamic terrorists have used the wide-open Mexican border for more attacks on the United States. The following video reference is from a Muslim leader detailing how radical Islamists are planning to bring terrorist material into the country through the open borders.[C3-1]

For many years Saddam Hussein was a principal supporter of the leftist rallies, riots, and communist movements throughout the world. Even after his death by execution, he is one reason why more than 2 million Muslims have been and are being indoctrinated with hatred for the U.S. Those millions of terrorists, essentially communists disguised as followers of Islam, are continuing to work and devote their lives to their hateful cause of death and destruction.

Saddam Hussein should have been killed or Iraq invaded 20 years earlier, but ignoring the threat for two decades was yet another mistake by our American leaders. The 3,000 victims of 911 are only one proof of our leadership failing to keep their solemn oath to protect and defend America.

The ruling majority of American public figures are afraid to take offensive action because the enemy has had so much success creating panic in our leaders, our political figures, and our government officials. Others are confused by socialism and simply turn a blind eye as our country is being sold into slavery. As for me, I'm a believer in James O'Keefe's technique of using the communists' own tactics against them. He has proven by the downfall of ACORN that it works. In order to take back our country before it is too late, we also have to equally counter the communist agenda while staying within our moral boundary:

- We must intimidate their leaders by exposing their real agenda.
- We must teach our youth the true, positive and patriotic way of living in a free American system.
- We must instruct our younger generations on the radical differences between Christian society, and a communist society.
- We must change bad laws and support organizations that combat the evil of communism.
- We need to support organizations or countries that agree and collaborate with us in our efforts to overcome communism.

While America was founded on Christian principles, our country has welcomed other religions to freely worship. How then has our core belief in the God of our fathers been relegated to the dust bin by so many, while others, some preaching our destruction, are given control much of our thoughts and actions?

The removal of prayer in public venues, the attack against Christian symbols and holidays, the criticizing of Jesus Christ and His followers are all intended to foster disbelief. The biggest problem is that they have been very successful in changing America's way of thinking; how we look at political figures, the way we believe in God, and the faith we have in our guiding principles.

Liberals who are able to make conservatives look like the bad guys will often win among the uniformed, the followers of socialism, the illegal aliens, and those who believe they are entitled to be taken care of by the taxpayers.

Our children must be taught how the people under communism live and how much they suffer. They must be shown that, in contrast, America is a land of compassion and understanding. The truth is that we represent the strong family structure and unity, while the communists represent hatred, hunger, and slavery. Moral religion is based on love; material religion is based on greed, power and hate. Christians are givers—Communists are always takers.

Americans and other freedom-loving people of the world have to learn how to fight back, how to protect our moral principles, and how to preserve our honor and our way of life. If conservatives don't stand and fight this evil force, our problems with communism will not only continue, they will expand and get worse.

The United States has to be careful about getting caught up in wars. Some trouble areas of the world are stirred up in order to get us involved in a conflict in which we can never be victorious.

When we send our soldiers into battle and they take casualties, the World Communist Media propaganda that follows makes our population vulnerable to their cause through confusion and division. Their agenda is always to make conservatives look bad, and to confuse the masses.

We have to know what kind of evil people we are dealing with, and after we understand how they operate, we must use their same propaganda tactics against them.

We have the technology, and the military power to silence any menace against America in any part of the world. That being true, all we really have to do is follow the example that Ronald Reagan did with Muammar al-Qaddafi. Reagan's mere threat to have Qaddafi killed, silenced the dictator for over 40 years. The threat was done completely in the open, without any cover up or concerns for world opinion.

Our leaders must, in the same way, let the world know that we will not stand for the kind of disrespect we have received from Chavez of Venezuela, Kim Yong-IL of North Korea, and Mahmoud Ahmadinejad of Iran. Only then will we be shown the respect that we have earned. Even so, we still have to be ready and willing to act without regard to world opinion that will always be manipulated by the Communist World Media Pressure.

Hollywood vs America

The constant bombardment of communist propaganda by the movie and television industry has caused many American families to lose their beliefs, their moral foundations, and their basic family solidarity.

In his book *Hollywood vs. America*, radio personality, Michael Medved, makes this observation:

> "America's long-running romance with Hollywood is over. As a nation, we no longer believe that popular culture enriches our lives. Few of us view the show, 'Business Capital' as a magical source of uplifting entertainment, romantic inspiration, or even harmless fun. Instead, tens of millions of Americans now see the entertainment industry as an all-powerful enemy, an alien force that assaults our most cherished values and corrupts our children. The dream factory has become the poison factory."

That poison factory and alien force that Mr. Medved mentioned in his book is what I see as becoming so widespread that you can find it in every corner of American society.

If we don't unite and do something about it soon, the American dream will quickly become the American nightmare. We have to recognize that we have a dangerous enemy within our borders. This adversary will never stop trying to destroy us, corrupt our society, and ruin our economy. We have an obligation to our future generations and ourselves to eradicate this poison factory from our country as completely and as soon as possible.

In the 1960's and 1970's, American communists established their revolutionary presence on a number of different fronts. For example, Students for a Democratic Society (SDS) was one of the first such organizations. The student communist movement in the United States was the main front organization here for the communist party. They flooded college campuses around the country in search of new members, ostensibly to protest the Vietnam War, a timely and convenient cause for them.

Another of their organizations was known as the Weather Underground. Cloaked in anti-imperialist, feminist, and Black Liberationist rhetoric, the group conducted a campaign of bombings through mid-1970. They aided in the jailbreak and escape of psychedelic drug advocate Timothy Leary (1920–1996). The Weathermen's first public demonstration held on October 8, 1969, was called "Days of Rage," which turned into a riot in Chicago.

The group even issued a "Declaration of a State of War" against the United States government. They were responsible for bomb attacks targeting government buildings, along with several banks. Their targets were to have included the bombings of the United States Capitol, on March 1, 1971, the Pentagon on May 19, 1972, and the Department of State Building on January 29, 1975.

The organization known as "The Revolutionary Youth Movement" (RYM) was a faction of SDS. The name was also the title of a position paper they distributed at an SDS convention in Chicago in 1969 calling for a "white fighting force" to be allied with the "Black Liberation Movement" and other radical groups to "destroy

United States imperialism and achieve a classless society." Interesting terminology used by the communist ideology all around the world.

Among the founders of the RYM were political organizer Mark Rudd, and Bernardine Dohrn, the former leader of the Weather Underground. Dohrn was also the former director of Northwestern University's Children and Family Justice Center, and is currently an Associate Professor of Law at Northwestern.

Other founders include William "Bill" Ayers, husband of Dohrn, co-founder of the Weather Underground (and a close friend of President Obama); John Jacobs (1947–1997), an anti-war activist who advocated the use of violence to overthrow the U.S. government; Terry Robbins (1947–1970), a radical leftist activist who led the first militant student uprising at Kent State University in 1968; and Jeff Jones, an environmental activist, and a leader of the Weather Underground. Most of the living founders are reportedly good friends and comrades of President Barack Obama.

After mid-970s the RYM radicals threw away their bombs and arms, and became involved in education. They advocated laws to make people government dependent, environmental laws to cripple the United States' economy, and actions to keep America reliant on foreign oil. They also began to take control of thousands of non-profit organizations.

While Jimmy Carter was president, communists in high-ranking government positions, and many left-leaning non-profit organizations were able to achieve impressive growth in the 1980's.

The communists quickly turned our institutions of higher learning into propaganda mills, used to indoctrinate hundreds of thousands of our children and thousands more professionals willing to come to the defense of their cause. In essence, they became part of this heinous plot to destroy the Christian America society and to ultimately thrust the world into a period of misery, hunger, and despair.

Liberal instructors through cultural hegemony teach socialism as a kind of heaven on earth, but in reality, socialism only delivers widespread agony and destruction as history proves.

Our federal government must be stopped from supplying taxpayer money to their organizations including public broadcasting, so called "non-profit" religions, and front associations that hide behind banners of peace, humanitarianism, environmental protection, etc.

It is past time for us to form an *army of troublemakers*, perhaps called the "Real People Pact," to do unto them as they have been doing unto us for decades. That means confronting them to remove their indoctrination materials from our schools.

At the same time, we need to make it possible for the Department of Education to teach students the truth about communism, the danger that it represents to our capitalist society, and to return Christian values to our curriculum. We need to bring back God to our government buildings and schools. In short, we need to take our country back to the way our founders intended it to be.

In the 1980's and 90's communists succeeded in getting student loans for left-leaning students, the vast majority of whom were minorities. Since then, the universities have indoctrinated hundreds of thousands of those who may never have otherwise entered their classrooms. With entitlements, comes a sense of loyalty to the donor. Tragically, few recognize that the givers are simply redistributing the wealth of those who make capitalism work.

Large numbers of professionals who have openly declared and acted upon their communist ideas have graduated from such prestigious universities as UCLA and Harvard on federal loans and grants.

Yet nobody questions why many universities are so involved in politics even as one typical institution claims to be the "Nation's guardian of liberty, working daily in courts, legislatures and communities to defend and preserve the individual rights and liberties that the Constitution and laws of the United States guarantee everyone in this country."

Clearly, we need to make it illegal for universities and other organizations to mingle in politics and at the same time receive federal grants. The question is a matter of ethics and the avoidance of a conflict of interest.

ACLU and Communism

The American Civil Liberties Union is involved in hundreds of lawsuits that tend to be anti-conservative, anti-Christian, and even anti-American. Here's a quote from ACLU founder, Roger Baldwin, "I am for socialism, disarmament, and, ultimately, for abolishing the state itself... I seek the social ownership of property, the abolition of the propertied class, and the sole control of those who produce wealth. Communism is the goal."

Letting them speak for themselves through their letters and documents reveals that they are a true communist organization in action. Even the U.S. Congress has affirmed that fact.

In 1931, just eleven years after the ACLU's inception, the US Congress convened a Special House Committee to Investigate Communist Activities. The report on the ACLU stated:

> "The American Civil Liberties Union is closely affiliated with the communist movement in the United States, and fully 90 percent of its efforts are on behalf of communists who have come into conflict with the law. It claims to stand for free speech, free press and free assembly, but it is quite apparent that the main function of the ACLU is an attempt to protect the communists."

Noted author Paul Kengor has unearthed declassified letters and other documents in the Soviet Comintern archives linking early leaders of the ACLU with the Communist Party.

Kengor found a May 23, 1931 letter in the archives signed by ACLU founder Roger Baldwin, written on ACLU stationery, to then American Communist Party Chairman William Z. Foster asking him to help ACLU Chairman Harry Ward with an upcoming trip to Stalin's Russia.

The letter suggests that Ward intended to visit the Soviet Union to find "evidence from Soviet Russia" that would undermine the capitalist profit motive.

Today the communists have over two thousand non-profit organizations using socialistic indoctrination tactics in nearly every aspect of our society, all disguised behind communist doublespeak as they claim they are involved in humanitarian causes.

Communism's main goal has always been to seize control of America, the only country with the strength and morals to wreck their global ambitions. This nation of freedom and prosperity represents the complete opposite of everything they stand for.

Their well-planned communist agenda began in the 1970's after the visit of the Soviet Union leader Nikita Khrushchev to America. Meeting with American communist leaders, and using their knowledge of our laws, our tolerant freedoms, and the innate compassion of our people, Khrushchev and his advisors' masterminded the takeover plot and encourage American Communist leaders to use Antonio Gramsci "cultural hegemony," to change the American society ideology...

They began with the elimination of overt protests and terrorist activity inside America. The idea was to remove attention from the socialist movement, and to lull American into a sense of peace. That paved the way to implementing the next steps of develops a systematic culture transformation.

1) **Arranging Free Education and Indoctrination.** Since the seventies many universities started providing free scholarships for leftist leaning students including many of the minorities. By the nineties the expenditure on education through grants and donations multiplied 600 times. Hundreds of thousands of young people have been indoctrinated with taxpayer money.
2) **Demoralizing American Society:**
   - First they attacked the family by claiming that disciplining and punishing our children caused mental and emotional trauma. Driving a wedge between parents and the younger generation would prepare the youth as candidates ripe for socialist ideology.
   - Second, they promoted violence, immorality and other depravity through the movie and TV industry, and in our schools.

- Third, they "legislated legal" rights for young people in homes and schools. Under the threat of law, parents and educators began losing control over our children.
- Fourth, they began promoting a culture of disobedience and cruelty through the "legalizing" of abortions and the use of pornography.
- Fifth, they "normalized" homosexuality, a massive attack on the nuclear family and on natural relationships between male and female.
- Sixth, they created an anti-religious bias among the young generation. Without a moral or family-based compass, the youth would look to communist teachers and leaders for guidance.

3) **Elimination of Christian Fundamentals**. They began in the seventies to form pseudo Christian churches to distort Biblical beliefs concerning God, Jesus, family, sin, and morality. They attacked prayer, religious ceremony, and the display of monuments and statues. The teaching of Christian beliefs and values were banned from education, while beliefs of other cultures, false sciences like the Darwinist theory were made a key part of the curriculum. The purpose was to confuse believers, distort the family structure, and encourage the acceptance of sin as being a normal part of life.
4) **Changing and Legislating new laws.** They use environmentalists to impede American progress by:
   - Blocking domestic oil drilling (keeping us dependent on unstable foreign oil)
   - Increasing the cost of manufacturing goods
   - Creating shortages leading to eventual inflation
   - Using agricultural products to make fuel instead of food
   - Diverting taxpayer money to fund thousands of communist organizations
   - Obstruct the construction of pipelines, businesses, and communities

- Using fake global warming science to gouge and control the economy. This and similar legislation, often disguised as humanitarian, is really designed to confuse, to create docile dependency and conformity, to recruit minority and illegal voters through entitlements and amnesty, and to maintain power over our citizens.

6) **Corrupting the Political System**. Working to elect their own socialist candidates, communists have grown in power to make and change laws through congress, and to get funding for their organizations, but with the addition of the White House, they have been able to corrupt and undermine all three branches of government: executive, legislative, and even the judicial through liberal judges.

The ultimate goal is to bankrupt America by causing an economic depression and political instability until capitalism is destroyed and the people are subjugated.

Ronald Reagan's strong leadership forced a huge set back in their plans and resulted in the breakup of the Soviet Union. Nevertheless, thanks to enormous amounts of money generated by American-based communists from alleged non-profit organizations, grants, donations and forced contributions, the leadership was shifted to the underground, and the New World Order (NWO) was advanced—all with American taxpayer money.

Over the last 35 years, the United Nations, the World Bank, *The Bilderberg Group, NGO's* (Non-Governmental Organizations) and many other world groups have been getting stronger with the addition of manpower and funding from America. More and more world leaders have joined up, and, today, most of the royal families belong to the NWO and the Bilderberg Group. These self-styled elites are convinced that the world has to unite and change, falling right into the agenda developed and established by the communists.

Since 1970's the communists in American have taken control of many non-profit organizations. Reportedly, they operate over 2,100 non-profit organizations such as with acronyms like: ACORN, CEC, AIW, WUO, WFT, UOC, RCP, PLP, MIM, AACRAO, FSP and

SEIU, to foster their socialist agenda. ACORN has more than 360 affiliate organizations to work on their communist agenda. The purposes for having these shelter organizations are:

- To have thousands of communist dedicated 100% to their cause.
- To strengthen one another while to working to elect their liberal candidates.
- To institute riots and protests, to intimidate, and to influence public opinion.
- To brainwash the leadership into passing legislation favoring their ideology.
- To establish laws that will cripple our economy.
- To intimidate religious leaders and local public officials.
- To build a standing army ready to control the population when needed.
- To payroll hundreds of part and full-time lawyers to defend criminals and terrorists, and to attack anyone that gets in their way.
- To acquire operational funds through donations and grants
- To brainwash Americans to the end that today more than half of us polled have favor opinion about socialism and/or an unfavorable opinion about the American system.

CHAPTER 7

Tools of Communism

How effective are the communists at their assignments? Remember the poll showing 62% of Americans have a favorable opinion about socialism? Consider the normalizing of homosexuality, the spreading of the abortion murders, the banning of Christianity from schools and public events, and the list goes on.

How strong are their personal attacks against conservatives? Former Republican Vice Presidential candidate Sarah Palin has had dozens of lawsuits filed against her at the time she resigned as Governor of Alaska. The intent was to make her damaged goods should she decide to challenge Obama in 2012.

Many of the communistic tactics have been honed to a fine edge over the decades. Conservatives can learn to use the left's momentum against them just as in martial arts. Instead of telling the big lie, however, we must tell the bigger truth. Rather allowing them to falsely accuse capitalism of being an evil system, we must relentlessly uncover the atrocities they have done, and expose what they really plan for our country.

The consciousness of the American people must be awakened to see how communists operate, how they have already changed our country, altered our children's behavior, influenced our churches in preaching of Word, corrupted our political system, and how they have infiltrated our legal system.

One of the techniques communists use is appearing to work on behalf of oppressed people, such as "non-whites." They are unanimously in favor of affirmative action, not because they care for the recipients, but because those who benefit from such reverse discrimination become indentured supporters of the left.

We may not be able to form thousands of organizations as they have done, but we can muster hundreds of thousands of individuals to combat their propaganda with one voice and one goal on every front.

We can introduce school curriculum materials, which will teach our children the truth about America and the truth about communism. We can encourage pastors, religious leaders, and Christian schools to teach and preach about the threat of communism.

Communism and its followers must be identified and publicly condemned for what they stand for, what they doing, and what they intend for our future. We must clearly and forcefully demand the abolition of communism in America.

According to Lisa Rosenberg and Shelly Rodgers of the American Association of Collegiate Registrars and Admissions Officers (AACRAO), one of hundreds of communist organizations supporting the University of Michigan's affirmative action policies:

> "Some 60 friends-of-the-court (amicus curiae) briefs supporting the University of Michigan's affirmative action policies have been filed by more than 300 organizations from academia, major corporations, labor unions, and by top former military and civilian officials. Such broad-based action attests to the reach of affirmative action policies across every sector and public policy issue today, reports the Chronicle of Higher Education.
>
> "On February 14, AACRAO urged its support for permitting U of Michigan to devise its own admissions policies in briefs coordinated by the American Council of Education (ACE) and filed on behalf of 54 national higher education associations. As detailed in an ACE news release, the amicus briefs argue 'first, that the preeminence of American higher education resulted from a long-held government tradition of non-interference. Second, that leaders of every type of college and university hold student diversity to be educationally valuable, and that there is ample evidence to

> support this brief. Third, that the government has a compelling interest in the quality of higher education, and by extension, diversity, and therefore should not bar the pursuit of racial and ethnic student diversity in higher education.'"

Clearly, this is a case of indoctrinating the educational system. According to the above statements, briefs, and petitions by all these organizations and interested parties, the elimination of the bourgeois class in America started a long time ago.

The middle class in America, burdened by the high cost of education, doesn't have much of a chance to register their youth in a university. Even if they apply for a grant or loan to study, they don't qualify in those universities dominated by the communists because, frankly, middle class students represent an impediment to their agenda. As a result, students admitted are frequently liberal leftists influenced by socialist indoctrination.

Look at the amount of money the government has spent in the last 30 years on education, and you can easily conclude that something is wrong. The United States does not need the number of professionals (lawyers for example) that have graduated.

The money granted to sustain indoctrination and affirmative action comes from the working taxpayers, whose children are often the ones without funding or favor to attend any university.

Further insult comes from the fact that universities are granting free or reduced scholarships to foreign students as well as minorities. A clear case of discrimination against the working middle class.

International Students and the SAT

Look at these statistics taken from the SAT Internet site: "Last year, over 200,000 students took SAT program tests in 175 countries outside the U.S. The SAT and SAT Subject Tests are offered overseas six times a year: in October, November, December, January, May, and June."

International test takers can choose from more than 1,000 international test centers listed online in the student area of the website. A list of international test centers is also provided in *The SAT Codelist, International Edition.* Listed are the SAT International Representatives who distribute test materials to test centers and students in the Middle East/North Africa, Africa, Asia, Australia, and Europe. Occasionally, supplementary test centers are opened on request where and when necessary.

It is absolutely incredible what the communists are doing in this country. Can you imagine over 1,000 international test centers set up to bring left-leaning students to this country for free education, while many bright American middle class students have the university doors slammed in their faces. Who needs those foreign freeloaders? Are they interested in learning the American way? On the contrary, they are too often set on the destruction of America.

When we compare groups of people, from a family, to a corporation, to a government, their security depends on how well they are organized, and how united they are in accomplishing their goals. When communists infiltrate the government, they create division, confrontation and laws to destabilize the country resulting in malfunctions throughout all branches of government.

From that point on the people are divided into different fractions, with each looking to follow their own agenda. That, unfortunately, is where America stands right now.

The communists want to take over and subjugate our country; Muslims want to convert us to Islam; liberal black leaders believe they can run the nation better that whites; 15 millions illegals want amnesty to become legalized Americans, and will support any party or person that will promise them citizenship, and the working class are the only ones working and paying for all this.

Conservatives of any race are attacked from all directions and feel helpless to fight as communists accuse and punish anyone for hate crimes if they protest or stand up against them. Being sued, fined, or even jailed often silences the patriot and the Christian majority.

Note that the socialist liberals are promising moderates and leftists in the different factions whatever they want in order to use them as pawns in their take over. How few realize that they are disposable after the elites win power. All this confusion and disorganization is purposefully causing disintegration of our government and the American system, literally won with blood, sweat and tears over two centuries.

Immigration is out of control; our welfare system is open to whomever wants it; our spending is no longer focused where intended or needed; our education is not based on the three "R's" but rather on programming young minds; our foreign policies are no longer aligned with our allies but are based on an ideology and master plan to dominate the world; our industries are over regulated rather than being allowed to operated in a free market system.

America is being turned upside down, which of course, is in keeping with the communist master plan. Warnings are being sounded every day, and if Americans do not act soon, we will be sitting ducks for the final coup de grâce by the communists.

This is so tragic, and even many of our conservative leaders seem to be naive about the danger to our liberty. Much of the blame falls on the communistic media, political correctness (P.C.), and our unwillingness to get involved.

Wake up, America! This is the best country in the world and one that we must not lose to the "evil empire" so aptly named by President Reagan. Take the time to view the references listed in this book and do your own additional research. America needs to be shocked awake and driven to clean house of these tyrants and parasites.

There is no other country on earth with as many freeloaders and fraudulent *non-profit* organizations per capita: it's like an epidemic. Whole segments of the population, both dedicated communists and those who are ripe to be recruited, hope to be supported by taxpayers through government entitlements and other handouts.

To buy their votes, politicians (especially liberals and moderates) spend more time looking for ways to tax producers than they do tending to their constitutional duties. The working citizen must use the time to earn a living, and has little time left to monitor what is being done to them and their freedom.

If your idea of a standard of living is above that found in those countries where the bicycle is the main transportation, standing in line for food and other necessities is a way of life, and the fear of a midnight arrest and punishment without trial exists, then join me in defeating our insidious enemy.

Through a "Real People Pact" and other such anti-communist organizations, we unit to work for the same goal. We all have to take action, to change people's opinions, and to get people involved.

I feel very optimistic in the last six months, but especially after the last mid-term elections. We have witnessed more resistance to communism than in the previous forty years put together. More followers of different anti-communist and anti-political movements were elected than ever before. The fledgling *Tea Party* has created a big difference by making people more conscious of the problems.

But all of our organizations, factions, and groups have to be united in one big movement bent on recovering America in the 2012 elections. After taking back our nation, we have to clean the government from the bottom up so there are no more communist agendas in our classrooms, in our government branches, and in our elected leaders.

Intimidation Communist Style

More than 200 leftist organizations have joined together to persuade Attorney General Eric Holder, Jr. to name a special prosecutor (or persecutor, to be more exact) to bring to trial ex-President George W. Bush and his Vice-President, Richard "Dick" Cheney.

Here's the wording of the outrageous petition submitted by liberal activist and blogger David Swanson:

> "We urge Attorney General Eric Holder to appoint an independent non-partisan Special Counsel to immediately commence a prosecutorial investigation into the most serious alleged crimes of former President George W. Bush, former Vice President Richard B. Cheney, the attorneys formerly employed by the Department of Justice whose memos sought to justify torture, and other former top officials of the Bush Administration.
>
> "Our laws and treaties under Article VI of our Constitution are the supreme law of the land, and require

the prosecution of the crimes that strong evidence suggests these individuals have committed. Both the former president and the former vice president have confessed to authorizing a torture procedure that is illegal under our law and treaty obligations. The former president has confessed to violating the Foreign Intelligence Surveillance Act."

That's how they work: their main tactic is intimidation of our leaders through a well-entrenched Communist World Media Pressure. They use similar tactics to ask for donations; they try to bully banks and big organizations in particular. These aren't new techniques, but rather are those that have been occurring for decades. Only by banding together to support those we elect to serve us, can we fight these outrages. [C3-2]

How fascinating that President Obama approved the killing of terrorist Osama Bin Laden by using information gleaned from the same "waterboarding" interrogation approved by former President Bush's administration. Does the left now dare to continue with their plan of prosecuting the men who made it possible to find and eliminate the mastermind of 9/11?

America's conservative talk media is pushing back at liberal radio, TV and newspapers, capturing their audience, stealing their thunder and keeping them off balance. We must increase that conservative pressure and do even better at fighting back. We must organize and create an unstoppable tsunami to drive them from our government, our schools, our churches, and, if necessary, our land.

Here is another unbelievable example of leftist/liberal/socialist action. In these United States, more than 400 organizations and individuals have called for freedom for Ahmad Sa'adat, a Palestinian militant and the Secretary-General of the Popular Front for the Liberation of Palestine (PFLP). Sa'adat is the man that Israel has accused of organizing the assassination of Israel's General, politician, historian, and Tourism Minister, Rehavam "Ghandi" Ze'evi. [C3-3]

Why would any true patriotic lover of freedom call for the release of this murderer? It's who they really are and whom they consider their heroes—heroes that will rule over us if we let them.

They use the state controlled media to enable thousands of criminal militants around the world, including Fidel Castro in Cuba, Hugo Chavez in Venezuela, Nelson Mandela in South Africa, Josef Stalin in Russia, and Adolph Hitler in Germany, to wreak havoc upon innocent people in their countries. The manipulation of the communication media is nothing new to me for I have lived through and battled against this den of cowardly wolves for almost half a century—first in Cuba, then in Venezuela, and now here in America.

No matter in which country you travel, you'll find the same educated, well-spoken criminals who have the same attitudes, the same desire for power, and the same lack of real compassion. Throughout the decades, they have all been the same evil creatures. Never forget that these are the people who have killed 94 million ordinary human beings across the face of the earth. For them, there are no national borders, no different races, or no language barriers. Their country is the world, and they want total control of every nation on the globe.

The video referenced here shows how united, and without borders they are. It also proves their need to teach Darwinism, knowing the affect this has on the younger generation. These are the people we need to silence or at least blunt their impact so that their mass attacks, which they call "action alerts," are ineffective. [C3-4]

Through the "Real People Pact" or any other conservative organizations or means, we will work together to concentrate on bankrupting these ruthless organizations. Without money, they will be crippled, the same way we crippled Osama bin Laden and other tyrants when we cut off their bank accounts and disrupt their ability to collect donations or to transfer money from the United States.

When there is proof that there are communist sympathizers in key positions in certain corporations and organizations, then we must send a strong and unmistakable message by boycotting their products and services. That being said, a major source of money for these groups is our own federal government. That must be stopped through conservative representation.

ACORN—A Twisted Communist Tool

Committee investigators have documented ACORN's wrongful use of charitable contributions. They found secret transfers of donor funds to pay for losses and other nefarious activities. Not surprisingly, this is a common practice among this army of leftist organizations. They regularly commingle bank accounts of federally funded affiliates with politically active affiliates.

Thanks to a convenient lack of sufficient oversight to safeguard taxpayer and donor interests, they often get away with it. Their activities show a total disregard for both federal and local laws. ACORN alone established 361 profit and non-profit organizations to try to cover their lengthy and twisted trail of wrongdoing.

Here is another example of their activities. Over 400 different organizations and individuals endorsed a call to free Ahmad Sa'adat and all Palestinian prisoners. On July 8, 2009, the Campaign to Free Ahmad Sa'adat sent a letter addressed to UN Secretary-General Ban Ki-Moon demanding that, "...he and the United Nations uphold their responsibilities to protect the rights of Palestinian prisoners and secure their freedom."

The letter claimed that over 400 organizations and individuals had endorsed and supported the message, and urged Ki-Moon to distribute the letter widely, link to the website of their Campaign, and continue to do the U.N.'s important work. [C3-5]

This was a clear demonstration of the Communist World Media Pressure technique of attack, perpetrated by youth, student and workers' unions, solidarity organizations, lawyers' associations, political parties, human rights groups, and numerous activists, academics, and supporters from around the world.

While not all of these people and organizations are necessarily communists, the majority are arguably so. They have learned many of the communist attack techniques used for over a century, and put them into play wherever and whenever possible. An important hallmark of their groups is to continually form little non-profit organizations, all of which become part of the World Communist Media Pressure, a powerful tool for mass indoctrination.

It is estimated that there are more than 3,000 communist organizations with 3.3 million members worldwide. They work together despite national borders, language barriers, ethnicities, colors, or nationalities. They have the same goals, use the same tactics, and act the same way. Thousands of communists and communist sympathizers have been freed from jails and thousands more have been elected to important government positions.

They use NGO's or Non-Governmental Organizations to control this association of pirates. They claim to be independent from any government, but the Soviet Union has over 277,000 members. NGOs emphasize humanitarian issues, developmental aid and sustainable development.

The communists have become skilled "artists" of political pressure and raising money. That is why we have to create laws that prohibit them from raising more money. And when they break the laws, we have to be there stop them and to prosecute them.

They use their state-controlled media to elect or appoint leaders, putting leftist communists in key positions where they direct donations, grants, money transfers, and contributions, to communist groups. They persuade people, organizations, and banks, to help them to get something they need approved or to force somebody to do what they want.

After the beginning of the war actions in Iraq, the Bush administration was almost paralyzed by the World Communist Media (WCM), repeating the playbook as they had done to bring an end to the war in Vietnam years before.

They lead the American people to believe that the main problem is between the left and the right; it is not. Whether they are communists or are Democrats who don't even want to be categorized as socialists, they attempt to bamboozle the American people into thinking that communism doesn't exist anymore. The New World Order is becoming real, and that due incessant and unabashedly biased WCM pressure.

The secretive Bilderberg Group, Bilderberg conference, or Bilderberg Club is described as a yearly, unofficial, invitation-only meeting of approximately 130 guests, who are influential people in their fields. While the names of attendees are made available to the press, the meetings are closed to the public and the press and no informational media releases are ever issued.

Historically, attendees at the conferences are bankers, politicians, military leaders, directors of large corporations, and heads of state. With its secrecy and refusal to issue news releases, the group is considered to be a part of a political conspiracy.

With an attendance that includes royals, communists, and influential political figures, I believe the Bilderberg group is the brain behind the socialist plot to establish a world government. World domination is not a new concept and has been attempted since earliest recorded times. The difference is that there are weapons, communications, and other tools available today that could make it possible.

America Cannot Tolerate Communism

The only way we can eradicate the influence of communism in this country is to eliminate their practices in this country; there is no other way to stop this poison factory. Until we realize we can no longer share this country with communists, we are never going to stop them.

Socialism represents a complete contradiction of everything America stands for: to live peacefully, to work hard and be productive, and to prosper and develop new ideas, inventions, and innovations. That's how America revolutionized the world through the last century. Communism represents misery, hunger, and atrocities around the globe.

Nobody described the communist influences better that Winston Churchill in one of his notes: "Communism is a philosophy of failure, the creed of ignorance, and the gospel of envy; its inherent virtue is the equal sharing of misery."

If we are to become serious about combating this poison factory, then forget about apologizing for our success, stop assuming that others respect our good behavior, and wake up from our apathy. We have to trust and support other God-fearing Americans, not our enemies.

Chili, Freed from Communism

When Augusto Pinochet overthrew the government of Salvador Allende, the free world was shocked at his killing of over 20,000 people. During the coup, 5,000 were killed in the battle, and during the next five years another 17,000 were charged with being communists and followers of Allende, and then were tried and executed.

He was compared with dictators like Hitler, Lenin, Stalin, Mao and Fidel. But unlike those tyrants, Pinochet's enemies were those who had enslaved his beloved country.

During his rule, he often said, "The day my people don't want me to run this country, I will call for elections and step down."

After the United Nations protested against Pinochet's régime, the country's military government held a national referendum, and asked the Chilean people if they supported Pinochet's rule. The "Yes" vote won with 74%. Years later, when the day arrived, he called for elections and peacefully handed over power. No communist controlled nation can say the same for one of their leaders.

For over 30 years up to today, Chile's economy has been a model for South American countries. The reason is because they no longer have the communist poison factory within their borders.

Think about this: Chile doesn't have environmental communist pawns operating under government grants to block their economy by interrupting their industries—as we have in America. Chile doesn't have ACORN, which used its 361 profit and non-profit organizations to indoctrinate our American people and generate confusion and distrust in our society.

Pinochet's bloodbath deservedly brought the wrath of world media down on his head even though communists have done the same and much worse in carrying out their agenda.

He could have jailed, exiled, or banned the communists from his country. He could have even been right to execute those who were proven to be criminals. The lesson here, however, is not in the method used, but in the results of a nation scrubbed of a satanic ideology.

The world watched on television as the Chilean miners were rescued in 2010. The country was united to save those men. What a different outcome it would have been if Pinochet had not freed Chile from the grip of communist rule.

Compare that with Russian and Chinese miners who are not considered important enough to work under stringent safety regulations or valuable enough to rescue when disaster strikes. Proof of that lies in the fact that communist countries have the worst records in mining accidents. To Darwinists, the lives of the miners are worthless, replaceable, and expendable.

Incidentally, for those who still brand Pinochet as nothing but a criminal, and believe that Salvador Allende was not a communist, let them read this quote from Allende during his interview with French Journalist Regis Debray in 1970. Allende said, "The answer is the proletariat. If it wasn't so I wouldn't be here...As for the bourgeois state, at the present moment, we are seeking to overcome it...to overthrow it...Our objective is total, scientific, Marxist socialism."

Been There, Done That

If you want to continue living and sharing with your family and enjoying this country's superior standard of living, then please listen to me, a person who has barely survived communist takeovers in two countries. This is the moment to stop them, to encourage them to leave, to throw them out, or we will suffer the dire consequences.

For over half a century they have been undermining the American economy, trying to make it collapse. I have seen many of my fellow countrymen working 10 to 12 hours a day or more for decades to build a business. It's a sacrifice I know well. I often slept in my car despite having money in my pocket, just to save enough so I could build my business. The majority of entrepreneurs have done similar things.

In the last couple years, I have watched many of those hard working individuals lose everything they built with their sacrifices. It is pitiful and heart breaking. When they follow the American dream and give all they have only to lose everything, then America suffers a loss along with them. As this happens to more and more people, it will soon be too late to do anything; we will join the defeated.

Much of this not so subtle loss of our freedom has happened at a time when President Obama made it possible for 86,000 black farmers to illegally receive $1.25 billion from the federal treasury for discrimination that they supposedly suffered.

How could that happen? Statistics show that there are only 39,000 black farmers in America; how can 86,000 get funded? Why was that money not given to help small businesses where new jobs are really created? Approximately 75% of private sector employment is found in small business ventures. Unfortunately, Obama's gift of $1.25 billion of your taxes was wasted without any positive results for the country.

And that is only one way that this administration has been spending your taxpayer money. Billions of dollars went to support the communist agenda. Just a few months after Obama was elected, ACORN was granted $8.5 billion to promote communism in this country, to get communists elected, and to put communists in key positions in the government.

It also went to help export their communist agenda to other countries and to maintain an incredible 361 communist organizations that help to cover their trail of wrongdoing. I know the media didn't report it that way, but by now, most alert citizens are fully aware of the ACORN agenda.

If they impose communism on us, one third of the American people are not going to survive. The same high standard of living we have enjoyed for decades will be gone forever and so many people will simply be condemned to death.

We are not prepared to live in a communist state. By the time we learn to survive under communist rule and a sustainable society, for the majority it will be too late. I know because I am a survivor of the bourgeois class extermination by the communists.

A Warning for Christians in America

For the past forty years, but especially in the last 20 years, communism has demoralized our family values and our Christians faith. The communists have tried to dishonor and humiliate Christ, Christians, and God-fearing conservatives. They purposely work to turn Christians against homosexuals, Muslims, blacks, Hispanics, and the New Popular Culture. Then they publish accusations of homophobia, racism, and lack of compassion. They also create fake religious organizations to confuse Christian beliefs.

They can succeed if our wobbly and moderately conservative Americans are made to blame their growing disbelief on the lack of Christ in their lives. In part, those who are insecure are probably right, but the solution requires more than self-flagellation. Perhaps fifteen percent of the Christian population is vulnerable as targets for the communists. It is vital for every patriot, for every conservative, for every Christian to know and discuss the menace that communism represents, and to advance the ideas in this book to combat that threat.

It is time to stand up and declare, "We don't have to be rethinking Christianity, which has spread the good news that Jesus died for us on the cross, so that we can be inheritors of eternal life. We know that He is the Son of God who came to save us, and we will not allow any communist to tell us how to think about our beliefs."

We have "professed" Christians who are anything but in their words and actions. For example, a racist white-hater like the so-called "Reverend" Jeremiah Wright, Jr. and his mega-church in Chicago. Who will ever forget his rant from the pulpit, "God bless America…no, no…God d**n America!" Wright also happens to be the same preacher that President Obama considered his pastor and a mentor for 20 years.

Groups like Wright's are just another way to attack the American system and to corrupt our citizens. So far they have apparently done a very good job. How shocking is the revelation in a recent poll that 62% of Americans claim to have a favorable opinion of socialism: a system that has been responsible for more than 94 million human deaths--a total greater than all of the world's wars put together.

Today we have Christians divided, confused, and disillusioned; they are lost in a world that doesn't want to understand them and doesn't want to accept or acknowledge their way of life and beliefs. Until recent times, this Christian-based nation grew, prospered and welcomed countless thousands of hard working immigrants into a unique society that declared itself to be "...one nation under God."

Now we have a bunch of free riders that have come along, wanting not only to destroy what we have built, but to label us as imperialists as well. In truth, they are the imperialists who are working to take over this country and destroy our capitalistic system.

The U.S. is a country unsurpassed by any other for the contributions we have made to the well being of the world and humanity, yet today we are being called imperialists and greedy people. Sadly, this isn't just from the leaders of communistic countries, but from American communists... citizens of this free land.

Discrimination Against the White Race

Let's look at our nation from another perspective, that of the oppressed of the white or Caucasian race in this country. Today whites in America cannot say anything negative about blacks, Hispanics or Muslims without being accused of racism. Yet many of these non-white groups can insult or denigrate white Americans with total immunity. How can that be just, legal, or fair?

A white American is denied the right to rent a house to whomever he wants in a supposedly free country. White Americans are pressured to hire a certain number of minorities, whether or not they are right for the job, or be sued for discrimination. Non-white group leaders make unjustified demands, and lecture about rights, equality, and tolerance.

The white entrepreneur, who sacrificed and worked to build a business, is helpless to operate with people that he knows can help create success, and then is blamed when the business is forced to close and everyone is out of work.

The real tragedy is that white Americans don't have the same rights, the same freedom of speech, the same tolerance at work, or the same right to obtain government help, as do minorities. What if the situation involving an entrepreneurial black were reversed?

There's the United Negro College Fund, but no United White College Fund; there's a Miss Black America, but no Miss White America; even in Congress, there is a Black Congressional Caucus but no White Congressional Caucus. How is this fair and equitable? Discrimination is discrimination regardless of who is targeted and by whom.

Our Illegal Alien Problem

Let's focus on the illegal alien problem in America. Liberals want to confer amnesty and even citizenship on those who enter this country illegally. Taxpayers are forced to educate, medicate, and integrate those who creep in the back door. Why is this being allowed to happen? No mystery there. In the last election, leaders who favor amnesty received 67% of the Hispanic vote.

Statistics prove that legal and naturalized immigrants, often result in more educated, law-abiding, and productive group of future citizens, compared with illegal aliens coming in now from the same countries. Many illegals have criminal backgrounds and come here to sell drugs, build crime organizations, form street gangs, and/or collect welfare benefits paid for by working Americans.

There is an argument that seems to be repeated again and again that illegals take jobs that Americans will not take. The problem is that is only a half-truth. If the illegals were not here to take those low paying jobs, employers would be forced to raise their compensation levels to attract the Americans. Illegal workers depress pay scales that would otherwise rise. Its simple economics, but such employers are playing into the hands of socialism.

No matter how we look at the flood of aliens coming across our boarders, it is harmful to our society. I ask myself, who are these people in Washington working for? Are they trying to benefit the American people or are they encouraging the inflow of foreign invaders to swell the ballot box in their favor, and to then be indoctrinated? This scheme is not just a left-wing political idea, as many believe. No, it is pure communism in action for a much larger objective…the permanent takeover of America.

Beyond the danger of power grabbing through bogus elections, there are the overwhelming costs associated with having so many illegal aliens within our borders. Consider this readily available information (I have included the referenced video URL's for verification of these facts):

- Between $11-22 billion is spent on welfare to illegal aliens each year. [C3-6]
- $2.2 billion per year is paid for food assistance programs such as food stamps, WIC, and free school lunches for illegal aliens. [C3-7, C3-8]
- $2.5 billion a year is expended on Medicaid for illegal aliens. [C3-9]
- $12 billion per annum is used for primary and secondary school education for children here illegally who cannot speak a word of English, so communicating with them raises the costs. [C3-10]
- $17 billion a year is spent educating the American-born children of illegal aliens, known as *anchor babies*.[C3-11]
- $3 million per *day* spent to incarcerate illegal aliens. [C3-12]
- 30% of all federal prison inmates are illegal aliens. [C3-13]
- $90 billion per year is used to supply illegal aliens with welfare and social services. [C3-14]
- $200 billion a year in suppressed American wages caused by illegal aliens. [C3-15]
- Illegal aliens in the U.S. have amassed a crime rate that is two-and-a-half times that of legal citizens. Of special concern are anchor babies that could grow up to add future crime problems for the country. [C3-16]

During 2005 there were between 4 to 10 million illegals crossing our southern border with as many as 19,500 illegal aliens being from terrorist countries. According to the Homeland Security Report, millions of pounds of illegal drugs, cocaine, meth, heroin, and marijuana were brought into the U. S. across our border with Mexico. [C3-17]

The National Policy Institute estimates the total cost of a mass deportation of illegals would be between $206 and $230 billion or an average annual cost of between $41 and $46 billion over five years. [C3-18]

In 2006, it was reported that illegal aliens sent $45 billion in remittances back to their countries of origin. [C3-19]

Roy Beck in his 1996 book, *The Dark Side of Illegal Immigration*, points out that nearly a million sex crimes have been committed by illegals. [C3-20]

Communists want this illegal immigration to continue creating problems for us. Statistics show that a large percentage of illegals represent the level of delinquency and outlaw qualities that are appropriate for the communists' purposes.

Do I mean to say that all illegals are bad people; of course not. There are a great many who are trying to raise their own standard of living, but there are legitimate ways to come to America. Immigrants who made legal application, followed the rules, and became naturalized citizens, as I had to do, are welcome to our American family.

On the other side of the coin, are the outlaws, delinquents, criminals, and non-producers often with a lack of education. They are the targets for recruitment into the communist cause.

Overall, the total annual cost of this tsunami flood of aliens is a stunning $338.3 billion per year. Never forget that we are talking about money taken from you and your family!

A visit to the video reference below reveals that in 1973, our immigration policy was allowing 250,000 people per year to come into the U.S.A. In the last several years, we are now allowing more than a million people per year inside our borders, both legal and illegal.

If we look back, one of the prime reasons for the great economic success of the U.S. in the past 50 years was that immigration was under control; it was an immigration of basically decent, productive people and our country was able to absorb and welcome those who came to contribute to and benefit from our way of life.

The numbers of individuals we allow in today represent an enormously different caliber and quantity, and that has created tremendous infrastructure problems for our cities in regard to schools, housing, utilities, welfare, health, and other services.

The website, *Numbersusa.com*, presents evidence that continuing to allow a million immigrants in this country every year, in twenty short years will bankrupt this nation. Permitting increasing numbers of immigrants into this country, or accepting illegals as a humanitarian gesture will not resolve the world hunger problem, one that is estimated to involve more than 480 million people. But, what a huge difference one million people a year is going to make. Overwhelming our resources and economy is still another tried and true communist tactic.

Communists say they want each country to determine its own destiny, yet they have not been able to solve the enormous problems their ideology creates. That is why, after years of destroying their own nations, their system collapses leaving the citizens desolate and the infrastructure in chaos.

Americans often work 8-10 hours a day to attain and maintain our high quality of life. Communism takes from those who produce and gives to those who do not. My father used to say, "Don't give rice to the poor; teach them how to grow it." The world hunger problem has to be resolved from inside each and every country. We must teach and help the hungry nations to grow their food, not shower them with money that never reaches those who really need it. [C3-17]

Another Look at ACORN

ACORN is not a uniquely American idea. The organization is made up of people that are exactly like those that I saw in action Cuba and Venezuela. They have the same kind of criminal mindset, and they are working to run this country. Let me rephrase that: they are the ones who are working to *ruin* our country.

They have over 150 thousand supporters of socialism working for them, and recent sting operations have revealed what kind of people they are and what they do. Videos taken by Andrew J. Breitbart, an amateur video producer and researcher, show the lack of any scruples in immoral and even criminal activities within ACORN.

Like those who infiltrated Cuba and Venezuela, they are people who believe the end justifies the means. Their infectious doctrine demoralizes and desensitizes every human being exposed to their poison.

One of Breitbart's video clips (referenced below), was secretly recorded at the ACORN headquarters in Maryland, and shows a woman posing as a prostitute and a man posing as a future congressional candidate. The couple wanted help getting a housing loan for a brothel where they intended to keep underage girls trafficked in from El Salvador. They claimed they wanted to avoid federal tax laws and detection by law enforcement, so they would be able to launder the money from their business to help the man get elected to congress.

The couple in the video asks ACORN employees to advise them on a variety of illegal issues. They show no signs of surprise or alarm in regard to the couple's proposed business venture. Tanja Thompson, ACORN Tax Specialist, advised that they classify prostitution as "performing arts" on the 1090 tax form. She pulled together tax write-offs equaling $7-8,000.

The "candidate" asks about filing taxes for the underage girls who will be engaged in prostitution. Ms. Thompson responded that they aren't legal citizens anyway so he cannot file taxes for them, and so he should not worry about them. She advised that the girls could be claimed as dependents. Besides, she pointed out, if the girls are under 16 it is illegal for them to work in Maryland so no one should know about it. She concluded, "They don't exist." [C3-22]

Thanks to undercover videos and congressional investigations, ACORN has allegedly gone belly up. Communism doesn't work that way. Exposed organizations sink out of sight and reemerge later under different names, but with the same malevolent goals.

In my Cuban homeland, one writer asked, "How can we allow this bunch of swindlers to take over this country, ruin the economy, and kill, incarcerate, or force so many of us to flee? Are we not doing anything about it?" In Venezuela, I saw very similar articles.

Communists all come from the same school of programming. While still in Cuba, my family, friends, neighbors and I never thought that within our country there were people who could be so cruel; we were utterly wrong. Public firing squads executions became commonplace. They were so frequent that they became almost a circus, a party—while it was happening, we couldn't grasp the horror of it.

Researching the incredible atrocities of communists around the world, you soon learn that they follow the same evil and immoral pattern whenever they are in control. From one who knows, it won't be different if they are allowed to take over the United States.

Stories released on television document that there are concentration camps being built and equipped in America for future use against citizens who rebel against the government. The news is downplayed now to avoid stirring up concern, but accept the fact that they are preparing in the belief that sooner or later the American people will need to be controlled. Communists intend to be well prepared. [C3-23]

Control Through Oil and the Environment

In the last 40 years, communists have been able to ram bills through Congress resulting in hundreds of regulations to sabotage our domestic oil industry. For example, take the Interstate act of 1987, and the Sherman Ant-Trust act of 1990.

These two acts aided the Anti-Industrial Revolution using a communist revolutionary principle. Former Federal Reserve Chairman Alan Greenspan explained, "The effective purpose, the hidden intent, and the actual practice of the antitrust law in the United States have led to the condemnation of the productive and efficient members of our society because they *are* productive and efficient."

The idea is to prevent America from becoming self-sufficient in oil, which resulted in detrimental consequences by creating and maintaining instability and unpredictability in every industry.

Thousands of companies have moved offshore or closed due to restrictive government regulations, plus criminal unions made it difficult to compete with foreign manufacturers.

In the 1970's President Ronald Reagan proved that he knew exactly what the communists were doing. The majority of these constricting laws exceeded the requirements of safety and good sense; they needlessly overburdened our industries.

In a 1973speech Reagan said, "…it seems no matter how we do, there is still a very active fringe element in the environmental movement that never seems to be satisfied. Orderly progress in a way that does not paralyze the economy is not enough."

Again, these are people who believe that the end justifies the means, no matter how painful or destructive to our nation. They are manipulating us; indeed that is their goal.

Be sure of one thing, if we don't do something now to stop this poison, it is going to be too late for future generations of Americans. Our children, our grandchildren, and their children, will be condemned to live a much poorer standard of life. [C3-24]

Thought Control Through the Media

The dangerous unbridled power of the television networks and greedy advertisers has created a culture of compulsive buyers in sharp contrast to the basic teachings of Christianity. Our younger generation cannot be themselves anymore. In order to feel socially acceptable, they feel the need to buy a particular brand name shirt or jeans or use a brand name watch or cell phone and drive the most popular car.

Over the past years, viewers have seen a parade of unrealistic families, individuals, and celebrities who are perfect in every way. Portrayed are faultless mothers and wives, exceptional fathers and husbands, and exemplary and super intelligent kids. For the last five decades people have been on a mindless quest for such perfection for themselves.

Those who are less than the ideal are often scorned, persecuted and bullied. The list of the imperfect is endless: the obese, ugly, disfigured, or otherwise deficient. It doesn't matter that they are honest, respectable, and sensible people; they are still rejected by society. Our society must change to be more understanding, merciful, and humble. We cannot allow TV, movies, or other influence to create impossible to reach illusions and dreams. [C3-25]

Politicians and their machines have used the TV networks to desensitize and demoralize our people. They often use outright lies and half-truths to dupe us into trusting them in order to convince us of their qualifications and worthiness to be our leaders. In truth, they are only interested in achieving their own selfish goals.

Somehow, Americans allow a small minority to decide who gets elected. How amazing that so many of the majority who believe in the Constitution and conservative values, stay home from elections believing that others will elect the right leaders, or that their one vote doesn't really count that much.

So, the political machines get more and more adept at spewing out a series of meaningless lies and promises to convince the few who will actually vote to elect them to important offices. Too many politicians simply do whatever it takes to win the election and then become our masters, instead of being our representatives or servants.

Rather than spending time looking for better ways to govern, they look for ways to feather their own nests by passing bills that expand or generate new taxes. We are made to believe that what they do is in the public interest when they are actually assuming unauthorized control over citizens browbeaten into submission. As a final insult, these charlatans refuse to leave office or to set constituents free of their abuses.

If we believe in freedom then each of us needs to get involved to assure that our people will always have peace, security, and harmony. But, if we sit silently by then we blindly become accomplices of those who speak out against our values and accomplishments as a Christian, conservative nation.

The old saying is still true, "If you are not part of the solution, you are part of the problem."

CHAPTER 8

Acorn, The Obama Connection

In 1970, Wade Rathke and Gary Delgado, Ph.D., founded ACORN, an acronym that stands for the *Association of Community Organizations for Reform Now*. As innocent as the name may sound, ACORN is a communist-based organization that advocates social and labor union problems, and the fraudulent voting registration of people who support their socialistic agenda and ideology.

At its height, ACORN had over 400,000 members and more than 1,200 neighborhood chapters in over 100 cities in the U.S., as well as in Canada, Mexico, Argentina, and Peru. It was a complex collection of 361 related profit and non-profit organizations which change and influence laws and regulations, voter registration, health care, and environmental and other social issues.

ACORN pursued its goals through demonstrations, Sol Alinsky style attack tactics, community organizing, indoctrination, lobbying, and voter participation.

An address by the ACORN's former CEO, Bertha Lewis, paints a startling clear picture of a true communist, one who is full of hatred and fixation on American racial problems as she sees them. Her statements also reveal the way she and all the other communists plan to achieve their radical goals. The following quotes are excerpted from the video clip referenced below:

> "First of all, let me just say that any group that says 'I'm young, I'm democratic, and I'm a socialist' is all right with me. The reason you have to build your organization and make

> it as big and powerful as you can is because you need to get into real battles. And here's what I think you need to do: you need to make sure that you get into this battle. The next big battle that's coming, whether healthcare lives or dies, is immigration. The next big battle is immigration, immigration, immigration.
>
> "My challenge to black folks and to people of color and civil rights folks is this, the face of immigration needs to be a lot blacker than it is. Because they can frame the immigration debate as [being] about Latinos crossing some mythical border, when in fact we have second and third generation black folks in this country who come from immigrant families. But they're not standing up and marching with their Latino brothers and sisters, and saying 'I am an immigrant too.' So young Democratic Socialists, join this immigration war. Black people, young black people put in the vast vat of 'African Americans,' JOIN. Don't march along side, don't march in back, be right out front." [C4-1]

It is incomprehensible how she can accuse others with phony accusations about racism and provoking violence and hatred. If there is anything that will lead to racial violence and civil unrest in this country, it's the attitude and audacity on display here.

This is the immigration agenda of real communists in action. It also happens to be the apparent agenda of our president. That aim is to turn blacks, Muslims and Latinos against whites in a racial war of hatred.

Trust me when I say from experience that President Barack Obama is a product of his socialist environment. He has exposed and perjured himself on many issues, but principally his involvement with ACORN and the Service Employees International Union (SEIU). Obama, ACORN and SEIU, were dominant forces in Chicago's New Communist Party. Another active participant was Madeline Talbott, Obama's closest ACORN contact and a key New Party supporter. [C4-2]

To get a sense of where the New Party stood politically, consider some of its early supporters: Barbara Dudley of Greenpeace; Steve

Cobble, political director of Jesse Jackson's Rainbow Coalition; Frances Fox Piven, coauthor of the Cloward-Piven strategy and a leader of the drive for the motor-voter legislation; economist Juliet Schor; black historian Manning Marable; historian Howard Zinn; linguist Noam Chomsky; Todd Gitlin; and writers Gloria Steinem and Barbara Ehrenreich.

At one point, writer and editor Micah Sifry describes the New Party's goals as social democratic. I lived through all the names used to hide the true nature of these types of organizations. The New Party clearly stands for the same principles of communism, which are shared by a large number of those inside the Democratic Party. [C4-3]

James O'Keefe III, famous for his 2009 ACORN investigation where Hannah Giles and he produced the blockbuster undercover video of ACORN, revealing systematic corruption in offices nationwide that documented aid for child prostitution, human trafficking, and tax evasion.

It shows by their actions, the communist attitude that the end justifies the means. Those ACORN workers were demonstrating was exactly how communists operate, how they do business, and how in governing they run everything.

When they saw the corruption, the U.S. House and Senate quickly voted to stop funding ACORN and the U.S. Census Bureau cut all ties with the group. ACORN was ultimately forced to shut down. James O'Keefe and Hannah Giles are really heroes. If you haven't seen that remarkable piece of undercover work, check out this video. [C4-4]

This next video reference shows Barack Obama inviting ACORN people and their friends to the White House to have them help him shape his presidential agenda. It is no wonder he has been able to wreck our country in only two short years. [C4-5]

Another clip suggests that Obama, ACORN, had full knowledge of election fraud. This one is a video compilation of various news stories regarding the president, the communist activist organization known as ACORN that he joined and chose to work with, and the massive voter registration fraud they perpetrated over the years. [C4-6]

The next video records how workers blew the whistle on SEIU election fraud, a further disgraceful act by the Obama administration and its cronies. Compare their actions to warning from our second U.S. President, John Adams, who said in his 1797 inaugural address: "We should be unfaithful to ourselves if we should ever lose sight of the danger to our liberties, or if anything partial or extraneous should infect the purity of our free, fair, virtuous, and independent elections." [C4-7]

This video reveals how SEIU-ACORN links put the integrity of the 2010 Census at risk. Republican U.S. Senator Mark Kirk of Illinois commented: "I've already called for a criminal investigation of SEIU operations in the Lake County voter fraud. And with these links, I think caution should govern our policy to sever links with this organization."

Interestingly, the president of SEIU is one of the people on the list of those who most visited the White House since Obama took over. [C4-8]

This next is a report on an investigation conducted by the U.S. House of Representatives to determine whether ACORN was internationally structured as a criminal enterprise. It is a shocking look at communism in action: "The end justifies the means." It's always the same with communism. [C4-9]

This report is one of the most repulsive I have seen concerning any organization that is close to a U.S. President. Its hundred pages are filled with illegal and communistic activities and procedures.

Labor organizations, unions, and other tax-exempt groups used Chicago-style political exploitation and back room plots in national, state and local elections. According to the investigation, Ohio ACORN directors drafted a political plan, which exposed their scheme. They targeted three competitive congressional districts and six state representative contests within the districts. This is a description of their mission:

> "Our electoral work will mobilize and educate voters. Our paid professional canvassers will execute tightly managed Voter ID and GOTV canvasses moving our core constituency of base and swing voters to the polls to vote for the candidates who most closely align with a progressive Working Families Agenda."

ACORN also ignored its own corporate guidelines by loaning funds without adequate legal documentation, ignoring its corporate bylaws, misappropriating corporate money, and terminating members without following the processes called for in its Articles of Incorporation. Further, ACORN did not comply with IRS or ERISA requirements.

Voter and Lobbying Fraud

Another legal question concerns subgroups of Project Vote such as CCI, Citizens Services Inc. (CSI), Communities Voting Together (CVT), and other non-profit, IRS 501(c)(3) certified organizations. Their mandates were to promote desirable governmental policies and legislation consistent with ACORN's objectives.

Regrettably, or maybe deliberately, ACORN and its affiliates could not differentiate their non-profit 501(c)(3) work from their profit-making activities. Apparently those individuals made strategic decisions about which groups did non-profit or profit-making voter registration work.

Lobbying was a major part of what ACORN did. It endorsed Democratic Senator Sherrod Brown of Ohio and Democratic Congress people Albert Wynn and Donna Edwards, both of Maryland. Reportedly, ACORN also kept donor records from the Clinton, Kerry, and Obama campaigns with the intent to use that information for prohibited communications.

In addition, the organization faced a series of alleged failures and indictable crimes: an Arkansas employee was arrested in 1998 for falsifying voter registration documents, while in 1999 about 400 voter-registration cards submitted by ACORN in Philadelphia were flagged for investigation when a judge noted that "a cursory look would have suggested that they were all in the same hand."

There is a great review in Claire Suddath's *A Brief History of ACORN,* published by *Time* on October 14, 2008. [C4-10]

According to a July 9, 2008 article in *The New York Times*, Dale Rathke, the brother of ACORN's founder, Wade Rathke, "...embezzled nearly $1 million from Acorn affiliated charitable organizations in 1999 and 2000." The Times further reported that

Dale Rathke embezzlement was, "...carried as a loan on the books of Citizens Consulting, Inc. which provides bookkeeping, accounting, and other financial services."

No one can deny that ACORN engages in politically partisan activity. *The Wall Street Journal* noted that ACORN had direct involvement in the Obama presidential campaign. According to reporter John Fund, Citizens Consulting, Inc., which controlled ACORN's finances, was paid $832,000 by the Obama campaign for get-out-the-vote efforts.

Note, the rules clearly state that non-profits participating in partisan activity are expressly barred from receiving federal funds; yet ACORN received $53 million in federal funds since 1994 and except for the landslide turnover in Congress to block payment, they almost received up to $8.5 billion more.

In March 2009, ACORN became a national partner with the U.S. Census Bureau to assist in recruiting nearly 1.4 million workers to go door-to-door to count every person in the country. According to *The Wall Street Journal,* ACORN was selected to assist the Census Bureau in "reaching out to minority communities and recruiting census enumerators for the count next year."

ACORN used its complex organizational structure to facilitate fraudulent and illegal acts. Piercing ACORN's corporate veil in order to determine which individuals owned or controlled the organization was a necessary step for stopping waste, fraud, and abuse of federal funds. When ACORN committed illegal acts, the individuals who were harmed were the low to moderate-income workers, the very people ACORN was founded to protect.

This video entitled, *Lessons Learned from the 2008 Election,* taped at a hearing before the House Committee on the Judiciary, 111th Congress, reveals how ACORN and its fellow travelers operate.
C4-11

There are far more examples. For instance, ACORN workers in Pennsylvania were charged with forging 51 signatures and violating election laws before the 2008 presidential election. Then, in March 2008, an ACORN employee in West Reading, Pennsylvania, was sentenced to up to 23 months in prison for identity theft.

In July 2008, three ACORN workers were convicted of voter fraud in Kansas City when they overwhelmed voter registration rolls with over 35,000 false or questionable registration forms. In May 2009, two ACORN staffers were prosecuted in Clark County, Nevada for paying bonuses to workers who registered over 21 individuals per day.

ACORN's Criminal Enterprise

If all of that isn't enough, there's the 100-page report of the Committee on Oversight and Government Reform, which is filled with evidence that ACORN is intentionally structured as a criminal enterprise. The report details thousands of violations in political advocacy, fraud, lobbying, misuse of funds, voting fraud, and 361 affiliated profit and non-profit organizations that ACORN used to cover their trail of illegal activities.

Americans should find it shameful, dishonest, stupid, illegal, and lacking in ethics for the President of the United State to even associate with these kinds of people. But it is a not just an association; these are people the President brought into the White House to help set his presidential agenda. That is also preserved on video. [C4-12]

But after all, this is precisely what communism is all about. Within his close group of cronies, Obama is not going to find people with ethics, scruples, or dignity.

I have spent almost half a century combating this poison factory, and understand that this is "business as usual" for them. The results of the administration's wrongdoing are exposed in this report, which clearly tells how communists conduct their business in this country: with no respect whosoever for the law, humanity, or our nation.

Just as the Bereans of Biblical times, each person is responsible for checking the truth about what he or she sees or hears, and then keep what is true.

These videos and other sources will indeed prove that only by eradicating communism from the U.S. will we destroy the cancer that is killing our great country.

Communism Can Only Win Through Fraud

When I discuss ACORN and the problems with communism in the U.S., I am not talking about left or right ideology, which is what the communists want us to be focusing on and talking about. We need to determine what is communism and what is not.

Some readers may judge me as a right-wing extremist, but I am not. I am a staunch, 100% anti-communist and a 100% pro-American. I have been fighting against this poison for 49 years. Just like General George Patton, I know that these evil people are only stopped by raw aggression, by brute force.

When Michael Medved called this communist movement the "poison factory," he was completely right. I pray that Americans will never have to live under their tyrannical system, and be forced to learn what Medved and I are saying.

Communists have already demonstrated how they need to exploit distrust and hatred between the social classes. Don't be surprised if they again try to have two or more Black Panther intimidators at each polling location in future elections. Citizens and law enforcement must be prepared to counter their outrageous behaviors; if we do not, it will not matter if we have the majority because they will win through fraud.

We have heard about every imaginable type of voting fraud and outright intimidation in the past elections; there was double voting, electronic machine fixing, and vote swapping intended to arrange the election of leftist candidates.

After several indictments were served on people accused of interfering with local elections, Republican Texas Attorney General Greg Abbott stated, "Voter fraud is occurring on a large scale when viewed statewide and consequently, our state elections are significantly impacted."

A former career Justice Department lawyer, J. Christian Adams, resigned to protest political interference in cases he worked on. Testifying before the U.S. Commission on Civil Rights, he claimed that Associate Attorney General Thomas Perrelli, an Obama appointee, overruled a unanimous recommendation by six career

Justice Attorneys for continued prosecution of members of the New Black Panther Party on charges of voter intimidation.

But Adams leveled an even more explosive charge when he said that Deputy Assistant Attorney General Julie Fernandez announced to attorneys in Justice's Voting Rights section that she would not support enforcement of a key section of the federal Motor Voter law, Section 8. That law requires states to periodically purge their voter rolls of dead people, felons, illegal voters, and those who have moved out of state.

Former ACORN Las Vegas field director, Christopher Edwards, pleaded guilty to voter registration fraud. While Nevada law prohibits paying canvassers for registering voters, he admitted to "a scheme to pay canvassers who were told they had to register at least 20 voters a day to keep their jobs and an additional $5 for getting 21 or more." Edwards agreed to testify against ACORN in return for a lighter sentence.

If they could do all that with the Republicans running the U.S. government, imagine what they can do being in complete control. It's the very same thing as in Venezuela where Hugo Chavez won the last five rigged elections. With everything being exposed in these pages, no clear thinking person can deny that this bears a frightening similarity to Venezuela. We have been very ineffective in fighting against communism right here in our own country.

Our Enemy Has a Head Start

It is truly alarming how the communists in this country are acting as if they have nothing to fear, creating laws favoring their views, changing laws to suit them, and changing everything and anything to facilitate their take over. It is frighteningly clear that we have been generally incapable of offering any resistant to their efforts. They have already tampered with our Constitution, our political system, our education system, and our legal system. Unless citizens and their representatives act quickly, much of what is taking place will be a done deal, quite legal and already approved.

Today the communists are fully prepared to take over; they can institute martial law and use the militia to force citizens to do as they are told or end up in a concentration camp. By controlling the justice system, every part of their plan will be made legally and physically feasible to take over our once great country.

We could easily find that we have an even larger fight with the Spanish-speaking and black people of this country. They have been carefully and expertly manipulated and agitated by communists inside the Democratic Party. The near future could be very ugly because the minorities are blinded to the reality of what is happening and the danger of what they are being provoked to believe and do.

Every single American must learn to clearly differentiate between the communistic and democratic systems. Through books like this, videos like those referenced herein, public speakers, and conservative media, our free peoples need to understand what the communists have done throughout the world and what they are likely to do here.

No matter how difficult the fight we face to stay free, we have to resist, or the “poison factory” will win, resulting in a drastic lowering of our standard of living, the annulling of our freedoms, the destruction of our infrastructure, the complete control of our educational system, and, don’t doubt me, the very real possibility of arrests, imprisonment, and executions.

Supporters of this administration may continue to accuse conservatives of racism in the next election. Our candidates and our own media must be strong to prove that true racism comes from the Left that has long used (and abused) the minorities to gain and keep power.

The proof is plentiful, but we need representatives who have the backbone to tell how Republicans have been the party that supported and recruited minorities while the Democrats, like the late Senator Byrd (a Klan member) often stonewalled black Americans who dared to succeed.

Fortunately we have the Tea Party. They are doing a great job of keeping the constitutional movement alive, and by making people aware of the problems that our socialist government officials apparently want to create. The Tea Party has the quality and the vision to fight the battle, and have already demonstrated their strength in creating a force capable of winning elections. The rest of us must unite to win back the country.

If our people insist that future elections are not to be like those in the past, we will be well on our way to being a force to be reckoned with. We can win elections on a regular and consistent basis; we will win the respect of politicians, of military leaders, and of the public. Then we can maintain and build on the system we treasure, and restore a strong and just government, one that for more than 230 years has made the U.S. the country in which everybody in the world wants to live.

From my perspective, the mid-term election of 2010 was the first time we had a full-scale resistance to communism; the members of the Tea Party deserve much of the credit. Now it is time for the rest of us to believe in the same conservative goals and to keep the momentum going.

One essential action is to be well informed. Read articles and books and stay up-to-date on unbiased news that reveals what the communists have done all over the world. For example, Kitty Werthmann, an Austrian-born survivor of the Third Reich, and now a U.S. citizen, wrote how the Obama administration is doing exactly what Hitler did in Germany: [C4-13, C4-14]

We have to publicize many articles and videos like these from actual eyewitnesses. Americans need to see, read, and understand not only what is taking place right now, but also what they should expect to happen, as has already occurred under similar attacks in other countries. The most difficult task facing us is to convince people that there is a cruel satanic movement alive today right here in America.

"We are dealing with a culture of corruption," writes conservative blogger and author, Michelle Malkin. She lays out the details in her book entitled, *Culture of Corruption: Obama and His Team of Tax Cheats, Crooks, and Cronies*. Their unlawful, immoral, and authoritarian behavior, found in the aspects and procedures of communism, is now in evidence all over America. For further confirmation, enter "*2008 voting fraud*" in Google search to find hundreds of cases of fraud.[C4-15]

One report showed that the Obama campaign donated $800,000 to an ACORN affiliate. This should come as no surprise as Obama was a key player in the organization as a trainer of their leaders, as a representative of ACORN in court, and in his funneling of funds to them. This same organization was investigated in more than 14 states for massive irregularities during the recent elections.

ACORN, like any other communist organization claimed that its priorities included better housing and wages for the poor, more community development investments from banks and governments, and better public schools. The same communistic tactic they use whenever they are trying to seize a country.

Voting Machine and Voter Registration Fraud

There is a video clip, referenced here, that shows how the Diebold voting machines are incredibly easy to compromise, without leaving evidence of what has taken place. Amazingly, it was a reporter from the very liberal CNN who interviewed a Princeton University professor. He easily demonstrated how the machines could be compromised in mere moments.

He used a simple "logic and accuracy test" to show how elections could be manipulated. Any of the machines could be accessed using an identical key. Then the compromising program could be passing from machine to machine by simply removing the memory card and using it in private at a voting headquarters: [C4-16]

Millions of Americans should be asking themselves whether the implications of this situation would be catastrophic. Is the integrity of the whole voting process completely undermined? Who actually put our current leaders in office? What is their agenda? Can this dangerous, faulty system be corrected before the next elections?

The complexity of what is involved in the fraud is so enormous that I don't believe anybody will completely supply the answers. But you can know for a fact that the communists are diligently working on a New World Order to enslave the U.S. and the rest of the world.

Since the 1960's, communists have fought to remove every trace of our Christian and Constitutional foundation. Consider how much has already been brushed aside in policies that govern our schools, courts, and federal facilities. Rewritten history and falsified science is used to indoctrinate hundreds of thousands of our children in our schools. Now, America has elected a socialist thug from Chicago as president. [C4-17]

Medved's aptly named poison factory uses dozens of tricks to derail election results in our country. One of the most blatant tricks was to steal the senatorial election of Republican Sharon Angle of Nevada when she confronted the powerful Senate Majority Leader Harry Reid. Reid was just too important for the communists to allow him to lose. Even with all the major polls showing Angle ahead or in a dead heat, and with Senator Reid acknowledging he was in serious trouble, Reid survived a ferocious challenge from the Tea Party star.

Compare the Nevada outcome with the results of a pre-election poll with a 99% accuracy rating and it becomes evident something fraudulent took place to overturn the election results.

In a video report featuring conservative political columnist for *The Wall Street Journal*, John Fund, he declares his conviction and commitment to combating communism. He also authored a book entitled, *Stealing Elections*.

Fund holds out the hope that the guilty will come forward, explain what they have done, and pledge to clean up their act. From my experience, that is being plainly naive to expect any communist to confess, explain, and clean up his act. They will never confess, yet they must be exposed and punished. [C4-18]

I admire Mr. Fund for his courage and dedication, and regret using his well-intended writings as examples. Unfortunately, his way of thinking is one of the biggest problems that we have in making Americans believe the reality of the time in which we are living.

As a former communist, I know how they act, think, and function. I know their code of ethics and procedures, and I know how to combat them as well. The way Fund thinks is the same way that many Americans do. Christians may quote scripture about turning the other cheek, but there is also the scripture that reads, "...an eye for an eye." Sooner or later we may be faced with a deeper understanding of that passage.

Check out this next video where a local news team was sent out to verify new ACORN-provided voter registration addresses. It includes a small portion with an ACORN registrant trying to prove that he is a female. You must see the audacity to believe it. [C4-19]

In this video, CNN's Lou Dobbs and his investigative team examine reports of ACORN's fraudulent voter registrations in Indiana and unveil the $800,000 Obama connection to ACORN. [C4-20]

The following video includes a Fox News interview with Congressman Bill Shuster of Pennsylvania noting the widespread voter fraud committed by ACORN in different parts of the U.S. The important thing to notice is that lawmakers across the country were beginning to get involved to see this criminal exploitation. [C4-21]

This short clip is a TV commercial by the McCain for President Campaign detailing Barack Obama's involvement with ACORN and the voting fraud scandal. [C4-22]

During the election, a federal judge ordered Ohio's top election officials to verify the identity of newly registered voters by matching them with other government documents. The next day a Sixth U.S. Circuit Court of Appeals set aside the federal judge's order. The ruling ignored testimonies like this one recorded on video. [C4-23, C4-24]

Communism seeks to rule the world and America is, perhaps, the last great barrier to their plan. The key is not spending more and more money, but electing leaders who can form a clear, workable plan to undo the damages and to force out the enemy. Then we must be dedicated to make that plan work, even if it requires an "iron fist."

The United States is the predominant super power of the globe, but that has zero significance if we don't use that power to make a better world. The battle against communism will be a long one to win back what our founding fathers established and our brave military has sacrificed to save.

Victory will only come when our society moves in a positive direction, and then only when the socialistic poison is eradicated from our schools, television, movies, churches, governments, armed forces and from our country as a whole. Only then will we see a new perspective and make the right moves to stop the destruction of our liberty.

CHAPTER 9

The Real Barack Obama

Mr. Barack Hussein Obama, the man that practically nobody knew in America, became president in a very short period of time. The day after the election, along with millions of others, I could not believe what had happened. I had read as much about him as I could, and never would have thought a person with his record would ever have a chance to win. But it happened and from that day on, he was my president, too.

Delving into Obama's history we can discover who he really is. His mother, Dr. Stanley Ann Dunham (1942–1995), was an anthropologist who specialized in economic anthropology and rural development and worked for a considerable period of time in Indonesia. She was also an American left-wing social activist (a communist), a dedicated atheist, and a liberal.

While Ann was still a child, her family was relocated to Mercer Island, Washington *specifically* so she could attend Mercer Island High School. Was there something very special about Mercer Island High School for a communist family? *The Chicago Tribune* explains: "In 1955, the chairman of the Mercer Island school board, John Stenhouse, testified before the House Un-American Activities Subcommittee that he had been a member of the Communist Party."

Barack Obama's father, Barack H. Obama, Sr. (1936–1982) was a senior government economist in Kenya and a stanch communist. He met Obama's mother in a Russian language class in Hawaii. In 1965 he published an important article in the East Africa Journal called "Problems Facing Our Socialism," where he said:

> "Bring down all the rich guys by the power of the state, confiscate their land, property, raises taxes as high as you want–100% if necessary, and obtain their wealth through fiat and legislative piracy. The rationale is that the wealth is not rightfully theirs, in the first place, but had been ripped off from the poor."

What a statement from our president in his book about the dreams of his father, a person who influenced his thinking and character.

The senior Obama abandoned his wife and young son when Barack was only two years old. After obtaining a divorce in 1964, Ann married Lolo Soetoro (1935–1987), an Indonesian oil manager and a Muslim, whom she met at the University of Hawaii. Soetoro returned alone to Indonesia and fifteen months later in late 1967, Barack and his mother moved to Jakarta.

Soetoro adopted Barack, Jr. and changed his name to Barry Soetoro. At age six, young Barry (Barack) was enrolled in first grade at an Indonesian-language school in Jakarta. According to his records, he was citizen of Indonesia and his faith was Islamic. Up to that point, he was the product of a communist and atheist mother, a Muslim communist father, and a Muslim communist stepfather. He was being raised in a strict Muslim country.

In 1971, Barry Soetoro was sent to Hawaii to live with his communist grandparents, Stanley Armour Dunham (1918–1992) and Madelyn Lee (Payne) Dunham (1922–2008). There, he attended the prestigious Punahou School. His grandparents arranged for young Barry's mentorship by journalist, labor movement activist, and communist party member Frank Marshall Davis (1905–1987).

This is the mysterious "Frank" cited as a friend and adviser by Barack Obama in one of his books. Obama has admitted attending social conferences and reading Marxist literature.

Dr. Kathryn Takara, another Obama friend and advisor and a professor of Interdisciplinary Studies at the University of Hawaii at Manoa, also confirmed that Davis is the "Frank" in Obama's book.

Reportedly, this Frank was the person to connect Obama with the right person inside the Communist Party USA where he allegedly obtained his controversial education.

After Barry left Hawaii, he purportedly attended Occidental College in Los Angeles. No substantial information has been offered to prove that he was there. There are no records that "Barry Soetoro" ever officially changed his name back to Barack Obama, and further, while allegedly at Occidental, he is said to have used the name Barry Soetoro, and was registered as a student from Indonesia. Of even more interest, California assembly records suggest that he received a state grant as a foreign exchange student from Indonesia.

Of his friends at Occidental, in his book "Dreams of My Fathers," Obama said: "I chose my friends carefully: the more politically active black students...the Marxist professors and structural feminists."

Also included among his friends are three Pakistani names: Wahid Hamid, Sohale Siddiqi, and Mohammed Hassan Chandoo. Obama and Hamid traveled to Pakistan in 1981; the reason for the trip is unknown.

Obama Is Hired by ACORN

After two years, Obama reportedly left Occidental and attended Columbia University in New York City. After his Columbia graduation, he moved to Chicago and became a "community organizer." There, he came into contact with more far-left political forces, including Students for a Democratic Society (SDS) and the Democratic Socialists of America.

Cliff Kincaid is editor for Accuracy in Media (AIM), which is a news media organization that describes itself as "a non-profit, grassroots citizen watchdog." Despite its assertion of political neutrality, the mainstream media often describes AIM as a conservative organization. Editor Kincaid asserts: "Among Obama's Chicago friends and associates were Mark Rudd, Bernardine Dohrn, John Jacobs, Bill Ayers, Terry Robbins, Jeff Jones and others who organize several fronts, including the SDS, Weather Underground, and the Democratic Socialists of America."

Barack Obama was hired by ACORN in Chicago to handle a lawsuit against the state of Illinois. Subsequently, he was to train community organizers and staff in the methods and tactics of community organizer and writer Saul D. Alinsky (1909–1972).

ACORN staged in-your-face intimidation protests in bank lobbies, drive-through lanes and even at bank managers' homes in an effort to get them to issue risky loans in the inner city or face charges of racism. Under the cover of the Federal Community Reinvestment Act (CRA), financial institutions granted what were called "Ninja" loans—no income, no job, no assets—to people who couldn't afford them.

In 1994, on behalf of ACORN, Barack Obama filed suit against Citibank under the CRA provisions. The purpose of the action was to force the bank to make questionable loans. The class action suit alleged that the bank had engaged in "redlining" practices in the Chicago area, and that they violated the Equal Credit Opportunity Act (ECOA), the Fair Housing Act, and the Thirteenth Amendment to the U.S. Constitution.

According to ACORN, Citibank rejected loan applications from minority applicants while approving loan applications filed by white applicants with similar financial characteristics and credit histories. In June 1995, Judge Ruben Castillo certified the suit as a class action and granted a motion to compel a review of the bank's loan application files. The case was named Buycks-Roberson v. Citibank Federal Savings Bank.

In his campaign for President of the United States, Obama told the group, "I've been fighting alongside ACORN on issues you care about my entire career." That is quite correct; Obama was fully aware of what the organization was doing with the money it received and expertise he provided.

In return, ACORN helped Obama from 1995 to 1999, while he was chairman of the Chicago Annenberg Challenge, a project designed to reform Chicago public schools. Bill Ayers wrote the initial grant application, which resulted in a $49.2 million grant. Reportedly, donors increased that amount even more.

The funds were spent, but not very well accounted for. Interestingly, the public schools did not improve and in the targeted Chicago neighborhoods more people were killed in gang-related incidents than were killed in the Iraq War of the same period. Where were the unbiased media reports on that statistic?

ACORN used intimidation, public charges of racism, and threats to use CRA to block business expansion and to bully hundreds of millions of dollars in loans and contributions from America's financial institutions. Barack Obama was their accomplice. Chicago's ACORN also used Alinsky's in-your-face tactics against Bell Federal Savings and Loan and Avondale Federal Savings.

In September 1992, *The Chicago Tribune* described the group's agenda as "affirmative action lending." Obama was instrumental in getting funding for ACORN when he served on the board of the Woods Fund for Chicago along with Weather Underground terrorist William "Bill" Ayers. The Woods Fund frequently gave ACORN grants to support its activities.

Politician Dr. Alice Palmer handpicked Barack Obama to succeed her in the Illinois State Senate. When Palmer was editor of the Black Press Review, she was the only African-American in the 27th Congress of the Communist Party in the Soviet Union in 1986.

Jeremiah Wright and Obama

Obama joined "Rev." Jeremiah Wright's "hate America church" and spent over 20 years as a member. The church's roots are founded in a Marxist and Leninist cult from South America in the 1960's. Many of the church members are communists, extremist radicals, and avowed haters of white Americans.

When he entered the White House as President, Obama could not hide his Marxist beliefs from people like me who have lived under communist leaders as they tried to hide their real intentions.

I took careful notice of the man who 62% of the American public doesn't seem to care whether or not he is a socialist. True to the communist pattern, he has already established a "sub-government" under the real government. He surrounded himself with 43 so-called czars, 120-plus lawyers, the largest White House staff in history, over

3,000 educators, more than 25,000 activists, and over 150,000 comrades working within 2,100 non-profit organizations. It's an alphabet soup: ACLU, ACORN, CEC, AIW, WUO, WFT, UOC, RCP, PLP, MIM, FSP, and SEIU.

If you still need to ask whether Obama represents our nation or a foreign ideology, then Obama's close ties with the Purple-Shirt thugs and highlights of his 2007 speech to SEIU members will perhaps convince you, as it did me, that this President is truly a Marxist Leninist Communist. The video record speaks for itself: [C5-1]

<u>Is Obama Another Hugo Chavez?</u>

When he encouraged and approved funds for the building of a million-plus man militia to *protect* Americans inside its borders, I knew we were about to have huge problems. This is exactly the same tactic used by Hitler, Lenin, and Hugo Chavez. That militia is not to *protect* Americans; no, it is to protect him and his cronies against America's anti-communists that he inevitably expects will confront his agenda. [C5-2, C5-3]

Compare what is being done here with what the communist Hugo Chavez did in Venezuela. He brought thousands of Cubans to Venezuela and created a sub-government under the legitimate government. This sub-government had different titles to disguise the real intentions. The Cubans began to take key positions in every cabinet post and every department including the police, army, and universities. They started screening all government workers, firing those that rebelled, and brainwashing the rest.

In just ten short years, through a process of indoctrination, activism, revolt, false elections, community organizing, and promoting envy and hatred among the social classes, Venezuela became a communist country hiding behind the iron curtain.

With a militia of more than 100,000 men to "protect" Venezuela, there are no freedoms or human rights. Chavez has systematically been closing all the non-government television and radio stations, confiscating most of the private sector, and putting all production and distribution systems, education, police, and the army under strict government control. No one has been able to stand up to the takeover.

Darwin's Theory—A Recipe for Murder

Remember the major influence that Charles Darwin and his theories had on communist leaders. That relationship between Darwinism and Marxism is very strong. Lenin became the first tyrant to put the Darwinist theory into practice when he arranged a famine that killed millions of his own people.

He watched what was happening with enormous pleasure. In his view, the famine was most useful; he calculated that it would help to destroy peoples' belief in God and religion, make them bow their heads to communism, and so make it a superior society. In the *Black Book of Communism* that sent shock waves around the world, the author wrote, "Lenin, indeed applied Darwinism to society, and mercilessly slaughtered whole societies he regarded as herds of animals."

Stalin was easily deceived by the superficial claims of Darwinism, and became an atheist. In that state of ignorance, he promptly joined the ranks of the Bolsheviks. The theory of evolution again formed Stalin's most important source of inspiration when he came to power.

He was especially eager to have the theory taught in Soviet schools, and declared his intention behind that: "There are three things that we do to disabuse the minds of our seminary students. We have to teach them the age of the earth, the geologic origin, and Darwin's teachings." Having established in his mind that humans are no more than higher animals, Stalin callously provoked the famine that killed millions of his own people.

Adolph Hitler, with his quotes and his barbaric records of the destruction of human life in masses, offers proof that he, too, was a Darwinist follower. He wrote: "Those who want to live, let them fight, and those who do not want to fight in this world of eternal struggle do not deserve to live.

"...Struggle is the father of all things. It is not by the principles of humanity that man lives or is able to preserve himself above the animal world, but solely by means of the most brutal struggle. If you do not fight, life will never be won"

Darwinism had such an enormous affect in China in the 20th century that the Harvard University historian James Reeve Pusey wrote a book on that very issue, *China and Charles Darwin*. According to Pusey's account, Darwinism's affect on Chinese intellectuals encouraged them to adopt a revolutionary worldview, and provided major ideological support for the development of the Communist movement in the country. In turn, that caused a famine that killed *60 million people*. Can we see a pattern here?

Obama is also a Charles Darwin ideology follower, just like Marx, Lenin, Hitler, and Mao. He is looking forward to teaching and reviving the Darwinism ideology here in America. [C5-4]

Celebrating the 200th anniversary of the birth of the President Abraham Lincoln, Barack Obama observed: "This day is also the bicentennial of Charles Darwin's birth. It is worth a moment of pause to renew that commitment to science and innovation and discovery that Lincoln understood so well."

In my 48 years of studying and combating communism, I have not found a single person who follows Charles Darwin's teaching that is not a devoted communist, and even fewer people remember his birth date. This astonishing revelation by the President is horrifying. Darwin himself expressed doubt his theory could ever be substantiated. Still, evil communist men have seized on his ideas to justify their actions. [C5-5, C5-6]

The previous videos show why prominent scientists of the time refused to take Darwin seriously. Only two people, Karl Marx and Friedrich Engels and their followers, adopted the theory of evolution as their scientific foundation. Why was Darwin's theory of evolution of great importance to the spread of Marxism among western intellectuals?

The theory depicted human beings as a species of animal, claimed that they developed by means of conflict; and most importantly, the Darwinian hypothesis denied the idea of creation. Those three great errors formed the basis of Marxism. Darwinism bears much of the responsibility for 94 million deaths cause by the communists.

I pray that I am wrong about the danger of losing out to this satanic ideology, for if I am right, we will surely have the same fate as Russia, China, and Cambodia. The courage to fight must govern our actions, for the risk of losing is too great. [C5-7]

Barack Obama has followed the same pattern of communist leaders in almost every action he takes. In his two years in power, he has overspent all other past presidents put together. He and his cronies have already made the federal government the country's largest creditor, debtor, lender, employer, consumer, guarantor, contractor, grantor, tenant, property owner, and healthcare provider.

If Obama is not stopped, such enormous spending is going to cause a catastrophe of unbelievable proportions in America, but totally in line with that which occurred in Russia, Cambodia and China.

In addition, Obama is blocking oil drilling all over America and its coastline while, at the same time, encouraging oil drilling in Mexico. To add salt to our wounds, the US Export Import bank has given a two billion dollar loan guarantee to Brazil to do their own offshore drilling. When the wells begin producing, however, the oil is aimed for the Chinese market, not for America!

Then, there is his inconsistent and apparently illogical approach to all our problems in the Middle East. One minute he is siding with the dictators of Egypt, Libya, Iran, Saudi Arabia and the next minute, making obligatory gestures of compassion to their long suffering populations.

His disastrous foreign policies include his participation in the dismantling of our only reliable ally in the Middle East, Israel.

Americans awaken daily to find that damage is being done as one destructive White House policy after other assaults the nation and its citizens. Obama appears to see himself as one of the great omnipotent leaders like Lenin, Stalin, and Mao who considered themselves super human beings. That kind of behavior takes leaders to an unreal world of fantasy and extreme cruelty where they all end up being reviled as devils. Obama apparently imagines America as an imperialist country that he has to repair. That is why he unnecessarily apologizes to Europeans and unacceptably bows to the Egyptian King. [C5-8]

It would also appear that Obama apparently desires to become the Global President through the New World Order. He already has acted as a world leader, hastening the U.S. downfall via the collapse of the dollar's value through increased debt. That is a major tool that will force America into becoming Marxist Communist through the natural mechanics of evolution. Such a government will then subjugate the people to the will of the "state" and eliminate God from society.

Those who are industrious and successful in our nation will be charged with various offenses against the state to justify confiscation of their property and the elimination of the free market system. America's new leader will be like the others who adopted Marxism, socialism, or fascism–Lenin, Stalin, Mao, Hitler, and now, maybe it will be Obama. Each of their regimes followed a clear pattern of brute force over the people.[C5-9]

Throughout my years of combating communism, I have not found any living person with better qualifications to be a Marxist/ Leninist communist than Barack Hussein Obama. Unfortunately, the American people don't recognize this because we have failed to teach the young generations the threat that communism represents; more importantly, we have failed to teach our youth what it means to be an American.

One of the biggest mistakes we have made is giving to our children everything they want, which teaches them to grow up being takers and not givers. Again, Christians are givers; communists are takers; so by setting the wrong example for our young people, we may be guilty of laying the foundations for communistic doctrines to mold our future generation.

I remember in the 1970's during a parent and teachers' meeting, we were being instructed on how to raise our own children according to statist guidelines. Back then, few parents understood that the enemy was engineering the new culture for tomorrow's communism.

Obama's communism comes well packaged from Hollywood. If we don't do equally as well in packaging our anti-communism, then even if we don't fight back with all our strength, we will lose. I don't know what people are reading these days, but what I am exposing here is all over the Internet. The facts can be found in the Recommended Readings index.

Those who have not lived through the experience cannot imagine how devastating it is to have been well established in your own country, only to have the communists throw you out with nothing. In the early 1960's, I saw hundreds of Cuban millionaires (including my own father) washing dishes to earn enough to eat in Miami and elsewhere around the world.

When Fidel Castro took control of the property and wealth of Cuba's most successful families, the remaining Cubans were left poor, extremely poor. I am convinced that this is exactly what Obama intends to do with America, and with all of us.

A Man Is Known by His Friends

In the following referenced videos, readers can witness Obama's views and identify his friends. In this clip, Obama contradicts himself, speaking about one America made up of black, Latino and white heritage. Later he claims that white supremacy is the cause of the world's problems. Being of mixed race—as much white as black—he conveniently adapts to either culture as the situation demands. [C5-10]

The next clip is about Malcolm X, one of the leaders of the Black Liberation Army. Obama mentions "X" as one of his inspirational models. Malcolm X is shown describing Islam as one of the great religions of compassion. He also states that Americans were the ones who invented slavery in the world.

He conveniently forgets to mention that slavery has been in existence since Biblical times. He also ignores the fact that since the 12th century after Christ, black Muslim Pirates have captured and enslaved millions of human beings on the coast of Africa. Viewers will note that Malcolm X proclaims that he never promoted hatred. Yet, compare that statement with his remarks about white people in this video. [C5-11]

People who spout hate like Malcom, confuse and stir up hatred and confusion in the black people of the world, and particularly in the United States. These same hate-filled beings criticize Dr. Martin Luther King, Jr. for his peaceful and benevolent behavior. Public figures who spread such venom are a cause of so much of a black person's problems today.

They are discouraging those of their own race from competing for honest work and for exhibiting lawful behavior. They are made to believe they have no chance to succeed. How do the hate mongers explain that even poor black Americans are among the most prosperous of their race in the world? [C5-12]

Obama's preacher, Jeremiah Wright, Jr., is another guilty of discrimination against whites; a true racist—an African-American racist. He preaches about the evil that white people do to his black brothers, but totally refuses to speak of the good that white people in American have done. White Americans have done more to lift up Black Americans than blacks have received anywhere else in the world.

Literally trillions of American dollars have been spent assisting blacks since the 1960s with welfare, food stamps, rent supplements, Section 8 housing, Pell grants, student loans, legal services, Medicaid, Earned Income Tax Credits, and poverty programs designed to bring the African-American community into the mainstream.

But Pastor Wright has repeatedly made it clear that he does not want to know that black-on-white rapes are 100 times more common than the reverse or that black-on-white robberies were 139 times as common as the reverse. [C5-13, C5-14, C5-15]

Castro Admits Total Failure of Communism

Recent mouth-dropping news: after 52 years of suppressing the Cuban people, Fidel Castro finally recognized the total failure of communism. According to journalist, author, and staff writer for *The Atlantic* Jeffrey Goldberg, Castro announced a startlingly assessment: "The Cuban model doesn't even work for us anymore."

We can only pray that Fidel's attempt to throw himself on history's mercy with his statement will be accepted as a word of warning for Barack Obama with his communist agenda.

Barack Obama's Approach as the World President.

The world still doesn't completely know who Barack Hussein Obama is. At first, many saw Obama as the most highly regarded U.S. President since John F. Kennedy; now he appears to be a president whose his every day policies are undermining the United States economic system, its long established foreign polices, and the fabric of American Culture. Meanwhile, the Middle East is crumbling under the weight of hate and violence driven by a world plan to put the region and then the entire world under communist rule.

Unlike a real American president, Obama sat on the sidelines or jetted off on his multiple vacations at taxpayer expense. He took on the title of leader, but without the experience, courage or instincts to lead. When he finally took action, it was not in the best interests of the United States, but rather in the interests of an ideology that resembles that of revolutionaries in Libya and the New World Order.

Some may ask why the president didn't act with the same determination in Iran and Egypt as he did in Libya. The answer is simple. Obama is acting in accordance with the plans for a world community. The attack in Libya has three purposes.

First: Obama is trying to show the world how authoritative and powerful he can be working together with the United Nation as world President. He was sending a strong message to the world when he said in Brazil "Gaddhafi has got to go."

Second: in the NWO plan to communize the region, Libya has the perfect living dictator to use as an excuse to bring the country under communist rule.

Third: Libya is one of the world's oil producing countries. A war in Libya will lead to higher oil prices at a time when the United States' economy is in deep trouble, which is what the New World Order needs. Once capitalism collapses, and panic sets in, the socialists will appear as saviors, seizing the government and the country without firing a shot.

This is not, as they say, rocket science. When history repeats time and again with the same result, intelligent people must understand and learn accordingly.

Time may sadly prove that I am right, and then the world will learn how destructive and powerful the New World Order will be if they succeed in winning over America on their way to world domination.

CHAPTER 10

Communism and Racism

We are now facing a very difficult era ahead. It could be one filled with hatred, treachery, treason, and horrible political instability. That's because no one stirs up more hatred between the social classes than the communists. For them, this period is the beginning of the termination of the bourgeois class here in America. They will use the New Culture, Muslims, blacks, and Hispanics to take over the country once they have built up animosity to a fever pitch between minorities and conservative whites.

President Barack Obama won the election with 53% of the vote. On Inauguration Day, he had an overwhelming 73% approval rating from the American people. That is probably the last time we are going to see that much unity in this country between the minorities and whites. The more the majority gives in to minority demands, legitimate or not, the more that the American haters demand.

The racial conflict that the President and his followers post on the Internet hundreds of times every day will create the worst boiling cauldron seen since the 1960's race riots. When Mr. Obama was campaigning in 2010, he said to the Hispanics, "The Spanish should punish their enemies, not their friends." He was telling them that the Republicans and whites were their enemies, playing to their fears and stumping for their votes.

Black Liberation Theology

Obama and all his friends come from the same evil ideology of hate, based on the black liberation theology (a name given to disguise its true Marxism and Leninism nature), a school of thought that began in 1969 with the publication of a book by the Marxist Dr. James Cone called *Black Theology of Liberation* a work that profess a moral superiority of black over white. All of the black supremacists, including Mr. Wright, have shared and preached the same militant racial communist themes adopted by Franz Fanon, Stokely Carmichael and Malcolm X. [C6-1]

Obama's involvement in the plot to subjugate America is nothing new, his life and his polices have been steeped in socialism from childhood. His friends and associates are communist radicals; his religious mentors practice the Black Liberation philosophy described by Dr. Cone, the pioneer of that ideology:

> "Insofar as this country is seeking to make whiteness the dominating power throughout the world, whiteness is the symbol of the antichrist. Whiteness characterizes the activity of deranged individuals intrigued by their own image of themselves and thus unable to see that they are what is wrong with the world. Black theology seeks to analyze the satanic nature of whiteness and by doing so, prepare all nonwhites for revolutionary action."

Here's another notable quote from Cone in his discourse about his Black Liberation Theology:

> "Black theology refuses to accept a God who is not identified totally with the goals of the black community. If God is not for us and against white people, then he is a murderer, and we had better kill him. The task of black theology is to kill Gods who do not belong to the black community ... Black theology will accept only the love of God, which participates in the destruction of the white enemy. What we need is the divine love as expressed in Black Power, which is the power of black people to destroy their oppressors here and now by any

> means at their disposal. Unless God is participating in this holy activity, we must reject his love."

Jeremiah Wright, Jr., Obama's pastor at the Trinity United Church of Christ in Chicago, has been known for many controversial statements regarding race and color. On April 13, 2003, he said in one of his sermons:

> "This government gives them drugs, builds bigger prisons, passes a three strikes law, and then wants us to sing God Bless America? No, no, no. Not God Bless America; G*d d**n America. That's in the Bible, for killing innocent people."

After the September 11, 2001 terrorist attacks in New York, Wright said:

> "We have supported state terrorism against the Palestinians and the black South Africans, and now we are indignant because stuff we have done overseas is now brought right back into our front yards. America's chickens are coming home to roost."

<u>Radical Islam and Black Theology</u>

Islam is another name given to disguise radical Islam's true Marxism and Leninism nature. One of the first ones to teach radical Islam in our country was Elijah Muhammad, who said:

> "As it was divine will in the case of the destruction of the slave empires of the ancient and modern past, America's judgment and destruction will also be brought about by divine will and divine power. Just as ancient nations paid for their sins against humanity, White America must now pay for her sins against twenty-two million "Negroes." White America's worst crimes are her hypocrisy and her deceit. White pretends to ask herself: 'What do these Negroes want?' White America knows that four hundred years of cruel bondage has made these twenty-two million ex-slaves too (mentally) blind to see what they really want."

Barack Obama embraces that same communist/Islamic ideology, which he and his radical friends have been practicing and planning for more than 30 years. In my book, that makes him a Marxist and Leninist.

Most public figures following the communistic ideology belong to a false Christian church or Islam temple, as a part of the plan to make them appear mainstream. Some fake Christian theologies preach a Jesus Christ described as a poor man of color living under an oppressive European white ruler (Romans during Biblical times.) They teach that He was as much about social change and bringing down governments as he was about spiritual liberation. That type of Jesus meets Dr. Cone's criteria for a God who supports black power rebellion.

Socialists have been indoctrinating minorities and people of the lower social classes for over forty years. Now they feel ready for the battle to take America. To win, they know that they must create hatred between the *Haves* and the *Have-Nots*, as did Hitler, Lenin, Mao and Fidel. In Germany it was good against evil, us against the Jews. Here in America it is going to be Blacks, Hispanics and Muslims against the whites, poor against the rich.

Instead of striving for equality among races, the hate mongers declare that blacks are the superior class, and therefore white America must pay for their crimes against minorities.

Hispanics believe that the western part of the United States belongs to Mexico. Puerto Ricans are told that white Americans are exploiting them, and that they should be free of the U.S. This, of course, ignores the protection and aid that they have gained as a U.S. territory.

The majority of Americans don't understand this communist process. The more we demonstrate that we want unity, the more the communists demand and provoke division.

Pigford v. Glickman

Andrew J. Breitbart is a Webmaster, commentator and a media genius. He proved that by his skillful handling of the ACORN "hooker" scandal, where he manipulated the leftist media, and forced the exposure of corruption in one of Obama's most powerful political support groups.

But Breitbart's handling of that exposé was minor compared to his ultimately brilliant disclosure of Shirley Sherrod's "white farmer" scandal. Sherrod was the Georgia State Director of Rural Development for the United States Department of Agriculture at the time of her address to the National Association for the Advancement of Colored People (NAACP).

Monday, July 22, 2010, Breitbart released videotape on his "Big Government" site with the country watching in shock and disbelief. The tape showed Sherrod, a black woman, laughing with a roomful of NAACP members as she related how she had ruled against a destitute white farmer, refusing to give him the financial aid he desperately needed. She told her delighted audience that she had sent him to a white lawyer, as she put it, to "one of his own kind," for assistance.

Sherrod immediately became the focus of a firestorm of controversy, which exploded throughout the country. Within a day of the release of that infamous tape, the head of the Department of Agriculture, spurred on by Barack Obama, demanded and received Sherrod's resignation.

Breitbart appeared to have won. But then his video seemed to explode in his face. As Sherrod protested, FOX News released the *entire text* of her NAACP speech in March. There on the tape Sherrod was shown repenting of her racism against a white farmer and instead she ran his campaign to obtain funds to keep his farm afloat. Within hours of that complete tape being revealed, the world turned against Breitbart.

Conservatives around the nation were outraged that he'd endangered their reputations by releasing "doctored" videotape. They accused Breitbart of dealing a fatal blow to the conservative media. However, it appears the real purpose for Breitbart's tape was to manipulate the media into exposing one of the most shocking examples of corruption in the federal government: a little known legal case entitled, "Pigford v. Glickman."

A North Carolina African-American farmer, Timothy Pigford, joined by 400 additional black farmer plaintiffs, filed a lawsuit in

1997. Daniel Glickman, the Secretary of Agriculture for President Clinton, was the named defendant.

The suit against the Department of Agriculture alleged that the farmers had been unfairly denied USDA loans due to racial discrimination during the years 1983 through 1997. It was a victory for the black farmers in 1999 when the government agreed to pay each farmer as much as $50,000 to settle their claims.

But that wasn't the end of it; in February 2010, something truly shocking happened with that 1999 judgment. Without revealing its actions, the USDA agreed to release a staggering $1.25 billion to Pigford plaintiffs. This was because the original 400 plaintiffs had now swollen into a class action suit to include 86,000 black farmers.

There was only one tiny, little problem. There are not 86,000 black farmers in the country. According to verified census data, the number of black farmers throughout the nation was only 39,697.

Of course, it is entirely reasonable to ask how 39,697 claims exploded into 86,000 claims. And, how did a $20 million claim ($50,000 x 400) burst into $1.25 billion...*62½ times as large*?

Well, the answer comes right back to the woman who spearheaded this case because of her position in 1997 at the "Rural Development Leadership Network." Interestingly it is the same woman whose family took home the highest single payout of approximately $13 million. You guessed it; she was none other than Shirley Sherrod.

It appears Ms. Sherrod exposed herself as the perpetrator of one of the largest fraud claims in U.S. history, a fraud enabled principally because she screamed racism at the government and battered them into meek submission. But it gets even more interesting when you probe further.

Ms. Sherrod has also exposed one of the powerful people who assisted her in this race fraud. The original 1999 judgment of "Pigford v. Glickman" only applied to 16,000 black farmers. But in 2008, a junior Senator from Illinois got a law passed to reopen the case and allow more black farmers to sue for funds. *That Senator from Illinois was none other than Barack Obama.*

Because the woman responsible for spearheading this legislation was an obscure USDA official, American taxpayers did not realize that they had just been forced to pay out more than $1.25 billion to settle racial claims...in the middle of a worldwide depression. [C6-2, C6-3]

There is a huge agenda ahead of us. We have to continue uncovering and examining cases like this one. This was not an isolated case; the reality is that this is happening every day all over our country. Remember, Washington D.C. is paying these immoral and illegal claims with your taxpayer money.

With endless variations of bigotry, our enemies are constructing a "house that is divided" from border to border and coast to coast. For example, the border struggle between the American Minutemen group and Mexico is nothing short of unbelievable.

A simple Google search finds hundreds of cases in which the police have had to intervene. Name calling between the factions frequently turns into skirmishes, battles, and even shooting deaths. Amnesty proposed by the moderates and leftists will result in even more drastic drains upon our economy, and our educational and medical systems. [C6-4]

The referenced video below shows how the communists use children to intimidate while creating a wide rift between the social classes. Whenever you see these tactics, with leaders united in phoning, speaking, or singing with one voice, that is typical communism in action. Not limited to the young, they also manipulate teenagers, adults, seniors, Hispanics, and blacks. Their followers feel they belong to something important, so they react and more racial problems are created. [C6-5]

What the communists want when they file cases like Pigford v. Glickman is to arouse public protests against blacks, while convincing minorities that they deserve payback for slavery. Few consider the fact that they are blessed by living in the greatest country in history, and that many black Americans have taken advantage of the opportunity to gain a higher standard of living than most of their race in other countries.

Those that spout hate conveniently cover up the history of black slave masters who kidnapped and sold their brethren into slavery around the world. While claiming that America was built on the backs of slaves, they ignore the fact that states involved in slavery were the poorest in the union and took longer to catch up to slave-free economies.

In any areas where there is no friction between the social classes, communism creates it. Eventually, discord between blacks and whites, rich and poor, citizens and illegal aliens will explode and create massive civil disruptions. Their methods of sowing discontent can be seen on this referenced website. [C6-6]

Divide and Conquer Tactics

Another example of how communists have agitated Mexicans and induced them to hold anti-American rallies is a matter of record found on the Internet. In retaliation, whites explode and protest back against Mexicans. Antagonism is stirred up between the minorities and social classes until communists hold majority power.

In Cuba, I was well trained in these tactics. I learned how to divide a society by pitting poor against rich, black against white, and evil against good. Hitler did that, and for a while was the world's strongest leader…and a mass murderer. [C6-7]

Today in America, this destructive work is still being done with your taxpayer money. Soon the black, Hispanic, new culture and Muslims will be the majority; this will allow the communists to win the elections. Help will be provided by a documented hoard of over 2,100 documented non-profit organizations that receive grants from our federal government. That means you and I are paying more than 150,000 full time communists who are working toward the unification of all those minorities against whites and conservatives of all races

President Barack Hussein Obama touts being a Community Organizer as one of his greatest accomplishment. Not only did he become a lecturer and teacher of his methods for ACORN members, but he was also responsible for putting pressure on banks and corporations to make bad loans and to donate to ACORN.

The last grant ACORN almost received, a few months after Obama was elected, was for $8.5 billion to spread their socialistic destruction across America, while employing, indoctrinating, and training thousands of communist workers. Additionally, communist controlled environmental organizations got over 14,000 federal grants used to hinder our industries and workers, and to prevent the United States from being free of foreign oil. All this has taken place within the past 20 years.

Unfortunately, none of the "old politicians" from either party noticed that anything nefarious was taking place in both houses. If Americans want to keep our democracy, freedom of speech, freedom of religion, and free enterprise, then we have to begin to take action right now. The alternative is to wait, do nothing and lose everything.

Broken Promises of Harmony

When Barack Obama was a candidate for the presidency, he had strong words for the black community that made it appear that he would work for understanding and harmony. Instead of harmony, however, he has created more friction between social classes, without regard for the racial consequences.

Obama and his administration deliberately passed up one of the best opportunities in our short history to bring about unity between races and classes in America. Why? Because Obama does not view those as problems but rather as his solution.

America has long been the best country in the world for black people. It was here that over half a million blacks were brought from Africa as slaves, and yet they grew into a community of millions of free people. Along the way, they were introduced to Christian salvation and reached the highest levels of freedom, education, and prosperity blacks have ever known in the world.

As with any group, African-Americans need good, strong leaders, like Dr. Martin Luther King, Jr. (1929–1968). What they do not need are instigators like Barack Obama who perpetrated hundreds of cases like *Pigford v. Glickman*, which, in reality, do nothing positive for the black community, but promote racism and anger. Sooner or later these injustices will have their consequences. It appears that Obama's leftist, liberal, socialist agenda of mutilating this country's economy far surpasses his love for his people.

Obama, who was elected through the support of millions of white as well as black voters, could have brought about an understanding and harmony between the races. Instead, he increased the rancor and division between races through distrust and hate.

Instead of the consideration and unity that Dr. Martin Luther King, Jr. envisioned, Obama became just one more purveyor of class and race envy. He and those like him see a golden opportunity to take advantage of chaos to advance their socialist agenda.

Whites understand that African-Americans have had a very painful past; but this is the present and the only way blacks will overcome their past and rise to prosperity is to work on the future. Being government-dependent doesn't have any opportunities for hope. Children learn from their parents, so with an example of endless dependency, black children will be sentenced to meaningless lives of government dependency as well.

Hispanics as Useful Pawns of Communism

On the Hispanic side, we find almost the same problem. They are so nearly identical, that anybody could make an educated guess that the tactics are from the same school of social paralysis. In others words, you can find the same agitator, with a slightly different mask and approach, but aiming for the same results.

Hitler enacted a terrible purge against the Jews, ranting that they (the Jews) were the ones who controlled the majority of the businesses. The Nazis relentlessly drummed their ugly slogans of "rich against poor, good against evil, and us against the Jews." And, tragically, they won.

What our homegrown communists are doing in America is similar, only with different players. Here it is to be Muslims, Hispanics, and Blacks against the white majority, and the poor against the rich. How tragic it is that only a handful of liberal socialists have been able to do more damage to this great nation than 200 years of attacks by foreign countrics.

Anyone who reads or listens to the news knows about the black hate preachers and the Muslim hate clerics. Now add to the mix, the rising up of new Hispanic dealers of hateful rhetoric. The poison factory has no borders, language barriers, or racial limitations. No matter what the nationality, color, or language spoken, communists are the same unscrupulous, tyrannical, and criminal individuals willing to do whatever is necessary to attain their goals.

There are a growing number of Hispanic leaders educated and trained with American taxpayers' money and through "non-profit organizations." These leftist-sponsored free riders are agitating and creating chaos. Here are examples of their South of the border ranting:

Augustin Cebada, of the Brown Berets de Aztelan, a paramilitary group said:

> "Go back to Boston. Go back to Plymouth Rock, Pilgrims. Get out. We are the future. You are old and tired. Go on. We have beaten you. Leave like beaten rats you old white people. It is your duty to die...through love of having children, we are going to take over."

What this person chooses to ignore is that the people he is attacking are the ones who built this country to what it is today. Rabble-rousers like Cebada should be sent to Cuba to enjoy all the "wonders" of communism. Notice his claim that by having more children, Latino families will eventually outnumber whites that are more likely to use birth control, and blacks who have the largest percentage of abortions.

Richard Alatorre, a member of the Los Angeles City Council: "They (Native Americans) are afraid we're going to take over the governmental institutions and other institutions. They're right. We will take them over . . . We are here to stay."

Excelsior, the national newspaper of Mexico City: "The American Southwest seems to be slowly returning to the jurisdiction of Mexico without firing a single shot."

All that the Mexican illegal aliens and their mouthpieces are doing is earning the hatred and disdain of Americans. History will prove that their allowing communists to represent Mexican people against the U.S. will bring down a worse disaster on their own heads. Once these Hispanic pawns have served the purpose of tearing down our democracy, the communists will dispense with them as if they were spent ammunition.

Jose Angel Gutierrez, an attorney and professor at the University of Texas at Arlington: "We have an aging white America. They are not making babies. They are dying. The explosion is in our population . . . I love it. They are shitting in their pants with fear. I love it."

The last mid-term elections prove that the American people are not ready to fold up their tents, and still have the power of the ballot box. I could almost feel sorry for people like Gutierrez and Alatorre; it is obvious they have not studied communist history to discover how subtly their masters are using them.

Art Torres, a gay politician and, formerly Chairman of the California Democratic Party: "Remember 187–the proposition to deny taxpayer funds for services to non-citizens—was the last gasp of white America in California."

We can thank the liberal California court for attempting to nullify the legitimate passage of 187 by a fed-up majority of Americans.

If communist agitators hadn't found a non-profit organization to provide their free education in exchange for indoctrination, they may today have had a successful career working for a private company in the country they wish to destroy.

After WWII if we had invaded the Soviet Union, and eradicated the communist ideology, we may have avoided the peril we find ourselves facing today. Remember, it was General Patton who wanted to turn our might on Russia after the defeat of Germany. He warned that they were our next and greatest enemy. He was ignored and our leaders of that time are responsible for allowing his prophetic future to happen.

Further proof of his words is that Chile has had 40 years of prosperity that would never have happened if they hadn't evicted the entire communist population from their country.

America has spent billions of hard-earned taxpayer dollars to train and educate hundreds of thousands of people, only to have many of them become our enemies. We have appeared soft and weak because of lack of oversight, and our overly benevolent way of thinking and trusting. Now we are paying the consequences for allowing that to happen.

Today in Cuba there are two generations condemning us for allowing Castro to impose communism on the island. Thousands of young Cubans have drowned trying to cross 90 miles of open sea to find the freedom that they lost in their own country.

If nothing is done to stop the poison factory, and we allow them to take over, future generations in our own country will blame the present generation for their loss of freedom. They will be right to do so.

Conservatives who are too busy to vote, too disinterested to pay attention to the news, too self-centered to think beyond their own well-being will be no different than a guard sleeping on duty as the enemy slips through the gate.

As a naturalized American, I feel shamed that our representatives do not stand up to people who talk trash, treason and sedition in this country. As Spanish descendent, I am embarrassed when someone of my heritage speaks out against the America I love so much. This book is my voice crying in the wilderness: the continuing of my fight through the press and other media.

You must join me whether you are a Muslim, a Black, or Latino who understands the value of America as a bulwark against communism in all its forms. Express your repudiation and indignation toward this evil system, and especially toward those of your own culture who are bent on destroying your personal standard of living and your freedom as well.

CHAPTER 11

Post Obama

After Obama vacates the White House, I pray that we will be smart enough to craft and establish a plan to bring back America's values, integrity and economic stability. As a nation, we have been declining in most aspects of our society for the last thirty years. We have lost the ingenuity and productivity that we used to have which made our country the greatest in the world. The honor, pride, and fierce patriotism taught at the turn of the twentieth century do not exist in the curriculum of our children anymore.

Fortunately, Christianity has survived this bombardment of contradiction, new culture, new ways of thinking, and communism. Nevertheless, the Christian religion has also suffered a great setback, fashioned in a large part by the destructive movie and television Industries.

To turn this country back to the right direction, we must be determined, persistent, and courageous. Refuse to participate in damaging political correctness, deny false science like global warming, overrule liberal environmentalists whose true concern is for power, and then we must conquer our own apathy and timidity.

In his 2009 book, *Heaven and Earth: Global Warming—The Missing Science*, Australian geologist Ian Plimer makes the following points:

- There is little to no geological, archaeological or historic analysis on what is causing climate change.

- Greenland was once a green land because of natural occurring global warming. During medieval times Earth was several degrees warmer than it is now.
- Climate has always changed but it is not because of industrialization.
- Atmospheric CO_2 has been far higher than it is now.
- The hockey stick graph that charts global warming as the result of manmade CO_2 emissions is fraudulent.

President Barack Obama is gambling America's future on "green" energy while ignoring these truths. A few weeks ago in a major policy address, Obama announced that America would continue to pursue green energy solutions from wind, solar, biofuels and nuclear power. He is pushing costly unknown projects while refusing to authorize drilling for our own domestic oil.

Bad Laws Must Go

Americans must demand that the Congressional Committee on Oversight and Government Reform conduct a thorough investigation of the laws passed over the last forty years. Eliminate the unnecessary and the restrictive ones that are stealing our standard of living and our freedoms.

One example is legislation that prevents America from becoming free of foreign oil by allowing us to extract our own oil with proven environmentally safe methods. Another example would be the politically motivated environmental and safety laws like those from OSHA and the EPA that prevent our industries from competing in world markets.

The Heritage foundation recently reported on an EPA regulation that would force dairies and other businesses that deal with milk to file a plan for handling catastrophic milk spills. They will have to train with cleanup protocol and build containment facilities similar to those needed for oil spills.

Hundreds if not thousands of these ridiculous and costly laws and regulations burden our businesses and families. In 2010 alone, the Obama administration issued 43 major new rules that will cost the private sector an estimated $26.5 billion. Obama Care has generated over 6,000 pages of legislative shackles and countless more are expected. These economy-destroying actions are not accidental. They come straight out of the communist playbook of conquering nations.

The Oversight Committee must move to adjust or rescind entitlement laws that make more and more people dependent on government. To turn the hearts of our children, our future leaders, back to our Christian roots, we must remove laws that have barred moral and Christian principles from being taught in our schools, while exposing the horrible truth of the socialist/communist ideology.

Another important need will be to establish a Commission on Political Qualification, where every candidate for political office and every high ranking federal appointee would have to apply, be thoroughly investigated, and have the appropriate clearances before being approved to run for or be accepted for office. This would include the President, governors, and legislators.

If the commission finds that an applicant is unqualified for the position he/she was seeking, that person would be unable to seek that office. If the commission approved the candidate, he/she would be able to start the political campaign. That campaign would be similar to the ones we have today but with one enormous difference: each candidate would not have to spend millions of dollars to establish their legal right to serve.

Further, public servants would quickly learn that if they don't follow through with their promises and obligations, they would not be eligible for re-election. We must understand that the important thing is not who we elect, but that the people we elect do what is right for our citizens and our nation.

This objective becomes far more critical when we consider that every member of the House of Representatives actually speaks for a population of about 560,000 people. Of that group, about 280,000 are registered to vote. Then only 140,000 to 180,000 actually exercise their right to vote. Those numbers startlingly underline the reality of what is happening in our elections; according to the statistics, the elections are often decided by less than 10% of the population.

We can create a citizen-based army of volunteers made up of housewives, seniors, and other interested and motivated voters in general. Then, we can arm them with cameras and papers and pencils to watch, record, and film any and all wrongdoing they witness.

America's future is not secure until the majority is able to exercise the right to vote free from fraud and bullying. Under the management of a neutral non-political organization, we can expose the malfeasance and bring renewed direction to our society and our people. Today, that direction is misplaced in the hands of public officials, politicians, police, judges, vocal minorities, and monopolies.

Only Troublemakers Need Apply

It will be something similar to what Rev. Dr. David Wilkerson, the founding pastor of Times Square Church in New York City and founder of Teen Challenge, said in a 1988 letter entitled, "Trouble Makers:"

> "We need an army of trouble makers who have become so full of the Holy Ghost they will stir up and trouble New York City and every city around the world, trouble their wicked institutions, challenge the established dead churches, and trouble the leaders, the mayors, the city councils, and the community leadership."

Fortunately we have laws established by our founders for the people to be the real voice in all aspects of our society. The American Constitution and the Bill of Rights are a series of road blocks designed to keep politicians from exerting power over the American people.

The problem has been that our leaders don't want us to have that power. With an army of motivated citizens, we can make our governmental leaders conscious of those laws so we can put our wants and needs first from small towns to the federal government.

Another thing that must be done is conduct a thorough search throughout the federal government to determine which departments and agencies are benefiting our society and which are no longer necessary. We need to know which agencies should be expanded or reduced, which are efficient and which are not. We need to improve efficiency, but without altering or distorting the smooth functioning of the government.

Non-Profit Organization Oversight

We need an apolitical committee to investigate all non-profit organizations' rules, regulations, laws, and procedures. They will make recommendations for regulating and controlling the abuse and misuse of federal funds. Certain types of nonprofit organizations should be subject to auditing to prevent funneling money to terrorist, communist, and other subversive organizations.

I believe that too many non-profit organizations today are too free to do whatever they choose with the money they receive, whether by grant or donation. When such organizations file their year-end tax returns and reports, they should be required to expose all their expenditures and employees' wages. There should also be guidelines on their executive salaries.

Of course, honest organizations should be allowed to exist and function freely as long as they comply with the governing laws. Nothing should interfere with their time and effort for social causes such as programs for youth, drug intervention, public safety and health awareness, and safe houses for abused women.

Abolish Communism

We should start to think very seriously about how we are going to abolish communism in every form from the United States. If we look at world history, we find that after throwing out a communist regime, only those countries that have totally abolished communism are the ones that have enjoyed freedom and prosperity for a long period of time. Look for examples at such countries as France, Spain, and Chile, among others.

Those who make the mistake of allowing communism and its followers to remain, find that years later the poison rises up once again, and it becomes clear that only a battle, and not the war, had been won.

I'm not espousing a radical response, but only saying we must fight communism with its own weapons. Trust me when I say from my experience, that you can't imagine how terrible it is when communist thinking and actions come to your country.

If you are a hard working person who is a well-established and productive member of society, that only makes you a target under communism. They can and will throw you out without a penny, or even worse unless you are lucky. You will be left with the feeling that you are an outlaw even though you have done nothing other than be opposed to their ideology, and are "guilty" of being successful and wealthy.

We are a people who will never be as evil and drastic as the enemy, but we must make them leave this country. Let them take their property, money and family with them, preferably to a country already infested with communism to open their eyes.

I can assure you that if they seize control they will do the same to many of us, as they did to me in Cuba and Venezuela. The bourgeois will be exiled or even thrown into a concentration camp. Don't doubt me. It is their way.

The time of mindless acceptance, apathy, and thinking we are different from other countries that have fallen under the rule of Communism or Islamism is long past. The enemy must be made to suffer their apocalypse or we will.

Those who refuse to accept the reality of a fading America today are part of the problem. The law has to be very specific in order to forbid any practicing communist to continue living in this country. Let them go where they are among their own, where they cannot hide among the innocent if retaliation becomes necessary. If they can't find a place to move, we might consider paying Castro in Cuba or some other communist leader to take them.

Remember, we are dealing with very sophisticated people and a very cruel doctrine that brainwashes people under their power. After a person has been programmed, it is very difficult to reverse the damage. In most instances, I have not found anything that qualifies them for deserving a second chance; it is simply not worth the risk. They are the pariahs of society and we would be far better off without them. We are slowly losing this country because our own behavior, benevolence, and tolerance. We cannot continue with this trend or we will be defeated.

You may find it hard to imagine that although you are well established in your own country, communists can come in and throw you out with nothing or they can imprison or kill you. As I wrote earlier, in the early 1960's, I saw former Cuban millionaires, who had fled to Miami, were now washing dishes to earn enough to eat. My own father was one of them.

The saddest thing is that all of these millionaires' businesses were destroyed with the goal of ruining their country's economy. The United States will not be any different; communism follows that same pattern in every nation they take over. *American Apocalypse* is a record of destruction that the followers of Marx have wrought.

Stéphane Courtois, editor of the "*Black Book of Communism*" said, "...Communist regimes...turned mass crime into a full-blown system of government." He cites the death toll from communism all over the world at 94 million. Can America honestly think that we are much smarter than all those millions who were killed by the communists?

Don't be too sure, for I can tell you that the majority of the people in those countries where the killing took place acted with more determination, more ability, and even more power than what we Americans have demonstrated up to now.

Realistically, we have done very little to stop this poison factory, this alien force that has been creeping in through leftist, socialist, liberal leaders and media. I remember that only a few years ago, the Republicans had control of the White House and both the Senate and Congress, and what did they do? Nothing.

They didn't make changes or pass any laws that would have allowed us to stop the liberal socialistic control of our economy, our banks, our industry, or our medical system. We are even slaves to foreign oil because we are prevented from drilling into our own incredible sources of energy.

I am convinced that the sooner we stop federal and state governments and corporations from giving communist organizations our taxpayer money, the sooner their activities are going to be slowed down and stopped.

Tragically, communism has invaded our children's education, taking God out of schools and federal buildings, and implementing environmental laws to cripple our economic and social laws to make more people government dependent. Following one of communism's basic tactics, they have been indoctrinating our youth through the universities and brainwashing the American people through the media.

Enough is enough. We must act now or our way of life will be destroyed. We cannot allow them to just win or barely lose an election because in two, four or eight more years, they will be even stronger and will have made many more people government dependent. If we allow it, more youth will be indoctrinated and their party will be even more militant.

Communists take advantage of any "crisis" or tragedy and twist it into a propaganda tool. For example, following the shooting of US Congresswoman Gabrielle Gifford and the murder of others in Tucson, Arizona, there were over ten thousand Internet and news media references against Sarah Palin who had nothing to do with the tragedy. How shocking to witness the irresponsible statements made by people apportioning blame on Palin for this terrible event.

Liberals are afraid of conservatives with backbone and they use media pressure to try to destroy them. Who can govern with that kind of power aligned against our conservative leaders? George Bush's administration was almost paralyzed by that power. Consider what happened in Wisconsin when the new conservative governor took on public unions. Teachers and their thug unions took over the capitol buildings and turned them into pigsties. Protesters were bused in from out of state to intimidate legislators. Thank God and Governor Scott Walker, their disgusting tactics failed. We need more victories like that.

Tea Party Express founder Sal Russo, during his interview with Newsmax, said, "This is the left's last stand to turn back the tide of what conservatives have been trying to do in the country over the last two years. So we can't fail there—it's ground zero. "Liberals are trying to say, 'Even if conservatives win the elections, as we did in a lot of states in 2010, we'll be able to frustrate and stop them and make it so difficult for them that nobody else will run like that in other states."

A person does not have to look far to see how much hatred, racism, and envy, communists have stirred up in our society. The only way we can be one big multiracial American family is by eradicating the communist influences from our country. This is the eleventh hour of our freedom, and we must take action before our liberty is taken away.

Obama's Messianic Syndrome

Viewers of the next referenced video clip will see a classroom in America where kids are learning to idolize President Barack Obama. It's exactly what has been done in every communist country in the world. It's the same indoctrination I received, from age 14 to 18 under Fidel Castro's "re-education" process in Cuba. If we don't intervene now to save our children from being the new-programmed generation, it will be too late. [C7-1]

Our youth and future leaders are being bombarded unceasingly from all directions. We are seeing more and more of our children indoctrinated by socialistic professors, and adults are being exposed to propaganda through all aspects of our society. Moral principles, honesty, and family structure will be a thing of the past. The honor and patriotism we hold in such high esteem will only exist in the history books.

Islam's Wave of Terror

Lebanese-American journalist and activist, Brigitte Gabriel says Islam deliberately keeps Arab countries backward, and teaches terrorism. Gabriel is an acknowledged authority on Muslim terrorism around thc world and the tactics they employ. She tells us about the indoctrination in our American universities and what she preaches is exactly what I have been saying for almost two decades. [C7-2]

The Muslim Invasion

President Barack Obama has funded a $20 million resettlement of Hamas refugees to the United States via H.R. 1388 (aka H.B. 1388), a bill apparently passed behind our backs in Congress. In the last two years, here in the United States, over two hundred new mosques have been built or are under construction.

What should be done about this invasion? Regardless of apologists, the Muslim religious philosophies and actions clearly fit our legal system's definition of hate crimes. How else can you describe teachings from their Quran that defines all non-believers, Christians, Jews, Hindus, Buddhists, etc.—as enemies and infidels who should be killed so that Muslims can earn their way into their idea of heaven?

Christians are not welcome in countries practicing Islam, and reports of believers being killed and their churches destroyed are too often in the news. Why then, should America tolerate a religion within our borders that teaches the killing of any person not believing in their god, Allah? Self-styled pundits argue that only radical Muslims are taught Jihad against Christians, Jews, Hindus, Buddhists, etc.

Perhaps those same apologists have never read the Quran, or Koran, which contains at least 109 verses that call Muslims to war with nonbelievers. Some passages are very graphic, with commands to chop off heads and fingers and kill infidels (anyone who is not a Muslim) wherever they may be. Muslims who do not take up the fight are labeled as "hypocrites" and warned that Allah will eternally condemn them if they do not join the blood bath. If you are not a Muslim, then the following quotes taken directly from Islam's Quran refer to you:

Quran 8:12

"I will cast terror into the hearts of those who disbelieve. Therefore strike off their heads and strike off every fingertip of them."

Quran 9:123

"O ye who believe, fight those of the disbelievers who are near to you, and let them find harshness in you, and know that Allah is with those who keep their duty (unto Him)."

Quran 48:29

"Muhammad is the messenger of Allah. And those with him are hard (ruthless) against the disbelievers and merciful among themselves."

Ishaq: 327

"Allah said, 'A prophet must slaughter before collecting captives. A slaughtered enemy is driven from the land. Muhammad, you craved the desires of this world, its goods and the ransom captives would bring. But Allah desires killing them to manifest the religion.'"

According to the website, www.thereligionofpeace.com, "The strangest and most untrue thing that can be said about Islam is that it is a Religion of Peace. If every standard by which the West is judged and condemned (slavery, imperialism, intolerance, women's rights, sexuality, warfare...) were applied equally to Islam, the verdict would be absolutely devastating.

"Islam never gives up what it conquers, be it religion, culture, language or life. Neither does it make apologies or any real effort at moral progress. It is convinced of its own perfection, yet brutally shuns self-examination and represses criticism. It is the least open to dialogue and the most self-absorbed."

This clear desire to dominate the world by whatever harsh means is nothing new for Muslims.

- In 633 AC, they conquered Syria. Shortly thereafter, they invaded Egypt, Palestine, Mesopotamia, and Persia.
- In 641, Muslims invaded and conquered Azerbaijan, Dagestan, Georgia, and Armenia.
- In 652, Muslims attached Sicily.
- In 669, the Muslims conquered Morocco.
- In 711, they invaded Afghanistan.

- Also in 711, they conquered what is now Spain and Portugal under the command of Muslim Umayyad general Tariq ibn Ziyad (689 – 720).
- In 731, they invaded France.

Thanks to military leader and politician Charles Martel (688–741), who was the grandfather of Charlemagne, the Muslim expansion was halted in 732 in the Poitier battle (also known as the Battle of Tours). But the Muslims continued to rule in Spain until 1492 when the Iberian Peninsula was re-captured by "The Catholic Monarchs."

In 1529 Muslims launched the second attempt to conquer Europe; the attack was stopped in Vienna, but they took a few countries, all of which were subsequently liberated one by one. The third attempt by Muslims to dominate Europe started just 50 years ago.

This time it was not by an invading army; instead it was an invasion of poor people looking for a better standard living. Today, Europe is shaking from the riots and demands of Muslims, who demonstrate absolutely no gratitude for being accepted in the various countries.

In the four largest cities in The Netherlands, Amsterdam, Rotterdam, Utrecht, and The Hague, Muslims represent the majority of the population less than 14 years old. The most popular name for a newborn in those cities is Mohammed.

In France, the Muslims represent 10% of the population. In the UK, Muslims openly preach hate, and Muslim fanatics and riots have become "old news." In Spain, there are over one million Muslims and the government is planning to build mosques for them and to teach Islamic thought in the country's schools.

The Muslims indoctrinated with communism, have found in the Islam religion something that Marx and Engels found in Darwinism. This combination of communism and Islam will bring the world to destruction unless free peoples stop them. [C7-3]

The fast-growing Muslim minority in this country makes millions of Americans worry that our traditional Christian culture is at risk. What if a Christian preacher tells his congregation that to enter eternal life they have to kill anyone who is an unbeliever? That idea for a

Christian is inconceivable, yet radical Islamic clerics teach this very thing in American mosques that are springing up everywhere.

Our country believes that if someone hits you in one cheek, you offer the other one. In context, scripture speaks of interaction between two individuals. It does not say that a nation must do nothing while the enemy kills its people and destroys its infrastructure.

In the Bible, we are told God sent His people to war many times with commands to leave nothing standing. Unlike Islam's god, Allah, however, the wrath of the true God of Abraham, Isaac and Jacob was not against those who were simply unbelievers. His anger was against those who were steeped in moral sin, or who fought against His chosen people, Israel.

The imposition of political correctness is silencing truth in America. The fear of hurting someone's feelings makes wimps of us all. Make no mistake, this flaw will be used against us. The freedoms we cherish and take for granted will be a weapon against Americans until those same freedoms no longer exist.

America is being attacked, and we have the right to strike back. Does the God of our fathers really want us to cower while evil men plot to overturn our government and our system? Think about the following statistics:

Saudi Arabia's $100 billion investment over the last 3 decades in over 60 thousand Madrassas or schools all over the Islamic world is finally paying off. While America was busy developing medicines, increasing life expectancy, decreasing human suffering, decoding human genes to find cures for cancer and heart disease, launching space shuttles, inventing the internet, working on new laws for human rights, and developing better economical models for a more prosperous world, Muslims were programming western world-hating terrorist murderers.

Regrettably, thanks to the help of our socialist leaders, we have been the biggest contributors to their creation. Islam's teachers say, "We will use the American's kindness, fairness, compassion, freedom of speech and non-discriminatory policies against them. We will stab them in the back." If we continue to sit back and allow their words to be true, we are finished. [C7-4]

No real Christian or free American would truly want to transform this country to the Islamic way of life and beliefs. Islam is a religion of violence especially for women, and their only law is from the Quran. The strict and unforgiving way of their belief keeps subjects under control through fear and unbending adherence to everything from prayer to dress.

Muslims are not allowed to choose what parts of Islam they follow. Islam teaches the Koran to be the direct word of Allah that descended from heaven. Those claiming to be moderate Muslims do not actively participate in the physical part of jihad, fighting, bombing, etc., but they do support the goals of Jihad and the terrorists. Even though they may hate the acts of Islamic terrorists, they have to agree with the ultimate goal, the conversion of the world to Islam.

Make no mistake, Communists and Islamists are all part of the same battle for America. The controllers, however, are the communists who use Muslims as disposable instruments of their agenda. Once in power, socialists have no use for minorities or religions of any kind, and they quickly eliminate them. History proves that to be a fact.

Islamic Pirates Then and Now

When American colonists were liberated from British rule in 1776, American merchant ships lost Royal Navy protection. With no Navy for protection, American ships were attacked and their Christian crews enslaved by Muslim pirates operating under the control of the "Dey of Algiers," an Islamic warlord ruling Algeria.

Because the pirates were destroying American commerce in the Mediterranean, our Congress agreed in 1784 to negotiate treaties with the four Barbary States. Congress appointed a special commission consisting of John Adams, Thomas Jefferson, and Benjamin Franklin, to oversee the negotiations.

Lacking the ability to protect its merchant ships in the Mediterranean, the new America government tried to appease the Muslim slavers by agreeing to pay tribute and ransoms in order to retrieve seized American ships and buy the freedom of enslaved sailors. Adams argued in favor of paying tribute as the cheapest way to get American commerce in the Mediterranean moving again.

Thomas Jefferson was opposed. He believed there would be no end to the demands for tribute and wanted matters settled "through the medium of war." He proposed a league of trading nations to force an end to Muslim piracy. Jefferson had an eye-opening experience with the Muslim and their way of life. [C7-5]

In 1786, Jefferson, then the American ambassador to France, and Adams, then the American ambassador to Britain, met in London with Sidi Haji Abdul Rahman Adja, the Dey of Algiers ambassador to Britain. The Americans wanted to negotiate a peace treaty based on Congress' vote to appease. Jefferson and Adams asked the Dey's ambassador why Muslims held so much hostility towards America, a nation with which they had no previous contacts.

Ambassador Adja answered that Islam "was founded on the Laws of their Prophet; that it was written in their Quran, that all nations who should not have acknowledged their authority were sinners, that it was their right and duty to make war upon them wherever they could be found, and to make slaves of all they could take as prisoners, and that every Mussel man (Muslim) who should be slain in Battle was sure to go to Paradise."

For the following 15 years, the American government paid the Muslims millions of dollars for the safe passage of American ships or the return of American hostages. The ransom payments and tribute amounted to 20 percent of United States government annual revenues in 1800.

Not long after Jefferson's inauguration as president in 1801, he dispatched a group of frigates to defend American interests in the Mediterranean, and informed Congress by declaring that America was going to spend "millions for defense, but not one cent for tribute."

As a result of intense American naval bombardment and on shore raids by Marines, the Barbary States finally officially agreed to abandon slavery and piracy.

Jefferson's victory over the Muslims lives on today in the Marine Hymn, with the line: "From the halls of Montezuma, to the shores of Tripoli, we fight our country's battles in the air, on land and sea."

Jefferson had been right. The "medium of war" was the only way to put an end to the Muslim problem.

First Muslim U.S. Congressman

Democrat Keith Ellison was the first Muslim United States congressman. True to his pledge, he placed his hand on the Quran, the Muslim book of jihad and pledged his allegiance to the United States during his ceremonial swearing-in.

Ellison, who was born in Detroit and converted to Islam while in college, said he chose that very unique copy of the Quran because it showed that "a visionary like Jefferson" believed that wisdom could be gleaned from many sources.

The Quran Ellison used was no ordinary book. It once belonged to Thomas Jefferson, third president of the United States and one of America's founding fathers. Ellison borrowed it from the Rare Book Section of the Library of Congress. It was one of the 6,500 Jefferson books archived in the library.

There is no doubt Ellison was right about Jefferson believing wisdom could be "gleaned" from the Muslim Quran. At the time Jefferson owned the book, he needed to know everything possible about Muslims because he was about to advocate war against the Islamic "Barbary" states of Morocco, Algeria, Tunisia and Tripoli.

Ellison's use of Jefferson's Quran as a prop illuminates a subject once well known in the history of the United States, but is today mostly forgotten. It was Muslim pirate slavers who over many centuries enslaved millions of Africans and tens of thousands of Christian Europeans and Americans in the Islamic "Barbary" states. This part of History was not apparently read by Muslim Louis Farrakhan who preached that Americans were the first world slave masters.

Author and lecturer Nonie Darwish says the goal of radical Islamists is to impose Sharia law on the world, ripping apart Western law and liberty, too.

She recently authored the book, *Cruel and Usual Punishment: The Terrifying Global Implications of Islamic Law*. Darwish was born in Cairo and spent her childhood in Egypt and Gaza before immigrating to America in 1978, when she was eight years old.

Darwish developed a skeptical eye at an early age. She questioned her own Muslim culture and upbringing. She converted to Christianity after hearing a Christian preacher on television. In her latest book, Darwish warns about creeping Sharia law, what it is, what it means, and how it is manifested in Islamic countries.

For America, she says radical Islamists are working to impose Sharia on the world. If that happens, Western civilization will be destroyed. Westerners generally assume all religions encourage a respect for the dignity of each individual. Islamic law (Sharia) teaches that non-Muslims should be subjugated or killed in this world. The ultimate goal is to set up Islamic law everywhere in the Middle East and eventually in the world.

While Westerners tend to think that all religions encourage some form of the golden rule, Sharia teaches two systems of ethics—one for Muslims and another for non-Muslims. Building on tribal practices of the seventh century, Sharia encourages the side of humanity that wants to take from and subjugate others.

While Americans tend to think in terms of religious people developing a personal understanding of and relationship with God, Sharia advocates executing people who ask difficult questions that could be interpreted as criticism. It's hard to imagine, that in this day and age, Islamic scholars agree that those who criticize Islam or choose to stop being Muslim should be executed. Sadly, while talk of an Islamic reformation is common and even assumed by many in the West, such murmurings in the Middle East are silenced through intimidation.

While America is accustomed to an increase in religious tolerance over time, Darwish explains how petro dollars are being used to grow an extremely intolerant form of political Islam in her native Egypt and elsewhere. In twenty years, there could be enough Muslim voters in the United States to elect the President by themselves.

In Murfreesboro, Tennessee, opponents marched to protest the construction of a new Islamic mosque. The march's organizer, Kevin

Fisher, said, "The people have spoken clearly that they don't want this mosque proposal that is before them."

The 52,960-square-foot mosque would include a 10,000 square foot area for prayer, as well as a gym, pool, offices, classrooms, sports field, pavilion, playground and a home for the imam. Courts ignore such protests even though the majority of Americans do not accept that the first Amendment should cover any professed religion that teaches the killing of anyone outside of their beliefs.

Tennessee is no different from any other state that does not want to be invaded by those who hate our way of life. Yet, Nashville, Tennessee has one of the fastest growing foreign-born populations of any major US city. According to the Federation for American Immigration Reform, "The 2000 data showed an increase of 210.1 percent in the immigrant population since 1990, which compared with a 6.5 percent increase in the native-born population.

Darwish said, "I think everyone in the U.S. should be required to read about Sharia law. It is too bad that so many are disillusioned with life and Christianity to accept Muslims as peaceful.... Some may be but they have an army that is willing to shed blood in the name of Islam... the peaceful support the warriors with their finances and their own kind of patriotism to their religion. While America is getting rid of Christianity from all public sites and erasing God from the lives of children, the Muslims and communists are planning a great change for America.".

Under the banner of Islam, "la, ilaha illa Allah, muhammad rasoulu Allah," (None is god except Allah; Muhammad is the Messenger of Allah) they murdered Americans and Jews, and massacred Christians in Lebanon, killed Copts in Egypt, Assyrians in Syria, and Hindus in India. They expelled almost 500,000 Jews from Muslim lands. Those "infidels" trapped in the Middle East paid the price then. Now "infidels" worldwide are paying the price for indifference and shortsightedness.

Al-Jazeera, a mouthpiece for enemies of the United States, aired a Moammar Gaddhafi speech praising Barack Obama and followed with a story depicting supporters of Sarah Palin as white, racist

Christians. The channel is subsidized by the oil-rich Sunni Muslim Plutocracy-dictatorship in Qatar.

Incidentally, Secretary of State, Hillary Clinton, said she would like to see Al-Jazeera news carried on American cable channels. Why would that be, Mrs. Clinton?

Lest Americans Forget

Too many Americans have become so insulated from reality that we imagine that America can survive defeat without any danger to ourselves. Think again:

- In 1972 at the Munich Olympics, athletes were kidnapped and massacred by Muslim male extremists.
- In 1979, the US embassy in Iran was taken over by Muslim male extremists.
- During the 1980's a number of Americans were kidnapped in Lebanon by Muslim male extremists.
- In 1983, Muslim male extremists blew up the US Marine Baracks in Beirut.
- In 1985 the cruise ship Achilles Lauro was hijacked and a 70-year-old American passenger was murdered and thrown overboard in his wheelchair by Muslim male extremists.
- In 1985 TWA flight 847 was hijacked at Athens. A US Navy diver trying to rescue passengers was murdered by Muslim male extremists
- In 1988, Muslim male extremists bombed Pan Am Flight 103.
- In 1993 the World Trade Center was bombed the first time by Muslim male extremists.
- In 1998, Muslim male extremists bombed the US embassies in Kenya and Tanzania.
- On September 11, 2001, four airliners were hijacked; two were used as missiles to take down the World Trade Center towers. Of the remaining two aircraft, one crashed into the US Pentagon and the other was diverted and crashed by the

passengers. Muslim male extremists killed thousands of people.

- In 2002 the United States fought a war in Afghanistan against Muslim male extremists.
- In 2002 reporter Daniel Pearl was kidnapped and beheaded on video by—you guessed it—Muslim male extremists.

Does anyone in Homeland Security see a pattern here to justify profiling? Do you? To ensure that we Americans never offend anyone, airport security screeners will no longer be allowed to profile certain people. Such utter stupidity is hard to imagine.

They conduct random searches of 80-year-old women, little kids, airline pilots with proper identification, Secret Service agents who are members of the President's security detail, 85-year-old Congressmen with metal hips, and the Medal of Honor winner and former Governor Joe Foss. Yet they leave Muslim males alone so as not to be found guilty of profiling. What other motive could there be?

How can it be that the Obama administration can eliminate the Christian day of prayer so as not to offend Muslims, while permitting the celebration of the Islamic day of prayer on our Capitol grounds? Where was America's "fair and unbiased" media when that took place?

Learn From Those Who Know

Brigitte Gabriel is an expert on the Middle East conflict and lectures nationally and internationally on the subject. She's the former news anchor of World News for Middle East television and the founder of *AmericanCongressforTruth.com.*

In a speech at Duke University, Gabriel had this to say about how the average American is unaware of the insidious nature of radical Islamists:

> "American is wallowing in a state of ignorance and denial for thirty years as Muslim extremist perpetrated evil against innocent victims in the name of Allah. I had a crash course in survival. Not in the Girl Scouts, but in a bomb shelter where I

> lived for seven years in pitch darkness, freezing cold, drinking stale water and eating grass to live."

Gabriel described how, at age 13, she slept in her burial clothes expecting to be killed in her bed. By the time she turned 20, Muslims had slaughtered most of her friends. Her family wasn't Americans living in New York, nor Britons in London. They were Arab Christians living in Lebanon. She continues:

> "As a victim of Islamic terror, I was amazed when I saw Americans waking up on September 12, 2001, and asking themselves, 'Why do they hate us? Simply put, they hate us because we are defined in their eyes by one simple word: 'infidels.'
>
> *"Yet apathy is the weapon by which the West is committing suicide. Political correctness forms the shackles around our ankles, by which Islamists are leading us to our demise. America and the West are doomed to failure in this war unless they stand up and identify the real enemies."* [C7-6]

Read that last paragraph again until the raw importance of what she said sinks in. Just as I speak from experience as a former communist under Castro, Gabriel is warning America about the Muslim mind. We must hear the alarm bells going off and act before it is too late.

Brigitte Gabriel warns that the constitution for the new Islamic Republics of EuroArabia and AmerIslamia is under construction, and that America had better be acutely aware of what the document writers reveal:

> *"We will fight the infidel to death. Meanwhile American laws will protect us. Democrats and Leftists will support us. N.G.O.'s will legitimize us. C.A.I.R. will incubate us. The A.C.L.U. will empower us. Western Universities will educate us. Mosques will shelter us O.P.E.C. will finance us Hollywood will love us. Kofi Annan and most of the United Nations will cover our asses."*

What she is saying is the truth, apathy, political correctness, and our misguided acceptance of enemy acts within America, empowers our enemies around the world. The video of her complete speech may be viewed on the Internet. [C7-7]

Their Numbers Are Growing

Communists, Muslims and terrorist sleepers, are getting funded, educated and even armed with your taxpayer money. The International organization SAT, with over a thousand recruiting centers around the world, is making it possible to bring Muslim and communist youth to our schools under full scholarship. There they can be educated and indoctrinated at the same time. Where are our representatives who are sworn to protect and defend those of us who are citizens and are paying the bills?

Adding insult to injury, as the people who make this country work are lowering our birthrate, the intruders are increasing in numbers by producing more and more children at America's expense. It is a largely unnoticed invasion that will soon overwhelm our country.

Under the influence of teachers steeped in socialism and families that follow religions of hate, their children will grow up filled with hate for America and its people. Even our own children are being encouraged to care more about Islamic interests, and socialist ideas than, in America's greatness and compassion.

The United States has long been a prime target for Communist, radical and Islamic hatred and terror. Communistic and radical Islamic actions have been as vile as their words. Since the Iran hostage crisis, more than three thousand Americans have died in a terror campaign unprecedented in its calculated cruelty against thousands of other citizens worldwide.

This is the ugly face of the enemy we are fighting, a powerful ideology that is capable of altering basic human instincts, that can turn a mother into a launching pad of death. A perfect example is a recently elected Hamas official in the Palestinian Territories who expressed great pride and joy about sending her three sons to death and offering the ones who are still alive for the cause.

It is an ideology that is capable of offering highly educated individuals such as doctors and lawyers far more joy in attaining death than any respect and stature life in society is ever capable of giving them.

Even the Nazis did not turn their own children into human bombs, and then rejoice at their deaths as well the deaths of their victims. This intentional, indiscriminate and wholesale murder of innocent Americans and other world citizens is justified and glorified in the name of Islam.

Know Your Enemies

America cannot effectively defend itself in this war unless and until our people understand the nature of the enemy that we face. Even after 9/11 there are those who say that we must engage our terrorist enemies, that we must address their grievances.

Those who think in that manner, do so in blissful ignorance, and are sheep among wolves. Their thinking includes such uninformed ideas about Radical Islamists as:

- Their grievance is our freedom of religion.
- Their grievance is our freedom of speech.
- Their grievance is our democratic process where the rule of law comes from the voices of many not that of just one prophet.
- It is the respect we inspire in our children towards all religions.
- It is the equality we grant each other as human beings sharing a planet and striving to make the world a better place for all humanity.
- Their grievance is the kindness and respect an American man shows a woman, the justice we practice as equals under the law, and the mercy we grant our enemies.
- Their grievance cannot be answered by an apology for whom or what we are.

Our attitude of not confronting communist and Islamic forces of bigotry and hatred whenever and wherever they raised their ugly head in the last 30 years, has empowered and strengthened our enemy to launch a full scale attack on the very freedoms we cherish in their effort to impose their values and way of life on our civilization.

We must wake up and challenge our Muslim and communist enemies, and take action against the practices of these ideologies within our country. If we don't believe in America as a country founded on Christian morals, we will pay a devastating price for our delusion. America's learning curve since the Iran hostage crisis is so shallow that it is almost flat. The longer we lay supine, the more difficult it will be to stand erect.

It is difficult to believe, but a man who has shunned our flag, supported communist individuals and organizations, and praises Muslims while looking down on Christians, became the President of this great country. How could this have happened? Apathy, ignorance, entitlement, and fraud…that's how!

With the record we have on dealing with Muslims, we need more people like Brigitte Gabriel, who is continuing to advocate a global campaign against Sharia Law. [C7-8]

Never forget that countries under the enemy's ideology demand that *their* beliefs are displayed publicly. Why should we allow our leaders and courts to restrict our freedom to do the same in America?

I say to those immigrants who follow Allah, this is our country, our land, and our lifestyle, and we would have gladly allowed you every opportunity to enjoy living here. But since your leaders complain, whine, and threaten us about our flag, our pledge, our Christian beliefs, and our way of life, I highly encourage you take advantage of one other great American freedom, THE RIGHT TO LEAVE.

Government Controlled Education

I believe that the present government controlled educational system is one of the most destructive aspects of our society. The way many of our children are being educated and trained will decide the conduct and the behavior of our future generation. Within the last 30 years there has been increasing indoctrination against family and Christianity in our education system. At the same time, Darwinism and multiculturalism is being programmed into young minds.

We have a huge task beginning with reeducating our children away from the communist indoctrination they've been receiving in public schools and universities. If we allow the present programming of our youth to continue, it will soon be impossible to take our nation back.

A recent poll showed that more than 70% of our children aged 13 to 15 years, have a poor opinion about the American system. How much more proof do we need to know that our school systems have to be changed?

In his book entitled *Storm Warnings*, renowned evangelist Billy Graham writes about our societal depravation and the bad consequences the wrong doctrines can cause:

> "The young Christians today have grown up in a discontented world, surrounded by distrusted people, and have seen that important people from our church fall in sin. Through their propaganda, this poison factory has our society living surrounded by violence, sex, homosexuality, satanic behavior and crime. A confused and disoriented young generation easily becomes vulnerable to their cause. All this antagonism and confusion creates persons who need guidance. A person with poor moral foundations is not looking for guidance from a church or his or her parents."

This referenced video illustrates some of today's educational programming taking place within our children's schools. [C7-9]

I cannot say that capitalism is perfect; like any successful venture, it needs constant correction. But I do say that what we have is 1,000 times better that communism. If we don't protect our future generation from the poison being spread through our schools, then in ten years, when our youth become the leaders, this bastion of freedom we call America will be destroyed.

The bottom line is that we are struggling against multiculturalism, socialist teachers and professors, drug dealers, false religions, unemployment, a bad economy, high taxes, foreign dependence for energy…the burdens are endless. All these problems have one common denominator: the communism spreading throughout our society, destroying families and our quality of life.

Traditional teachers must retake control of the classroom, and without humiliating or mistreating students, they must teach the basic fundamentals of math, language and writing. A lack of respect and discipline are major problems in today's schools. Students that are attentive and obedient are a must if America is to regain her standing in the world under future leaders.

American is still the best country in the world; let us join together to protect it. Through our foundation's Real People Pact, or any other organization, we will teach our younger generation what it takes to be an American. When I arrived in this country in the early 1960's, I was so impressed that I became indoctrinated with Americanism. Then, communism was outlawed in this country. Our predecessors knew that communism and capitalism are opposites and cannot exist together. How shameful that we have not taught that truth to our children.

Chile's Purge of Communism

As old adage tells us, "If we do not learn from history then we are doomed to repeat it." How true! During his coup of Allende's communistic regime, Chile's Augusto Pinochet killed 5,000 communist fighters. Over the next 5 years, he arrested and executed another 17,000.

He eliminated or drove out of Chile every communist that was arrested charged and convicted. That's a harsh reality, but Chile's economy has been booming for more than 30 years. That nation has become a model among South American countries, all because Pinochet cleaned house of the poison that Allende's regime had spread across Chile.

Chile doesn't have dozens of socialist environmental organizations that have been awarded thousands of federal government grants to interfere with business and construction and energy exploration as we have in America. There is no ACORN organization in Chile using their 361 profit and non-profit organizations to indoctrinate people and elect communist candidates. George Soros and his followers would not be allowed to do to Chile, what our "leaders" have allowed them to do to us.

The Communist World Media Pressure cannot cripple Chile's economy with lies and biased reporting. Only in America have they had the freedom to attack our system for over 30 years.

Obviously, I don't support Pinochet's ruthless methods. He could have jailed or forced them to leave the country. The only point here is that he rid Chile of communism and his country's safety and prosperity stands for all the world to see.

The hard, quantifiable fact is that the American's majority is too peaceful and too silent. Russians were also peaceful and silent as communists stealthily robbed them of their country. Under Lenin, more than 21 million "peaceful and silent" citizens were murdered. In the end, the complacent majority was irrelevant.

China's huge population was peaceful as well, but the Chinese Communists took control and killed a staggering 60 million people. The peaceful and silent majority was again irrelevant.

Are you getting the picture? Our American silent majority may end up condemning us and our young generations to the same destiny of suffered by our Russian and Chinese brethren.

Welfare Is Out of Control

I believe that the welfare problem is even bigger than the Health Care problem. Every civilized country must have some degree of welfare to help those who temporarily need assistance. But there is a big difference between helping the truly needy and our present system of entitlement that supports generations of able-bodied families as a way of life.

Socialists in our government are making more people dependent on the handouts and are creating problems of enormous proportions. This puts a tremendous burden on the taxpayer, while destroying families by installing low self-esteem, greed, and lack of ambition. The damage to minorities is especially heinous. Welfare makes it economically more profitable for unwed mothers with children.

That's a major reason why today the percentage of children without fathers has doubled among black Americans over the last 20 years.

Welfare has created a problem for the healthcare system too. There are numerous young adults on welfare that are also covered by healthcare, making them a burden on society, instead of being productive members paying their own way.

The children of these "permanent" welfare families grow up exposed to drugs, crime, prostitution, out-of-wedlock pregnancies, lack of education, depression, and continuing poverty. They are ripe targets for the false promises of communism.

Welfare's biggest monument is block after block of ghetto filled with hopelessness. Yet, beyond reason, those that vote still elect liberals who have placed them in their unhappy plight in the first place.

Let's look at the basic concept of welfare: a temporary hand-up rather than a way-of-life handout. Applicants should be accepted on the condition that they have six months to get back on their feet. Of course, extraordinary circumstances would be appealed.

Aid to Dependent Children should be limited to two per mother to discourage those on the program from having baby after baby without a supportive father and an independent means of support.

Money wasted on pork barrel projects or funneled to organizations should be awarded through the small business administration to create income-producing companies that employ those who want to work their way out of nanny government programs. Childcare and basic medical facilities could be provided.

I believe that 50% of the people on the welfare system are free riders; the majority are people capable of becoming productive citizens with a little help and encouragement.

All they need is a push. But it has become so easy to get welfare, and so widespread that everybody who is without a job goes to get help from welfare.

Equality Under the Law

Equality under the law is the third rail of America. Discrimination is morally and legally wrong and should not be tolerated. Regardless of race, creed, or gender, any person seeking employment should be considered on their qualifications only. However, employers should also have the right to hire the person they need regardless of race, creed, or gender.

Affirmative Action has become a Politically Correct term that means a business owner must hire according to quotas or government mandate, even if the person being forced on the employer is not as qualified as another. Am I wrong, or does that sound like discrimination?

Nowadays, a white person who sacrifices and works to build a business may find himself out of control of his own enterprise. If a minority is found unsuitable for a position and is let go, the owner can be sued for being guilty of hate or discrimination. The owner could lose everything including the ability to provide employment for his other workers. Does that sound like discrimination?

If a person works and saves to buy property to rent, does not he/she have an intrinsic right to decide whom to rent to? Not under current P.C. conditions.

There are Black America Pageants, Black Universities, Black History Month, Black Caucuses, but I have yet to see the word "White" placed before any of those items. Why is that not labeled as discrimination?

Illegal aliens flood across our border and are granted entitlements, education, healthcare, driver's licenses...the list goes on. Americans are even paying to have our official documents printed in two languages. What will we see next—translations for Vietnamese, Chinese, and German?

The Jesse Jacksons, Ralph Abernathys, and Jeremy Wrights here in America, foment hate between the races, ignoring the fact that it was the majority white population that helped elect the first black president, right or wrong though that might have been.

Louis Farrakhan is guilty of stirring up his own people with such pronouncements as this: "White America pretends to ask herself: 'What do these Negroes want?' White America knows that four hundred years of cruel bondage has made these twenty-two million ex-slaves too (mentally) blind to see what they really want." [C7-10, C7-11]

The great accomplishments of America in the first years of independence came from a sense of Christian brotherhood. There is nothing in Christianity to foment hate, envy, and ingratitude. We were about survival and growth before and after the Civil War.

Those that claimed that America was built on the back of slavery, overlook the fact that those states that were free of slave owners, were the most prosperous. It took the South decades to catch up to the rest. They also choose to ignore that most slave traders were blacks and Muslim pirates.

Productivity and equal opportunity to succeed according each person's abilities is essential to a free society. We cannot allow communism and Islamism to destroy this great nation with their hateful ideologies and hateful agenda that include economic destruction, communist indoctrination, Sharia law, and big government.

In order to home grow industry and business so that every person wanting to work and produce can find a job, there are definite steps to be taken.

1) Government must get out of our lives and off our backs. Their responsibilities are limited by the Constitution.
2) Citizens must take responsibility for their education and support. Affirmative Action and welfare must never interfere with free commerce and private interests.
3) There should be no labeling of citizens as Black, White, African, Asian, etc. If we are of America, we are Americans.
4) The Constitution bans the government from establishing a state religion. It does not give it the right to prevent the free exercising of Christianity or any other non-political belief.

Until we get back to the basics that made this country great, our jobs and our money, and our security will continue to leave our borders. Buying American is becoming increasingly difficult because our elected leaders are making it so. It is pitiful to see the most industrious country in the world, beaten by almost all other nations. We have lost the creativity we use to have that produced the inventions and innovations that, from 1935 to 1985, changed the world.

Until our people are fully conscious of how communists are purposely behind so many of these escalating problems, then they will get away with disguising themselves as Democrats, socialists, leftists, and even Muslims or people of *good will*.

CHAPTER 12

Cutting Costs

I really can't understand the people in our Government when they talk about cutting costs. Even many of the old school Republican politicians are so befuddled by the liberal media, the communist agenda, propaganda, and peer pressure that they believe that the only way to solve the deficit problem is to raise taxes and impose other penalties.

Socialistic ideology assures that no one will find good solutions. Politicians only seem to do a good job in raising their own salaries. As a result, they are among the few that haven't suffered from the recession in this nation.

They have created a mentality that only thinks about punishing the working class in America, the retirees, and the small businesses. They go after the easy targets, the most vulnerable, the taxpayers, and people who work and don't have time to defend themselves. The mentality extends past the Federal into state governments as well. In Florida, in one year alone, lawmakers raised driver registrations and license plate fees by almost 400%.

Recently, an obscure government official was caught after running up over $40,000 in charges on his government credit card for an Africa Safari. Allegedly, his only defense was that he produced over $12,000,000 a year for the government.

The men and women we elect to govern, often work harder to find new ways to tax or confiscate the taxpayer's money, than they do in working for the citizens who elected to be their representatives.

The Tea Party, as well all other such organizations, has to successfully find ways to force our lawmakers to fix our governance problems. We can't allow deficits to keep piling up to burden our future.

My company used to own a semi-truck for years. The Reagan administration made it easy in the 1980's, allowing us to buy a red federal truck's tag, good anywhere in the United States. That eliminated the requirement to buy a fuel permit in every state. That was one example of a great time and money saving law.

Not too long ago, the IRS got into the trucking permit business, and imposed an extra permit that cost about $300 per year to all trucks with red tags. Simply multiply $300 by 15.5 million trucks; that means the government is "taxing without representation" a staggering $4.5 billion from the small business owners' pockets. But that is not all the story; they now require disclosure of all trucking activities during the year.

That represents more unnecessary and costly impositions on small businesses. Between the high cost of transportation tickets, costly permits, and stifling regulations facing our trucking industry today, like countless other businesses, I was forced to sell my truck.

There are similar problems facing every industry. Economic news seems to indicate that we can expect a record number of small businesses to go bankrupt in the coming years. Government does not solve problems: they *are* the problems, just as former President Ronald Regan put it.

Government regulations, taxation, and unionism are responsible for the loss of millions of jobs over the last 30 years. In the meantime, echoing the communist mantra, Washington blames *unscrupulous* corporations, *greedy* capitalists, and foreign competition for our country's hard times. Let no one be fooled: politicians know full well that the restrictions that they have created are designed to slide all our industries downhill.

Cutting corners in the post-Obama America is going to be a difficult and painful process. Newly elected representatives must sort out every wrong-headed expenditure and pork barrel fraud that affects the American economy. Big and small businesses in every industry have to be unshackled from unfair regulations so that we are able to compete in the world market, and without damaging the environment.

By lowering the cost of doing business, our industries will be allowed to flourish, produce, compete globally, and generate the wealth that is, after all, the biggest source of government income. Millions of people will find jobs and be paying taxes instead of collecting welfare, unemployment and government (read that as taxpayers') assistance.

Communists have been following this playbook for so many years and are so well organized that the only way we can roll back the damage is to defeat their "World Communist Media Pressure," by contacting their sponsors, moving to conservative news sources, and, in general, cutting their funding. There is a choice we must make as a united and constitutionally free country to accept the idea of becoming a mediocre subjugated third world country or to fight to eliminate this toxic Maxis/Leninist presence in our government.

This poison has become so strong in this country that the new laws, the budget, the expenditures, and supposed savings that Washington is working on, are only aimed at achieving ruling class goals. Through liberal media, they dictate the legislation that controls what we eat, what we buy, what we drive, what we read, and, unless stopped, what we are allowed to send and receive on the Internet.

If the media is so fair and unbiased, then why are the following billions of taxpayer dollars being spent without being reported?

- Billions spent on non-profit organizations that are politically leftist/socialists.
- Billions spent on the United Nations, a major tool for the New World Order plan.
- Billions sent to other countries to gain favor for those generous with our money.
- Billions spent on the military for wars that we have the technology to win quickly if not for leaders without the courage to order it done.
- Wasteful spending on earmarks to buy votes for politicians in both houses.

- Billions spent on the Environmental Protection Agency because it is a major force that blocks domestic drilling for oil, but also roadblocks industry expansion and jobs.

The fact is none of the media is reporting about the big spending because in every bill that allocates funding, the communist controllers are getting their share. In addition, where is the once "fair and balanced" media in reporting and promoting pro-American action and spending, while exposing why communists are standing in the way of fixing our problems?

- Stories supporting the drilling of our own oil, and exposing how we are prevented from doing so because bankrupting America is part of the communist plan.
- Stories about fixing the welfare problem, and why that is not being done because communism needs more people dependent on government.
- Stories about how affirmative action is another tool used to make people beholden to the government.
- Stories about the flood of illegal aliens, and how they are being used as fraudulent voters, free riders to bankrupt our social security and medical programs, and indoctrinated pawns for a communist takeover.
- Stories about the Global Entrepreneurship Program (GEP), which is the Obama program focused on supporting and empowering entrepreneurs in Muslim communities around the world.

These are the real problems in America, not healthcare, retirees, or even the China trade deficit. Our tribulations stem from this government's over reaching, overspending, over regulating, multicultural divisions, a liberal and biased media, and increasing socialistic/communistic indoctrination.

Visit nearly any hospital emergency room, and you will see a young welfare recipient looking for free healthcare while carrying and using a cell phone that costs $200 or more, an IPod, an electronic ebook, expensive clothes, etc. They claim not to be able to buy medical insurance, but they can afford expensive attire and gadgets. The real problem is not a welfare problem as much as a cultural one.

Behind all of these problems, however, there is a much bigger issue—one that I have experienced firsthand. That is the enemy that is hidden within. It is not an over exaggeration to say that there are communist sympathizers inside every governmental department working to destroy capitalism.

Our population's general lack of belief in that domestic enemy has made it difficult to combat. To those whose eyes are open, however, the veil is lifting and the adversary is becoming more visible. The solution is to educate the rest of the population while there is time to do something about it. At present, the communists are divided as to what they believe and how to accomplish their goals. They are making some mistakes and we should take full advantage of their errors, and expose them to the public.

Massachusetts Democratic Senator Barney Frank shamefully allowed Fanny Mae and Freddie Mac's corruption and intentional bad handling of loans to people who either had no means or intention to repay. According to a report by Stephen Labaton in 2003, the Bush administration attempted to warn Frank and his cohorts of the problem, but was ignored.

Then the Bush administration proposed a new agency to oversee Freddie Mac and Fannie Mae, but the Democratic-dominated Congress rejected the proposal. Finally, the Frank housing problem caused the market to collapse. The financial earthquake reached around the world, and the economy tumbled like the proverbial house of cards.

The blame for the millions of job that have been exported to other countries also lies at the feet of government liberals imposing stifling regulation, taxes, forced unionism, and laws designed to strangle our domestic industries.

It was shocking to see Obama during his campaign for presidency, speak openly about his socialistic beliefs, and yet today, at least 50% of Americans don't believe that he is a communist. It is thought that communists and their followers only represent about 23% of the American people, but that percentage will continue to support and follow Obama and his kind until the end. Without intervention, their numbers will also increase.

Due to the weak and even the lack of resistance from Americans, the communists believe they are invincible and capable of convincing the undecided to help them win elections. They are hoping that in another decade, they will have majority support in this country, and believe me, if they are not stopped by conservative unity, they will.

Their biggest fear is that groups like the Tea Party, conservative radio and TV hosts, bloggers, and books like *American Apocalypse* will be successful in showing the independent and undecided voters the reality about communism. The last thing they want is for people to know the truth about the Obama administration's not-so-hidden agenda.

Even war hero, Arizona Republican Senator John McCain, Karl Rove and other moderate older politicians like then, are confused and fooled by the communist agenda. They have become unwilling dupes who overburden our cause due to misplaced political correctness and a lack of understanding of the dangers of "just going along."

When McCain told an anti-Obama woman in the crowd, that he was addressing, "No madam, Obama doesn't represent any danger to America," I knew that he would lose the election. We must elect leaders who are constantly aware of the importance of their words in the political arena. Too many conservatives are afraid of being crucified by the Socialist Media or of being branded as a radical and extreme rightist.

For freedom's sake, we must support those leaders who are not afraid of criticisms or threats. I'm speaking of tough leaders like Sarah Palin or Donald Trump, who are capable of confronting and fighting and making our enemies back off, as did President Ronald Reagan.

In 1961, when I arrived in Venezuela, 7% of the Venezuelan people were communists. They had been energized by Fidel Castro's victory, as were the majority of the communists across Latin American countries. At the time, the communists were attempting to build an anti-government guerrilla army in Venezuela, I personally witnessed the riots and protests throughout the country.

In the meantime, the United States was preparing a plan that would show the world what Fidel Castro was doing in Cuba. When Fidel declared that he would be a Marxist and Leninist Communist until the day that he died, the U.S. began to reveal the truth about communism.

One result is that in less than 15 years, Venezuela's communist membership began to shrink, and by 1976, their numbers represented only 2.2% of the population..

I believe that half of the American Communists are enamored by the communist system simply because they don't know the truth about their own ideology. Americans that vote radical liberals into office often believe the lies that the communists spread, or else they accept the fallacy that communism is dead. Many are fooled into thinking that their candidates are merely socialists, or leftists, or liberals, or progressives, but never communists. It is the job of Constitutional Americans, to pull back the curtain and show the informed their real plan.

Cutting the Government Apron Strings

If we Americans are serious about putting this country back on track in the right direction, the first thing we have to do is bring spending under control. Socialism (a.k.a. communism) uses dependency on government as a way to cripple the family structure and to create a continuing support base for the ideology.

In too many cases, a single mother with aid to dependent children cannot afford to marry the father without losing much of the government's largess. Without a limitation on the number of children receiving aid, a single mother is encouraged to continue giving birth without consideration to what the child's future will be.

The result is that the percentage of families without fathers has doubled over the last 20 years, especially among welfare recipients. Burgeoning welfare has also produced a problem for the healthcare system. Many of those on welfare are young people who should be productive members of society, but are, instead, a burden. Too many women on welfare suffer mental and other health problems due to inactivity, loneliness and boredom.

Their children grow up angry and often continue into adult life as welfare recipients on their own. Lack of hope, pride and ambition results in low self-esteem, exposure to gangs, out-of-wedlock births, crime, illicit sex, substance abuse, poor educational development, depression, alienation against authority, and makes them susceptible for indoctrination. It is no secret that our present welfare system is a major cause of intercity ghettos.

Those who have properly received and used temporary help while getting back on their feet are the only ones who really benefit. There is an old saying, "Give a hungry person a fish and they will be filled for the moment; teach them to fish and they will not go hungry again." The liberals in government see entitlements as taking from those who earn and giving to those who don't in exchange for voting support.

Welfare must become a system for temporary assistance, not a way of life. Applicants should be carefully screened and accepted only on the condition that in six months they find employment, or are being trained for a job, or have a health situation that requires further aid. A limit on the number dependent children would soon discourage birthing for dollars.

The Liberal Healthcare Myth

Healthcare does need improvement, but not through a 2,000 page power grab by the Federal Government. We don't need radical changes that pass into law before being read by Congress. That is, however, the way the administration jammed the Obama care monster down our throat against the will of the majority of the people.

What *is* needed is open competition on drugs and medical insurance to lower costs, severe sentences for those who commit healthcare fraud, and tort reform to stop the rape of the system by an overabundance of lawyers.

Liberals claim that Canada and England have a more economical and efficient healthcare system. It is interesting and telling fact, nevertheless, that a growing number of people seeking treatment, without the weeks and months of waiting, are coming to America from those countries.

A news clip showed a modern hospital in Cuba that rivaled the best and touted Fidel's superior medical program. As a Cuban native, I was not fooled. That hospital happens to be the only one of its kind. The rest are fifty or more years old and are without medicine, equipment and supplies. Go to http://www.therealcuba.com/ to see the reality of today's Cuba, including that island's highly touted hospitals.

Pork Barrel Waste

Let's enthusiastically help the majority of elected representatives who promise to shrink government, reduce spending, unshackle small businesses, and return to constitutional governing. Here are some of the ways to begin:

- Decrease government salaries to the level of private workers in similar employment.
- Public employees must contribute to their own pension and healthcare.
- Reduce government grants to non-profit organizations and conduct audits to eliminate fraud.
- Reduce America's contribution to the United Nations. Better still; organize democratic allied nations into a new block.
- Stop contributing funds to countries that demonstrate their disdain and hate for America. Spending should be used for building and maintaining a powerful military presence that will discourage the need to actually fight a war.
- The method Reagan used to silenced Muammar al-Gaddafi should be used in dealing with troublemakers in the world without risking lives.
- Eliminate earmarks. Webster defines the term as identifying an item for a specific use. In government, that means using taxpayer money to impress voters to keep a politician in power. A recent *Pig Book* report showed that Congress added 11,600 earmarks to bills in 2010, at a cost of $17 billion.

- Permit domestic companies to drill for our own oil under environmentally sound methods to reduce our vulnerability and dependence and on foreign oil.
- Eliminate affirmative action programs that are nothing more than blatant racial discrimination.
- Stop the illegal alien invasion, and deport those already here.
- Put an end to indiscriminate spending on pork barrel projects such as:
    - $211,509 for olive fruit fly research to be performed not in the USA, but in *Paris, France*
    - $1,950,000 for the Charles B. Rangel Center for Public Service … sponsored by none other than *Charles B. Rangel;*
    - $98,000 for a walking tour of Boydton, Virginia … a town of 474 covering less than one square mile *that can all be seen from one spot;*
    - $148,950 for a Sheep Institute in Montana and
    - $188,000 for a Lobster Institute in Maine.
    - $196,000 to renovate the historic post office in Las Vegas
- Roll back funding of the Environmental Protection Agency to the initial $900 million established in 1970, before reaching a level of $14.86 billion in 2009.

2010 was the second most pork-filled year since 1991, when the Pig Book was first published. The total cost of wasteful projects over the past 18 years exceeds $271,000,000,000.

CHAPTER 13

The New World Order

What I am seeing today, was inconceivable only three years ago, but after reading over 5,000 pages on the subject, and doing a full research analysis, I eliminated the few reports that were the least credible. Only those backed by hard facts and evidence were used as sources for what you are about to discover.

The majority of my research reveals that a large number of world leaders are organizing to establish a world government. They have done a disturbingly good job of convincing powerful figures to join them.

Their plan consists of using four main organizations to bring about the New World Order.

- First is the United Nation as the main body. The power that the U. N. already has is inconceivable, especially in the last decade. [C9-1, C9-2]
- Second is the International Monetary Organization, which is working today to have one World Central Bank with only one kind of currency.
- Third is a World Union to organize the working classes and unify the masses. This includes the World President.
- Fourth is the Anti-Christ Communist Organization—that is the one group spearheading this. All four organizations are working on a plan behind the scenes to use their powers and influence to take the major nations to a new level of world control and slavery.

After many pacts, agreements, and accords with the Soviet Union, most of which were never fulfilled, the present U.S. administration is now involved in this NWO plot with world leaders, many of whom are openly communist. They seek world governance with a global army. This means that our entire military structure would be placed under a foreign control, not regulated by American laws or morals. Whoever controls the army controls the nations, which, of course, is the evil intent of communism.

For the past 40 years, communists have guided and directed the U.N. The members of this tyrannical organization are obedient to the Marxist code of conduct, not only to achieve the main goal, but to also preserve their own position. They blindly ignore the fact that history has demonstrated the failure of their ideology time after time by war between their leaders for world leadership.

The World Central Bank will completely regulate the global economy with one universal currency. That means America will no longer have control over our own monetary system. That means the gold from all over the world on deposit in Fort Knox will be redistributed to other nations under U.N. direction.

Every nation will have to borrow from the World Central Bank and pay interest that will be used by the NWO to subjugate the world.

If we let them succeed we will watch our wealth disappear, our best in the world army under foreign command, and our constitution relegated to the scrap heap. World courts will dispense justice according to laws alien to our Christian foundations.

I can foresee America's future at the mercy of the NWO army, as it imposes dictatorial mandates already in place here in America. The "National Emergency Centers Establishment Act" (HR 645) calls for the militarization of FEMA, with over six hundred or more internment facilities (concentration camps), with a 2,000,000-man militia, supposedly to protect America inside its borders. Over half of those camps are already functional!

The World Union will be in charge of protecting and directing the working classes across the globe. The exact function of that organization has not been spelled out, but after they take power it is clear that they won't care about the plight of the working class.

Current domestic labor unions openly support socialist/liberal/communist candidates, who in turn help them to grow and maintain power. Expansion to a world power union, would give them control over production and distribution in a Marxist-Leninist world.

Barack Obama, Javier Solano, and Prince Charles, reportedly will be named as the three World Apostles. Then there is British Prime Minister Gordon Brown, who has repeatedly urged that the financial crisis should be used to make world leaders.

The Bilderberg Group, Bilderberg conference, or Bilderberg Club is an annual, unofficial, invitation-only conference of around 130 guests, most of whom are people of influence in the fields of politics, banking, business, military, and media. The original conference was held from May 29 to 31, 1954 at the Hotel Bilderberg, near Arnhem in The Netherlands. That and subsequent conferences are closed to the public and the media.

There is clear proof that almost all Bilderberg members and visitors are supporters of the New World Order. We do have a list of all the chairmen of the steering committee and the dates that they served: Prince Bernhard of Lippe-Biesterfeld (1954–1975), Walter Scheel (1975–1977), Alec Douglas-Home (1977–1980), Eric Roll (1986–1989), Peter Carington, 6th Baron Carrington (1990–1998), and Étienne Davignon (since 1998).

At the next referenced Internet site, you can see a full disclosure of all attendees, members, and the history of the organization; you can even view the information by countries and personalities. Be aware, however, that you will only see information that they want you to see. The majority of the real players are hidden in the shadows. [C9-3]

They use this club to secretly lobby, plan their objectives, gather information, and review innovations. They regularly invite world leaders to the meetings and then try to persuade them to become members or participants. When they convinced ex-president George H.W. Bush to join, his participation was a tremendous boost for the organization. Since then, the group has grown significantly. [C9-4]

Have you fallen for the Global Warming myth? Would you believe that using environmentalists as modern Chicken Little, "The sky is falling," alarmists to destroy a nation's economy was planned decades ago? Read on.

The uproar about the global warming frenzy made Al Gore a wealthy man, fueled the trade and cap/carbon footprint/electric cars/spiral mercury filled bulbs/windmill farms and other "green" frauds. In truth, global warning is only caused by the hot air coming from those who want to frighten the uniformed and the "useful idiots" into the arms of a cruel world government.

Joseph Goebbels, Hitler's propaganda minister, once said that if you repeat a lie often enough, people will start to believe it. That is the case with the global warming. Lenin calls those who swallow the big lie, "Useful Idiots." The "Obama '08" bumper stickers that are still on some cars will often identify them.

An "Inconvenient Truth" for Mr. Gore, Michael Moore and many of the N.W.O supporters of the communist agenda, is that they will not be running the show once the shadow leaders take power. The record shows that the power brokers behind the curtain have no use for those pawns that helped them gain the throne.

They should read the Communist Manifesto, which proclaims, "The friend of today will be the enemy of tomorrow that you have to kill." I wonder how many of today's *friends* will be those enemies of tomorrow. [C9-5]

Unfortunately, what we are able to learn is limited by what the real organizers of the evil communist plans want us to know. But one thing is quite clear; they are planning to reduce the world population by 23 to 33%!

Paul Ehrlich's book "The Population Bomb" brought his belief in anti-humanism into the main stream. Let's see what he said: "There are only two kinds of solutions to the population problem. One is the birth rate solution, in which we find ways to lower the birth rate. The other is a death rate solution, in which ways to raise the death rate–war, famine, pestilence...."

President Obama's Science Czar John Holdren is a co-author with Paul Ehrlich in "Ecoscience." Were they trying to perfect the killing machine with forced abortions and mass sterilizations—a "Planetary Regime" with the power of life and death over American citizens?

This is not the tyrannical fantasy of a madman; it is the mindset of the person in control of science policy in the United States. Compare that with the same evil thinking that Germany's experienced under Hitler in the 1940's.

These (among many other equally horrifying recommendations) were put forth by John Holdren, whom Barack Obama has recently appointed Director of the White House Office of Science and Technology Policy, Assistant to the President for Science and Technology, and Co-Chair of the President's Council of Advisors on Science and Technology, informally known as the United States' Science Czar. Like others of his ilk, he is a follower of Charles Darwin.

The agenda calls for bankrupting the world economic system so that the poor and weak will simply die of hunger from a manmade famine similar to the one that Lenin and Stalin orchestrated. As unreal as this may sound to a sheltered American, I believe if those 94 million human beings killed by the communists were living today, they would be witnesses to the inhuman brutalities that took the lives of them and their loved ones.

Communists are experts in military tactics, political strategies, espionage, and disguising the truth, and their shadow leaders will be true rulers of a global government. Those who are the visible puppets will only last as long as they are useful to the party.

The Internet video referenced here explains in detail what the NWO is planning to do and how it is going to be done. [C9-6]

Among the list of NWO participants and members, I found an odd mix. While it is easy to believe that most of those appointed to run the Obama administration belong to the New World Order, the same can't be true for other attendees of the Bilderberg Group's meetings. For example, what of the chairmen of the 100 most powerful corporations in the world, such as Daimler-Chrysler, American Express, Goldman Sachs, Coca Cola, British Petroleum, Microsoft and Chase Manhattan Bank?

While these people are obviously money driven and want to secure a place in the brave new world, the list of professed public servants is very disturbing:

- Vice Presidents of the United States
- Directors of the CIA and the FBI
- General Secretaries of NATO
- American Senators and members of Congress: Barney Frank, Nancy Pelosi, Charlie Rangel, Chris Dodd, Bill Richardson, Chuck Schumer, Dianne Feinstein, Maxine Walters.
- Top editors and CEOs of the leading newspapers in the world, such as: *The Washington Post, The New York Times, Time Magazine* and other large publications.

Some of these personalities have only visited the club once, and have not been further involved; while the majority are active members. As usual, I believe the communists are using, the wealth and influence of rich and powerful people to establish the New World Order. The names found on the list are the ones in control of the world's press and virtually all the banks and financial institutions. Many of those listed are also part of the anti-Christ Illuminati Communist New World Order. They screened and chose America's and other World leaders.

A paramount reason for crushing their plans is to prevent our American Army, Air Force and Navy from passing under their control. To fail to do so would be to hand over the future of our nation to a world dictator. This startling information was taken from these video references. [C9-7, C9-8]

Note this critically important quote from Bill Clinton's book, "My Life." In Chapter 24, pages 338-339, he writes: "I ended 1987 with my third speech of the decade at the Florida Democratic convention. I told the Florida Democrats, 'We have to do nothing less than create a new world economic order and secure the place of the American people within it.' The central arguments I made was 'We've got to pay the price today to secure tomorrow,' and 'We're all in it together.' " [C9-9]

A startlingly frank quote comes from David Rockefeller: "We are grateful to *The Washington Post, The New York Times, Time Magazine*, and other great publications whose directors have attended our meetings and respected their promises of discretion for almost forty years. It would have been impossible for us to develop our plan for the world if we had been subjected to the lights of publicity during those years.

"But, the world is now more sophisticated and prepared to march towards a world government. The supranational sovereignty of an intellectual elite and world bankers is surely preferable to the national auto (self) determination practiced in past centuries."

Rockefeller not only reveals the reality of this communist cruel plan, but also the malignant intention of their secret meetings. The events are accelerating because communists believe that the world is ready for the taking today. Their reasoning is based on the fact that America, signifying the biggest barrier, has demonstrated over the last 30 years a complete ignorance about communism, and their world conquering goals.

The more I research, the more creditable and believable I found the facts. Today, I am more convinced than ever that the core group secretly works for International Communism. The other powerful world leaders, I believe, have been fooled into participating by smooth lies like this quote from Denis Healey, a Bilderberg founding member and a steering committee member for 30 years.

> "To say we were striving for a one-world government is exaggerated, but not wholly unfair. Those of us in Bilderberg felt we couldn't go on forever fighting one another for nothing and killing people and rendering millions homeless. So, we felt that a single community throughout the world would be a good thing."

That sounds so familiar: "…save the proletariat, save the poor and needy, save the world." Ask those who have fallen for that deception after a decade or more under communism. Ask those who have lost loved ones in mass murders by their new rulers.

Who can be more believable to the masses than American presidents and ex-presidents, people like Prince Charles, Prince Carlos I, Prince Philip, members of the U.S. Congress, and top CEOs of leading big corporations, banks and news organizations?

Conversely, why are "useful idiots" convinced they should follow those who never have done anything for humanity and only think of themselves and their images? Is it because they want the government to shower entitlements and other freebees on them, or do Hollywood idols and those born with a silver spoon in their mouth leave them simply star struck?

The only problem was how to create a royal atmosphere of superiority and holiness where the royalties feel comfortable and where the communists can use peer pressure to convince them they are on a sacred quest. That has now been taken care of.

How interesting that I cannot find a single known communist leader identified as belonging to the Bilderberg club. Yet, their convictions, goals, and perspectives of a New World Order, and even their operational tactics are the same.

There is a reason. Communists are aware that most people would shun any organization with obvious socialistic ties. Like puppeteers, they manipulate trusted world leaders and the masses to move blindly toward a totalitarian "New World Order." [C9-10]

To understand the magnitude of what I am exposing, you need to research the references, read the suggested books, and follow your most trusted news sources.

Each of us must get to the truth behind the lies. If we collectively and individually do not get involved, then nothing will be done to prevent the inevitable victory of the communists, and the destruction of liberty.

Barack Obama "The Golden Boy"

When Barack Obama spoke at the Democratic Convention in 2004, he was seen as "the golden boy" they were looking for. All four branches of the New World Order turned to make him the leader they were seeking. Today, people are asking how an unknown like Obama could go to the top of the world leadership so fast.

The answer is simple; they enlisted the help of the world's most powerful organizations: the United Nations, Communist anti-Christ groups, world banks, labor unions, and, most importantly, an enslaved news media. All were skillfully focused in one direction, with one idea and one goal.

Barack Obama has identified himself with Christianity as a cloak for his political agenda. He followed the guidance of Saul Alinsky, the founder of community organizing, who regarded churches as the ideal places for advancing Marxism. To have credibility in organizing churches, young Obama joined Chicago's Trinity United Church of Christ, a mega-church headed by Rev. Jeremiah Wright, Jr. Obama claims he joined that church because he was impressed by the emotional effect of Wright's preaching.

Obama was reportedly tapped to be the first Apostle and the world president of the "New World Order." He was an unknown Marxist and Leninist figure just few years ago and arrived at the apex of power already with the idea of the "New World Order." This dangerous idea will bring the world horrifying political, economic, and social consequences. Unfortunately, Obama is a dreamer who could hurl this country backwards hundreds of years. [C9-11]

After the New World Order is in place, the Constitution of the United States will be meaningless and irrelevant because the laws will be rewritten under a worldwide code, developed and administered by the U. N. Just imagine what a different world we would have today if America had an idea like this one after WWII!

There is convincing evidence that the entire environmental "movement" and its concocted phony crisis of global warming was created to cause panic and to facilitate dependence on a world government. Amazingly, this isn't new since there are records of human, economic, and environmental destruction under communist ideologies with their central planning governments. With increasing urgency, we are moving decisively toward to a totalitarian "New World Order." [C9-12]

George Soros and the NWO

If America does not remain strong, with our military the most advanced on the planet, the rest of the world will force us to join the NWO One of their best-selling tools is to convince the rest of the world that is better to be a citizen ruled by a world government rather than to be a puppet of the United States.

One interesting development occurred on November 16, 2010, when businessman and key figure in a socialist takeover, George Soros, told financiers of the Democratic Party that "Obama must go." He said, "...if this president can't do what we need, it is time to start looking somewhere else."

Soros, in a recent Human Events' poll was voted the single most destructive leftist demagogue in the country. This is the man who would

like nothing better than for America to become subservient to international bodies. He wants more power for groups such as the World Bank and International Monetary Fund, even while saying the U.S. role in the IMF should be "downsized." In 1998, he wrote: "Insofar as there are collective interests that transcend state boundaries, the sovereignty of states must be subordinated to international law and international institutions."

He said that America is the only tool they have to establish the New World Order. They know that without the American military, they can't get anywhere. The rest of the World should be alert, because they are counting on American strength to subjugate the rest of the world.

U.S. Worst Polluter?

In the last United Nations conference on the environment in Rio de Janeiro, the largest applause was given to Cuban Fidel Castro when he denounced the industrialized countries saying they are guilty of most of the world's environmental problems. By blaming the U.S. in order to turn world opinion against us, they conveniently overlook the biggest polluting nation of all, China.

The people in Fidel's audience who applauded had to know how horrible the environmental problems are in communist countries. But instead of addressing their own shortcomings, they reacted sheep like to what their communist master wanted them to accept. Indeed, there is no doubt that they knew Castro's ranting were intentionally designed to incite hatred toward the U.S.

Such hatred is a contagious disease that is spreading around the globe yet many American citizens, conservative leaders, and millionaire business people continue ignoring the inevitable consequences as we trudge toward our own destruction.

Obama's ego and his dreams of becoming the world leader were well expressed in his Berlin speech July 2008 in which he called for global unity. A year later, President Obama became the first US president to address the Muslim world in a historic speech made in Egypt. Oddly enough, in that speech, he called for more freedom and democracy.

In fact, it was he who may have lit the fire that helped bring about the Egyptian uprising that overthrew President Hosni Mubarak, the second Muslim leader brought down in a very short time.

I have maintained for more than a decade, that the two million Muslims indoctrinated into communism under Saddam Hussein will bring about the world's biggest troubles in the very near future. Apparently, some of them were the driving force behind the two Muslim uprisings in Tunisia and Egypt. The revolt may allow the Muslim Brotherhood to further eliminate western influences as the domino effect continues throughout the rest of the world.

What's happening in Egypt has already been in process throughout Europe. The Muslim population is growing in England, France, and elsewhere on the continent. Communists will continue destabilizing the entire Middle East, South America and eventually the rest of the world using, as always, an endless supply of useful idiots. The Communist World Media Pressure is a willing tool in preparing the nations for indoctrination.

Is the World Ready for Messiah Obama?

Conservative Christian author Hal Lindsey declared in an essay on World Net Daily: "Obama is correct in saying that the world is ready for someone like him—a messiah-like figure, charismatic and glib. The Bible calls that leader the Antichrist. And it seems apparent that the world is now ready to make his acquaintance."

Civil rights activist and Baptist minister Rev. Jesse Jackson, Sr. commented: "The Messiah complex is a growing phenomenon."

During Obama's visit at the University of Texas, crowds sang "Obama-hallelujah" at his approach. Onlookers fainted at his speeches with alarming frequency.

Dallas, Texas columnist and culture critic, Mark Morford of *The San Francisco Chronicle*, began his June 6, 2008, column with:

> "Many 'spiritually advanced' people I know, identify Obama as a Light Worker, that rare kind of attuned being who has the ability to lead us not merely to new foreign policies or health care plans or whatnot, but who can actually help usher in a new way of being on the planet, of relating and connecting and engaging with this bizarre earthly experiment. These kinds of people actually help us evolve."

As a communist of the new era, what Mark Morford refers to here is how they see Obama as a kind of messiah who will be able to turn this America to communism.

Obama's involvement in reaching the New World Order objective is a compelling one. Throughout his life his policies have been socialistic driven. This is no surprise since Obama has proven to be a socialist all his life, and his friends and associates are communist radicals. By their own account, they are preachers of the Black Liberation philosophy.

That school of thought began in 1969 with the publication of a book by a Marxist ordained minister in the African Methodist Episcopal Church, professor and author Dr. James Cone. His work, "Black Theology of Liberation" professes a moral superiority of blacks over whites. Dr. Cone is the recognized pioneer of this "theology."

Obama's pastor for over twenty years, Dr. Jeremiah Wright, has shared and preached the militant racial communist themes adopted by Franz Fanon, Stokely Carmichael and Malcolm X. [C9-13]

It will be almost impossible for the world to avoid future tragedies unless it learns from the past. The majority of the leaders who advocate the "New World Order" are playing right into the hands of the Anti-Christ Communist plans. The New World Order is a satanically inspired system in which "America-first ideas" must be crushed, her people conquered, and enslaved.

From political fundraiser, restaurateur, and real estate developer Tony Rezko, a convicted felon who ripped off millions of dollars in housing projects, organizer Saul Alinsky, Pastor Jeremiah Wright, and his cabinet of czars, Obama has demonstrated his desire to destroy the American capitalist system, our religious values, and the entire social structure for the majority of Americans. These are the actions of one that would be chosen as an apostle of the New World Order.

His ego and arrogance was evident when he self-proclaimed, "We are the one we have been waiting for!" If he truly believes that, then Obama is just another demented leader like Lenin, Stalin or Mao. Regardless, we must realize that unless he and his cronies are defeated, they could become our masters.

At the beginning of his presidency, he suggested that he could talk to the leaders of Iran; but he failed to accomplish anything. Then he thought he could talk to the Russians; again he failed. In the Middle East, he sought to stop the Israelis from building new settlements on the West Bank to bring peace between them and the Arabs; all he brought about was the death of the peace initiative.

In the mid-term elections of 2010, the American people put a restraining order on many of his initiatives. From that standpoint, he has been a monumental failure, and to his puppet masters, a man with such failed accomplishments would hardly fit their image of world president. Who then would replace him? We may soon be introduced to whoever is picked as his successor.

The second NWO Apostle is Dr. Javier Solana Madariaga, who is a Spanish physicist and Socialist politician. After serving in the Spanish government under Felipe González (1982–1995) and as Secretary General of NATO (1995–1999), he was appointed as the European Union's High Representative for Common Foreign and Security Policy, Secretary-General of the Council of the European Union and Secretary-General of the Western European Union. He held these posts from October 1999 until December 2009, allegedly leaving to work on the New World Order.

Dr. Madariaga has been a leader in reshaping the political dimensions of Europe and the Euro-Atlantic partnership. He has spearheaded the European Union's declared goal to render a key contribution to world peace by community action based on common values and convictions.

How admirable that sounds. However, compare the New World Order's Madariaga with the Scriptures concerning the Antichrist, who will strengthen a peace agreement with Israel and the surrounding nations.

No, I'm not saying Solana is the Antichrist, but he could be an instrument used to do the works of that prophesied Wicked One. Look at Daniel 8:25, "He... shall use peace to destroy many." See how Luke refers to the time of the Antichrist in Luke 21:28: "And when these things begin to come to pass, then look up, and lift up your heads; for your redemption draweth nigh."

Javier Solana has helped broker peace agreements throughout the world. Initially, his role as High Representative was to bring Russia and the Caucasus regions closer to Europe. He was also heavily involved in the Middle East. He was a key player in bringing about Iran's suspension of its nuclear program.

The Meaning of 666?

The European Parliament is the parliamentary institution of the European Union (EU) and has been routinely described as one of the most powerful legislative bodies in the world. "Recommendation 666" is a declaration of the Western European Union proclaiming that it will be the "military muscle" of the EU.

Ironically, the WEU is made up of ten member nations...the exact prediction of the Scripture's Anti-Christ's one world government. Further, the WEU establishes the senior ranking High Representative who has the power to call a council meeting at any time and to execute the union's "emergency powers."

According to a report, "The EU's new glass parliament building is of the Space Age. The seats of its massive hemicycle are designed like the crew seats in the Star Trek space machines." There are 679 of them allocated to Members; however, only one seat remains unallocated and unoccupied. The number of that seat is 666."

Evidently Javier Solana is the world's new spokesman via the power and authority vested in him by the European Union, which as shown above, has significant correlations to 666 or the Antichrist. Solana's credentials for the position are quite impressive: he is the Foreign Policy Chief of the European Union having been commissioned in June 2006 (by foreign ministers of the USA, Britain, France, Russia, China, and Germany) to convey "demands" to Iran regarding their probable nuclear weapons production.

It's interesting that the current potential of a World War III resulting from the Israel-Iran conflict could do just the opposite and bring about greater worldwide peace compliments of the EU (which has been prophesied to come about during the first three and a half years of the tribulation under the Antichrist's one world government).

Further, if the EU is solely about monetary matters and not world control, why is it already mediating diplomatic matters such as the Israel-Iran crisis, and maintaining armies to enforce its directives such as EUFOR (European Union Force), Euro corps, and its European Union battle groups?

"Apostle" Prince Charles?

Another NWO Apostle is England's Prince Charles. Born in November 1948 with the name Charles Philip George Windsor, he is the eldest son of Queen Elizabeth II and the heir of the throne of England. He went to Trinity College, Cambridge and served for five years with the Royal Navy in 1971-1976.

What was really shocking for me was to learn who he really is. I had seen him as an heir of the royal throne, but could not understand why he was chosen to be one of the Apostles of the New World Order.

When I began to study his life and accomplishments, I discovered that he has an exceptional combination of powerful partnerships with governments and corporations around the world, with a unique concept. To my surprise, Prince Charles makes 30 to 40 speeches around the world every year, heralding the new world order. Here are just a few of his accomplishments and future goals:

- He wants to be the King of Europe.
- He heads the United World Colleges.
- He steers the environmental ethics and business agendas of over 100 of the world's largest multinational corporations.
- He is credited for the success of the Rio Earth Summit and thus the Kyoto Protocol, and he has spearheaded the push for enforceable environmentalism worldwide.
- He initiated the Global Security Program and its lecture series, for which Mikhail Gorbachev has become a spokesperson.
- He has partnered with the United Nations and the World Bank.
- He appears to be responsible for the initiation of the current Mideast "peace process" and has been directly involved since Yitzhak Rabin's funeral.
- His media exposure has exceeded that of every other man in history.
- He claims to be descended from David, Jesus, and Mohammed. He is launching a scheme to increase the use of alternative medicine in primary healthcare.

In Tim Cohen's book, *The Anti-Christ and a Cup of Tea*," he wonders if Prince Charles is possibly the man of the "666" resolution and the one to fill the vacant seat "666." We may soon see. [C9-14]

Cohen's book also details the British Monarchy's centuries-long conspiracy for a '"New World Order" using the Order of the Garter, which is the core leadership of the Priory of Sion, the Knights Templar, the Rosicrucian's, English and French Freemasonry, and the Illuminati, as well as the overarching "Committee of 300." This work is a fascinating read for anyone interested in the modern fulfillment of Bible prophecy.

Agenda 21 – The Sustainable Philosophy

I have studied Prince Charles and the environmental philosophy of sustainable development since the 1994 United Nations Conference on Population and Development-UNCED in Cairo, Egypt. I found that sustainable development was a philosophy behind the Program of Action called "Agenda 21." At the 1992 UN Conference on the Environment and Development-UNCED, the "Rio Earth Summit," Conference Secretary-General Maurice Strong stated: "After all, sustainability means running the global environment, Earth Inc. like a corporation: with depreciation, amortization, and maintenance accounts. In other words, keeping the asset whole, rather than undermining your natural capital."

In 1990, when the Brundtland Commission had just formulated sustainable development, it was Prince Charles who commended them for "bringing the term 'sustainable development' into everyone's vocabulary." Everything has to be self-sufficient.

In April 1991, fourteen months before UNCED, Prince Charles held a private two-day conference aboard the royal yacht, Britannia, while it was moored off the coast of Brazil. Reportedly, his goal was to bring together key international leaders in an attempt to promote harmony between the various countries. Former Senator Al Gore was present, along with senior officials from the World Bank, chief executives from leading companies such as Shell and British Petroleum, the key non-governmental organizations (NGO's), and other officials.

Prince Charles unveiled sustainable development at the 1992 UNCED conference. Interestingly, there was a very powerful corporate lobby called the World Business Council for Sustainable Development (WBCSD) that had come together to support this sinister agenda of control. This group still exerts great power and influence on the international stage.

The WBCSD has nurtured and expanded sustainable development all the way to the ten-year follow-up of UNCED in 2004 at the World Summit for Sustainable Development in Johannesburg.

One report states, "Agenda 21 still stands as the most comprehensive, most far-reaching and, if implemented, the most effective program of international action ever sanctioned by the international community. It is not a final and complete action program, but one that will continue to evolve."

Agenda 21 of the United Nations included an Official Development Assistance (ODA) aid target of 0.7% of the gross national product (GNP) for rich nations, specified as roughly 22 members of the OECD, known as the Development Assistance Committee (DAC.) Today Agenda 21 and ODA are flooding many countries in Africa with money.

Thousands of Africans have become millionaires and yet the plague of hunger continues just as it has always been. In the last several years, many African customers have come to my business in the United States bragging of their large houses and how well they had been doing. Yet, they readily acknowledge that the situation for the poorer classes in their countries has remained unchanged.

It is unfortunate for the countries where that new prosperity has come from, like the U.S. Here, many people are suffering from a lack of resources, and yet our leaders are focused overseas and would rather to give the money to African millionaires.

Since sustainable development was introduced, a communist scheme has continued with the false outward appearance of protecting the world's resources when the real reason is to control the use of them on a global basis.

In this country, the Communist agenda being put in place by the Obama administration has control as its core and is evolving rapidly. With the outright lie of "constant change," they continue with the evolutionary processes that began in Rio. One example is the Clean Water Restoration Act of 2007 (HR2421 and S1870). The changes that the Obama agenda are trying to do under this act come straight out of the agenda 21 goals.

The NWO's master plan is to bankrupt the world monetary system to force people to accept the global government. It is a repeat of the economic crisis of the 1930's that drove desperate and hungry people into the hands of the Nazis. If allowed to proceed, this plan could be the seed for World War III.

Agenda 21 establishes the global infrastructure needed to manage, count, and control all of the world's assets. Included among the resources are forests, fresh water, agricultural lands, deserts, pastures, rangelands, farmers' fields, biotechnology, in fact, every aspect of living, farming, production, manufacturing, research, and medicine, etc. That, incidentally, includes you and me.

The video references at the end of this segment will give you an idea how this sustainable system works. According to Russian sustainable economic authority Dmitry Orlov, the Soviets and their satellite communist countries have used sustainable economic techniques for self-sufficiency for years. How's that working for them?

The collapse of America's economy would automatically create a sustainable economy, not based on production, but rather based on using the available resources to the maximum. If that sounds like a workable system, consider this next revelation.

Orlov explained, the collapse of the economy will force families to live together, three generations at the same address. In turn, that facilitates the older generation taking care of the younger generation while the breadwinners can go and work. The struggle will make the generations more united and create a tremendous savings in heat, transportation, etc.

That would be a painful cultural transformation reversal for Americans, and would lead to the development of a new economy characterized by poverty and even slavery. Like everything else in the socialistic toolbox, the Agenda 21 initiative is communism made to look like something else.

The collapse of the economy will force people to look for ways to survive. In transportation, for example, they might have to use sailboats to transport produce, people, etc. That is how the principle of sustainable economy works: produce something without using any resources. Sustainable transportation, etc., is a phrase communists use to disguise the reality of the catastrophe with less impact to the public opinion. [C9-15, C9-16]

According to their school of thought they see the world as being divided between "intrinsic value" and "instrumental value." Cows, for example have "instrumental" value, because they produce milk, meat, and leather for our use. According to the communist ideology, their governing system provides instrumental value for the people, another proven lie.

Capitalism, in their twisted logic, is a cancer that uses up the earth's resources and must be eliminated. Those who are a part of capitalism represent intrinsic value, meaning they are self-sustaining and don't need a big government, and are therefore a threat that cannot be allowed to reproduce or even survive.

They know that capitalism is the exact opposite of what they are. The Communist sustainable communist society does not produce, and is therefore the true intrinsic government system.

I personally witnessed a *sustainable society* in Cuba, when the population's only means of transportation were bicycles. Once the omnipotent communist government was established, the loss of production resulted in a rapidly declining standard of living.

Darwinism reduces human beings to the level of an evolved lower form where only the fittest survive, and a man's life has no more value than that of a chicken. That takes away any moral conscience when communists seize property or commit murder.

Through advanced technology such as the Geographic Information System (GIS), the NWO can control, count, and manage the earth's assets. Reportedly, GIS can tell you what kind of birds and insects are in which kind of tree. It can also track you and me sleeping in our beds and living in our houses.

Such a gross invasion of privacy the U.N. calls transparency. For those of us with Christian values, this is the antithesis of what we believe; sustainable development is really pagan. It perverts Genesis 1, 2, and 3 by putting the earth as a dominant factor over man: the reverse of what God ordained from the beginning. This video will show you why you must refuse to have a microchip implanted. [C9-17]

Not happy with the Christian faith, Prince Charles turned to "Parapsychology," which some define as "dabbling in the occult." South African-born writer, explorer, and mystic Laurens van der Post (1906-1996) was a heavy influence on Charles. The prince was also influenced by James Lovelock, a British scientist who proposed the

Gaia hypothesis, which today is known as the worship of the earth, a belief based on the Greek goddess Gaia. Prince Charles agrees with the perversion of Genesis 1, 2, and 3.

Putin, Soros, and Solana, like the majority of the really big players in this New World Order plot, are nearly invisible; their environmental ideas never reach the headlines of major newspapers. Neither do their biographies explain their involvement, for there is basically a blackout on what they are doing behind the scenes.

David Rockefeller said the world was now sophisticated enough to accept global governing. I experienced his type of indoctrination and know that it changes our way of thinking, acting, and believing. It distorts belief in God, diminishes respect for parents, and colors our behavior as human beings. In fact, there has been such a recent transformation that communist leaders believe the United States is ripe for their take over.

Ken Ham in his book, *The Lie*, said, "Christianity cannot co-exist in a world community with relative morality as its basis. One or the other will yield. There are two worldviews with two totally different belief systems clashing in our society. The real war being waged is a great spiritual war. Sadly, today many Christians fail to win the war because they fail to recognize the nature of the battle."

I am not crying "wolf!" when I say time is running out to reverse these trends and to wakeup people who do not understand what is happening in this greatest of nations: this last hope of freedom.

In his Baden speech, Rockefeller revealed that he was talking in communist terms when he said the world now would prefer an international governing body of the intellectual elite and world bankers. This is a man who belongs to the corrupt elite that has been running the United Nations and Washington. Now they want to rule the world.

These elite, who declared that the World New Order is the only way to protect humanity from war and killing, are the same people that in May 4, 2004, elevated Sudan to full membership on the UN's Commission on Human Rights. A *New York Times* story from the same year detailed Sudan's ethnic cleansing of Darfur.

It reported that 1,000 people are being killed each week, tribeswomen are being systematically raped, and 7,000 families have been driven from their home. The newest member of the Commission on Human Rights even bombed those who survived the initial purge. This is a recent video released about Darfur. [C9-18]

November 14, 2007: the United Nations, with their sustainable mentality, praised Cuba as "a world model in feeding their population." In reality, Cuba is not producing anything, not even sugar. Before 1958 Cuba was the biggest producer. Empty store shelves tell the real story.

June 5, 2008: less than a year after Burma slaughtered thousands of monks and others pro-democracy campaigners, and less than a month after Burma allowed nearly 100,000 of its citizens to perish in the wake of a deadly cyclone, the United Nations elevated Burma's representative to vice-president of the UN's General Assembly.

June 19, 2008: the UN gave UNICEF's credibility to a Saudi-based charity linked to terror groups. The Islamic charity, with ties to Al Qaeda and the Taliban, is now linked with a new partner: UNICEF, the United Nations' Children's Fund.

I ask again, "Can we trust these people to run the world?" Dealing with communists requires understanding of their code of ethics, or at the very least, some firsthand experience. As Prince Charles continues as one of the major players in the affairs of the United Nations, the New World Order, and sustainable development, I doubt he has any idea of how risky and dangerous what he is advocating will be!

Born in Rome in January 1938, Rey Juan Carlos I, whose real name is Juan Carlos Alfonso Victor Maria de Borbón y Borbón-Dos Sicilias, is the reigning King of Spain. November 22, 1975, Juan Carlos was proclaimed King according to the law of succession put into place by Franco. He now seeks approval as an Apostle of the NWO

In his book, "The Antichrist King–Juan Carlos," Charles Taylor, who is also of Merovingian descent like Juan Carlos, provides significant information into the popular belief that King Juan Carlos of Spain was the coming Antichrist. From the age of ten, he was personally trained under Franco's direction, and graduated from all three of Spain's military academies. According to inside sources, Juan Carlos is a principal supporter of the satanic plot known as the New World Order.

There's even a New World Religion for the New World Order. In the middle of the boiling pot of communistic ideas and ideologies, this evil system seeks a unification of all religions—in their specific style.

Is it possible that all of these Royals, Presidents, Senators, Government Officials, Ministers, CEOs of big corporations, and bankers really believe there can be a Communist Divine World Religion that is pure in their way of thinking, if not divine? Or is this pseudo religion a pacifier to fill the vacuum left by the destruction of true belief in a Creator God? You can believe this, the world is in danger of being turned topsy-turvy by a satanic influence. [C9-19]

In truth, the New World Order that already has businesses worldwide operating under the same guidelines, is nothing more than a subtle technique for globalizing industry—more of the NWO agenda.

What if there were a computerized management program for production, distribution, and procedures is already on the shelf, waiting for the time to be implemented? Surprise! There is. Viewers of these next referenced videos will see their lies people working on standardizing every aspect of life in the new world. [C9-20, C9-21]

The next video reveals how the U.S. Army indoctrination with New World Order techniques has been accomplished. [C9-22]

As time allows, I urge you to visit each of the following websites. The videos following each introductory paragraph are part of my research sources. They not only indicate the range and depth of my studies, but will also expand on what is written on these pages.

This next video documents the ways in which communists use the misery of children around the world to advance the communist agenda, especially with the United Nations. To accomplish their criminal goals, be aware that the communists employ the fraudulent premise of helping children or doing something to improve the human condition. Non-biased accounting shows that less than 10% of the money collected goes toward alleviating a particular problem, but instead is spent to advance other communist agendas. [C9-23]

In the New World Order world, everything has a global aspect. In this video you will see how they are working to produce universal laws that will be executed in every country. If you know the laws of one country, you will know them for every country in the world.

To some, that may sound reasonable and even good. That is, until one realizes that there are societies with laws that would be outrageous in America or any other civilized country. [C9-24]

This next video defines what the new world order calls the Modern Laws of Global Life-Laws of Success. Please understand that this is vitally important. Compare what I've written about what I learned from my early life in communist Cuba with the agenda being promoted here. It's the same old communist lies, and the same attacks on the capital system. What you never or rarely hear is the explanation of why all those beautiful, well-planned programs have never worked in any of the countries that have followed a communist agenda. [C9-25]

It's the same collection of falsehoods about the new world's laws and how they will be applied in the new communist world. It'll be nothing more than the same propaganda and the same tired rhetoric about how through global development lawyers can bring positive change to the world. [C9-26]

In the next video, you can see how the U.N.'s military forces are training new leaders with more than 120,000 troops serving under NATO's International Security Assistance Force in Afghanistan. These are in addition to 30,000 troops under American command and the Western military bloc's recent confirmation that Malaysia has become the 47th official Troop Contributing Nation (TCN) for that war effort.

Never before have military forces from so many nations served under a common command in one country, one theater of war, or one war. Never before Obama has an American President handed over control of our troops to the U.N. These actions must be crushed very soon or they will rule the world. [C9-27]

The U.N. forces and the new world order are here to stay, making decisions, carrying out world policing activities, mostly with American taxpayer money. You and I have become cash cows, but our input doesn't count anymore. As in case in every communist program, they can only be stopped by informed majority effort as outlined in Chapter Ten, or by brute force

World Control of Your Money

This next video clip is one of a series on the world banking scheme, and it details the façade of what happens when Central Banks Rule the World. This is the lie they want us to believe, for the communists are really the ones who are going to rule.

To understand their plan to bankrupt world economy, pay attention to the details of how they are interconnected and directed at creating a tremendous financial crisis. With the Central Banking System propelling this crisis, we are at an extremely critical point in history and the amount of debt that we American taxpayers owe is nothing short of mind boggling, and that debt is ever climbing. [C9-28]

There is a reason. This credit crisis is a tool being used to remove one of the final barriers separating the entire world from being ruled by a world government. The credit crisis is better identified as "Creative Destruction."

At the very center of this crisis is a document prepared by Henry M. Paulson, Jr., Secretary of the Treasury. The document is entitled "The Department of the Treasury, Blueprint for a Modernized Financial Regulatory Structure." It's an eloquently benign name with absolutely cruel intentions.

We have been educated to believe that the world is ruled by and through governments. Even though there is lot of truth to that belief, it is actually the central banks and the powers behind them that shape and govern the world. The global credit crisis is how the remaining wealth and power of the world will be transferred.

Central banking, which really is a group of private corporations, started lending to governments back in the 1600's. Protective barriers were being broken down between countries with the Bretton Woods Agreements.

The Bretton Woods system of monetary management was established to provide rules for commercial and financial relationships between the world's major industrial countries. The system was the first example of a fully negotiated monetary order intended to govern financial relations between independent nations.

Now, nearly 70 years later, the National Regulatory Barrier is the one obstruction that stands between countries and the opportunity for central bankers and international bankers to control the world's assets.

It is so important at this point that these barriers be removed that Sir Evelyn de Rothschild was on television to say that each country must face up to regulations and teach bankers and investors to work within prescribed regulatory limits. The Rothschild family is typically secretive when it comes to family or business matters. So, it was unusual that he even made an appearance.

As President Obama was coming into power, Paul Volcker became one of the White House observers. He was the former Chairman of the Federal Reserve under Presidents Jimmy Carter and Ronald Reagan from August 1979 to August 1987. Volcker was reported to be in Obama's White House to "Mastermind what could become the biggest overhaul of the U.S. financial system in decades."

In the next video, you will see how the Federal Reserve lends newly printed money to commercial banks in the U.S., and therefore makes it clear that all balances on bank loans, mortgages, and credit cards, are ultimately owed to the Federal Reserve.

The Federal Reserve in Washington, D.C. does not pay taxes, nor does it issue an annual report. No one knows who the private shareholders are because there is no public record. Since its inception in 1913, the Federal Reserve Act has been amended 195 times.

In 2008, the Federal Reserve took control of the Federal National Mortgage Association, nicknamed Fannie Mae, and the Federal Home Mortgage Corporation, nicknamed Freddie Mac. Both have operated since 1968 as government sponsored enterprises meaning that, although the two companies are privately owned and operated by shareholders, they are protected financially by the support of the

Federal Government. They were established to provide local banks with federal money to finance home mortgages.

The Community Reinvestment Act (CRA) of 1977 mandated Banks to extend mortgages to low and moderate–income residents. But in the Clinton Administration, Henry Cisneros loosened mortgages restrictions for any first time buyers who could afford and qualify for loans through the CRA. Banks coming under pressure from ACORN, and under the threat of punishment from the Federal Government made risky loans that normal banking practices would have been turned down.

By legislatively mandating that banks make loans to high-risk lenders, the government empowered the communists to attack the economy, a major tool in their agenda.

Barney Frank, Chairman of the House Financial Service Committee, spoke during a hearing on H.R. 1479 Community Reinvestment Modernization Act of 2009. He pointed out that the purpose of the bill was to close the wealth gap in the United States by increasing home ownership and small business ownership for low and moderate-income-borrowers, and persons of color. It was the torch point that ignited the final touch of the financial crisis.

The Federal Reserve takeover involved $5.4 Trillion and greatly enhanced the organization with the transfer of wealth in the treasury. The ability to seize America's economy in secrecy must end by overturning laws that have protected and enriched the shadow masters of the Federal Reserve Bank while enabling the socialist agenda.

The following video reference is part II, a continuation of the bank crisis information. It includes reasons for more global banking regulations. In the opening, there is a G10 Chart showing the global banking network, which includes 33,101 banks with 337,406 branches. There is information on U.S. banks under control of the Federal Reserve, and a projected timeline for the creation of a world bank. [C9-29]

This third part of the Central Bank videos points out a disturbing issue. At present, there is only one limiting international regulation preventing the World Bank taking global control. If that international barrier were eliminated, the entirety of the world's monetary assets would be under the direct control of the banks. [C9-30]

Over the next two years, due to the socialist caused economic crisis, I predict that the Obama administration will print record amounts of new money to pump up the economy to help him win reelection. [C9-31]

This next video begins with information about the G-7 and the Asian Crisis. The Banking Act of 1933 established the Federal Deposit Insurance Corporation (FDIC) and introduced banking regulations, partially designed to control speculation. The Act is most commonly referred to as the Glass-Steagall Act after its legislative sponsors, Carter Glass and Henry B. Steagall.

Some provisions of the Act, such as having the Federal Reserve regulate interest rates of savings accounts, were repealed in 1980. The Gramm-Leach-Bliley Act removed restrictions that prevented a bank holding company from owning other financial companies in 1999.

Repeal of the Glass-Steagall Act effectively destroyed the separation that had previously existed between Wall Street investment banks and depository banks. Here are some of the actions that opening this Pandora's box accomplished:

- Foreign banks, insurance companies, and brokerage firms were allowed to purchase U.S. companies.
- All the protections were removed between investment and community banks.
- Opening those doors created the requirement for global regulations.

With the chaos created by the 2008 credit crisis, there was a perceived need to revamp the capitalist system. President George W. Bush said, "We live in a world in which our economies are interconnected. Financial turmoil anywhere in the world affects economies everywhere in the world."

Currently there are many separate agencies with diverse accountabilities for financial activities in the U.S.

- Securities and Exchange Commission (SEC) regulates the securities industry.

- Federal Reserve System controls the U.S. banking system.
- Office of the Controller of the Currency oversees federally chartered banks.
- Federal Housing Finance Agency supervises the General Services Administration (GSA) as well as Fannie Mae and Freddie Mac.
- State Insurance Departments regulate insurance operations in each state.
- Office of Thrift Supervision controls Savings and Loan Associations, also known as thrifts
- Futures Trading Commission oversees futures, options, and derivatives transactions.
- Federal Deposit Insurance Corp. (FDIC) insures bank deposits.

According to the Blueprint for Change put out by candidates Barack Obama and Joe Biden, these agencies will be under one roof with accountability and control shifted to the Federal Reserve. Few will take into consideration that if the wrong person is running the Federal Reserve or that person follows directives from this or any socialist President; the entire country could face bankruptcy. [C9-32]

This next referenced video site begins with charts showing the shift of assets across the globe. With the passage of the blueprint in Congress, comes a new Global Regulatory Structure.

Since then, the power brokers have been working on eliminating every international barrier that remains as obstacle between them and the domination of the World Banking system. Believe me, they had done a very good job.

The Tea Party movement and the 2010 midterm elections have slowed them down, but if Americans are not vigilant, the barriers will be history in another two years and the world's banking system will be changed for the worse forever.

Click on the next video reference and you see many of the current pertinent changes concerning monetary control. Further, you'll some of the key players who are making these Structural Changes. [C9-33]

Beginning with the U.S. Public Debt Chart, this video covers the 2001-2007-debt explosion and the results of the new structural changes that have been introduced. In the very near future, the monetary control system could shift to the Treasury/Federal Reserve. The Treasury Secretary will be a facilitator/changer agent, with the transfer of U.S. assets moving to the Federal Reserve. That constitutes a huge shift in power and a potential plan to destroy the value of our currency and to increase the use of credit to capture control of this country and the world.

During the bank bailouts, Treasury Secretary Henry Paulson set a new precedent by nationalizing the banking system with a new stability plan. Watch this video, which features information on bailouts, and what results come from them. [C9-34]

The following reference video opens with a discussion of the New Treasury Plan and the public/private partnership. The new Treasury responsibilities and those of the Federal Reserve are outlined.

As of October 2008, Congress no longer protects the pool of taxpayer's money. The Federal Reserve now has direct access to $2.4 trillion taxpayer dollars. [C9-35]

Americans are in bondage to the Federal Reserve and this should be stopped. Several examples of the Federal Reserve's control are shown in this video. Global regulations will lead the U.S. to adopt a value-added tax to pay for all of the bailouts. We learn that in a global world, if the dollar is replaced, it will not be a 1 to 1 exchange; instead we will be in a big trouble. There is a serious discussion on global taxation.

A final subject covered in this series of videos reveals that FEMA is building large compounds all over the country that could easily become citizen detention centers. Obama has ordered the Department of Defense to create a civilian workforce to deploy in support of combat operations by the military. Reportedly, the numbers involve a force of over 1,000,000 militia members. Their goal seems to be to keep people focused on the activities instead of the original, true agenda. [C9-37]

To my fellow Americans, I plead that you join me in reading to learn more about candidates before electing him (or her—think Pelosi, Boxer, Collins, Snow, et al) to positions where they can do so much damage to our country. Do not stay away from the polls because you don't believe your vote counts. Presidential elections have been won by the votes of less than the population of a small town.

To Obama followers, I plead that they read about communist history and how desolate (and dangerous) life is like in a communist regime. It's terrible, even for those who are in the elite classes. Lenin used to call people who follow a communist leader without any acknowledgment "useful idiots." Those are the ones who enjoyed temporary freedom and prosperity given them in exchange for their passionate work to destroy prosperity in order to enslave the masses. Once their usefulness is no longer needed…neither are they. Life is too short and complicated to spend it in constant fear of the midnight knock at the door.

To the minorities, I recommend learning to think American, not African-American. Many non-whites have refused government handouts that make them modern slaves. Those are the men and women who excel in business, in government, in family and community. They are the ones who refuse to place the race card, a pathetic and immoral tactic that only makes racists of any color a pariah of society.

To the Muslims, I recommend incorporating the riches of the American system and way of life if you wish to live here. If that is impossible to do as a Muslim, then this is not the country for you. One warning, after you have tasted freedom here, you may never want to live again under the harsh rules of Islam.

America welcomes our Latino friends who have clearly demonstrated that they are hard workers, are willing to follow the rules of becoming citizens, and understand that English is spoken here. Most of you are equally frustrated with the liberals' willingness to let criminals and illegal alien's short circuit the system through amnesty. You are valued as naturalized citizens; so don't let yourselves be manipulated by communists bent on destroying your adopted country.

To my brother Christians, I recommend reading Jeremiah 18:7-8 concerning God's word to nations:

> "Then the word of the LORD came to me: 'If at any time I announce that a nation or kingdom is to be uprooted, torn down and destroyed, and if that nation I warned repents of its evil, then I will relent and not inflict on it the disaster I had planned.' "

This once blessed nation has committed murder by abortion, immorality through unnatural sex, idolatry fueled by greed, blasphemy in denying the Creator, adultery through false religions, and the list goes on.

America, founded on Christian principles, was given special blessings by God. He claimed us as a people set apart to preach the gospel and to be a protector and provider to other nations. We have failed Him and no stretch of the imagination is needed to apply Jeremiah 18 to the U.S. Praise God that He promises in verse 8 that He will not inflict disaster on that nation that repents of evil and returns to Him.

As God used ancient Israel as His sword to punish evil kings and nations, so might He not use a humbled America to punish those who have attacked our nation in our sins? The recent American mission that resulted in the death of that arch-terrorist of 911, Osama Bin Laden, may have been a sign.

Dutch Renaissance humanist, Catholic priest Erasmus Roterodamus (1466–1536) said what we must do is to, "look for the words that unite us and not the words that divide us. The Evangelical light can't be turned off."

I learned to walk with wounded feet while I carried the sins that scarred my soul, as I looked ahead for the divine light to help me to persevere to the end. Now, reborn as a Christian, I live, no longer with the ignorance of secular life, but with the energy, sensibility, love, and compassion of a follower of Jesus Christ.

CHAPTER 14

How *You* Can Help Save America

The ideology founded and practiced by communists from the time of Marx and Lenin, and through socialist tyrants over the decades, employs a stealthy wearing down of people and ideas that are barriers to their conquering of a nation.

Like a predator, they lurk in secrecy, creeping in silent increments toward their prey. They are here in America, and they are engaged in a hunt for survival. Banks, including the Federal Reserve Bank, which are under their control, have accumulated the largest amount of money in history. Why? Whoever has the gold makes the rules.

Over the span of decades, communists have also infiltrated and gained control of unions, schools, entertainment, the media, the justice system, the economy, and the liberal side of Congress, and, in 2008, the White House.

We are living in very dangerous times. Over the past forty years of the American communist evolution, they have made huge advances that place them in a favorable position to take over America. Even so, George Soros has warned that if Obama cannot do the job to the puppet masters' satisfaction (i.e. tearing down the U.S.) then he will be replaced with someone who can.

Inconvenient Obstacles to Socialism

Today the Liberal/Socialist/Communist agenda is accelerating to take advantage of their planned economic collapse. However, they have encountered inconvenient obstacles in the form of alert and fed-up

Americans who formed the Tea Party Movement, our leaders, conservative governors, Internet bloggers, and talk show hosts. These and others have undoubtedly shaken this evil empire building ideology, but we have no guarantees that we have stopped them…yet.

Obama printed a lot of money to improve the economy, appears to have compromised with the GOP controlled house, and distanced himself from his more radical associations. But don't be fooled, for he still continues his agenda and makes speeches filled with socialistic code to communicate his intentions and plans to fellow comrades.

If you believe that these words are harsh and unfounded, then take time to view the video references. You may wonder why the call to action is repeated so many times in these pages. Just as communists repeat lies over and over to program those who run to evil, so we who believe in good must be convicted by repetition to push back to regain what so much blood was spilled to build. But if you still have doubts about what you have read, ask yourself how Americans who say they love this country can do these things:

- Deliberately cause an economic meltdown?
- Take Christianity out of the schools, Federal building, and from the education department's curriculums?
- Work to create the New World Order with its world subjugation agenda?
- Want to bring America down into misery with their Sustainable society?
- Open the borders to 100 of thousands of foreign students every year for free education?
- Give to the United Nations control of our Army, our laws and our monetary system?
- Allow the Federal Reserve Bank to accumulate vast amounts of your money, yet be exempt from paying tax or to even file annual reports?
- Permit ACORN to have 361 profit and non-profit organizations to cover to fund illegal activities?

- Consent to the building of hundreds of mosques and to the permit the immigration of hundreds thousands of Hamas Muslins to this country?

The obvious answer is that no true patriotic American could want to harm this nation by such actions. Who then are these people and how can we defeat their evil ideology? Read on and then take action.

What Can You Do?

Most of you, who are reading American Apocalypse, are NOT politicians, banking executives, industry leaders, pastors, or billionaires, but you have incredible power to recapture our nation, restore our free market system, and return God to His rightful place as the cornerstone of America. Each of us needs to understand that Communism's greatest enemies are:

- An unshakeable faith in the God of our founding fathers,
- An informed citizenry,
- An unbreakable family circle,
- Patriotic pride in one's country,
- The light of truth about them and their agenda,
- And elected officials grounded in the constitution and dedicated to conservative principles.

"America is like a healthy body and its resistance is three-fold: its patriotism, its morality and its spiritual life. If we can undermine these three areas, America will collapse from within.", so wrote Joseph Stalin. He, perhaps inadvertently, has given us the weapons that will defeat the enemy. But undoubtedly their advance has been incredible.

Writing as a former indoctrinated and trained communist, I am qualified to Show How to Save America. You have the weapons, but to accomplish our task, we have to be united in one voice:

WE MUST BE PREPARED

1) **Study to understand the truth about Liberalism/ Socialism/ Communism.** Only informed citizens are fully armed against brainwashing propaganda.
2) **Research to learn how countries were overtaken by communism.** Compare the agenda used by the enemy with what is happening now in America.
   - View the referenced videos, Internet and print sources.
   - Review your children's textbooks for revised historical facts.
   - Read non-fiction books written by former communists.
   - Compare current legislative actions against the Constitution. **Avoid obviously biased media reporting.** Seek balanced and trusted sources of editorials, news and articles. Don't depend on just one source for your news.
3) **Learn all you can before choosing your government representatives**. The freedom to vote is priceless, but in the hands of an uninformed electorate it is a two-edged sword.
4) **Learn all you can about the New World Order, agenda 21, NGO's, and thousands of communist organization around the world.** These are organizations with an evil agenda aimed at destroying America and establishing a global dictatorship.

WE MUST TAKE ACTION

1) **Having chosen candidates through diligent research don't neglect to cast your vote**. People who stay home because they believe their vote doesn't count are casting a vote for the other side. Opposing votes cancel each other out until the final ballots decide the winner. Countless elections have been won by the slimmest of margins, too often to the detriment of the governed.
2) **Campaign and donate funding for candidates who meet your criteria for serving.** Honest (and basically conservative) candidates are usually hard pressed for money and need you on the street to campaign against those supported by liberal backers.
3) **Share your research and concerns with family and friends.** Encourage them to take part in the rare privilege of being able to

choose their leaders. Millions have died throughout the ages to win such a freedom.

4) **Volunteer to monitor the voting polls.** Nothing deters voting fraud more than the gathering of vigilant citizens keeping an eye on proceedings. Become one of an army of reporters that expose and combat illegal actions at the polls. Upload videos to YouTube and other social networks of intimidation and unlawful campaigning during voting.
5) **Expose socialism wherever it has planted its deadly roots.** Help rid our schools and universities, "charitable" associations, environmental organizations, and even our law enforcement and legal systems. Write editorials, letters, and emails to make others aware of the evil.
6) **When you disagree with decisions being made in government that negatively affect your life and standard of living, write letters to the editor of your newspapers.** Stir up those of like mind to put pressure on the local, state and federal government to return to the Constitution. Remind them that they work for you and not the other way around. Be prepared to vote them out if they refuse to keep their campaign promises.
7) **Write, call, fax and/or email your representatives.** Praise them when they do right for America, and become a thorn in their side when they don't. Contact information is found on our www.saso2016.com (Save America-Save Ourselves before 2016) website. Hot topics to address when contacting your elected representatives:
   - Expose, defund and prosecute fraudulent communist organizations.
   - Overturn laws and regulations that favor socialism and that affect free market commerce, freedom of religion, and invasion of privacy.
   - Investigate federal departments and agencies and eliminate or reduce those that are no longer necessary, redundant, or impinge on states' rights.

- Demand a constitutionally balanced budget. If we can't afford it, we can't have it…just like those of us in the private sector.
- Read and be informed about the New World Order and Agenda 21 and do everything that is possible to stop it.

8) **Be sure you elect the next U S President capable to push communist back, like Ronald Regan did**. The only thing this country needs to become prosperous again is to be free from the communist influence, religion, and cultural distortion.

For our readers who believe in America's Christian foundation, there is another, and perhaps more important, action to be taken. The God of our fathers gave this unbreakable promise in II Chronicles 7:14:

"If my people, who are called by my name, will humble themselves and pray and seek my face and turn from their wicked ways, then will I hear from heaven and will forgive their sin and will heal their land."

Spread the Word. Throughout this book, I have exposed the many wrongful and destructive tools in the form of laws, regulations, and actions taken by the recent administrations: especially the current one.

Become an activist in applying the weapons listed above to fight the invasion working to destroy us. Take time to review what you have read and highlight the issues that you feel compelled to address, and then take corrective action.

Don't see yourself as a helpless pawn, for you are in reality part of the growing army of patriots who refuse to allow the bloodshed in the founding of the United States to have been spilled in vain. Help us to build banks of information and to expose everything is happening and who are doing it in this country.

If we don't act now to turn this ship of state around, then *American Apocalypse* will have failed as a warning, and will become merely an account of how we lost the greatest country in history.

May God bless America, and May America Bless Our God!

VIDEO REFERENCES

REF.	INTERNET ADDRESS
C1-1	http://www.youtube.com/watch?v=tleics8Jhuy
C1-2	http://www.youtube.com/watch?v=lPaz9ztzFTA
C1-3	http://www.youtube.com/watch?v=Fh0cPdKRZNs
C1-4	http://www.youtube.com/watch?v=JC3NGZ4dfrk
C1-5	http://www.youtube.com/watch?feature=player_embeddedandv=fsE1dVd56Ya
C1-6	http://www.youtube.com/watch?v=UoUJmSiixmE
C1-7	http://www.youtube.com/watch?v=LkWwdyqIK28
C1-8	http://www.youtube.com/watch?v=Wabimgh3Mk0
C1-9	http://www.youtube.com/watch?v=UWEgM63Uwy4
C1-10	http://www.youtube.com/watch?v=NJ4L8JEILNEandfeature=related
C1-11	http://www.youtube.com/watch?v=-XgxLgnpRYwandfeature=channel
C1-12	http://www.youtube.com/watch?v=ROSTsHs79wMandfeature=related
C1-13	http://www.youtube.com/watch?v=hc2XGHA7NK4andfeature=channel
C1-14	http://www.youtube.com/watch?v=W_w0-odySN4andfeature=related
C1-15	http://www.youtube.com/watch?v=bHltct8JY0Y
C1-16	http://www.youtube.com/watch?v=JZs423K7B5k
C1-17	http://www.youtube.com/watch?v=YsjZR7Ggn38
C1-18	http://www.youtube.com/watch?v=JZs423K7B5k
C1-19	http://www.youtube.com/watch?v=AY9F0fwDx2E
C1-20	http://www.youtube.com/watch?v=tphBPpvxtNc
C1-21	http://www.youtube.com/watch?v=v_GNsG0_jMMandfeature=fvw
C1-22	http://www.youtube.com/watch?v=N4tKfE8d8e8andfeature=related
C1-23	http://www.youtube.com/watch?v=JZs423K7B5k
C1-24	http://www.youtube.com/watch?v=fEMYLkpYxX8andfeature=related
C1-25	http://www.youtube.com/watch?v=Ry9fhMRk_Diandfeature=related
C1-26	http://www.youtube.com/watch?v=_GzCwgkgPc4andfeature=related
C1-27	http://www.youtube.com/watch?v=OJ9_Terlpdkandfeature=fvw
C1-28	http://www.youtube.com/watch?v=rhkLWRaxUJUandfeature=related
C1-29	http://www.youtube.com/watch?v=38mm4TimlLwandfeature=related
C1-30	http://www.youtube.com/watch?v=iL2AJBYjsZQ
C2-1	http://mediamatters.org/mmtv/200909240014
C3-1	http://www.youtube.com/watch?v=QLnATSxMYIE
C3-2	http://www.afterdowningstreet.org/prosecutorstatement

C3-3 http://www.freeahmadsaadat.org/
C3-4 http://www.youtube.com/watch?v=AY9F0fwDx2E
C3-5 http://www.freeahmadsaadat.org/bkmletter.html
C3-6 http://tinyurl.com/zob77
C3-7 http://www.cisorg/articles/2004/f/iscalexec.html
C3-8 http://www.cis.org/
C3-9 http://www.cis.org/articles/2004/fiscalexec.html
C3-10 http://transcripts.cnn.com/transcripts/0604/01/ldt.0.html
C3-11 http://transcripts.cnn.com/transcripts/0604/01/ldt.01.html
C3-12 http://transcripts.cnn.com/transcripts/0604/01/ldt.01.html
C3-13 http://transcripts.cnn.com/transcripts/0604/01/ldt.01.html
C3-14 http://premium.cnn.com/transcripts/0610/29/ldt.01.html
C3-15 http://transcripts.cnn.com/transcripts/0604/01/ldt.01.html
C3-16 http://transcripts.cnn.com/transcripts/0606/12/ldt.01.html
C3-17 http://tinyurl.com/t9sht
C3-18 http://www.nationalpolicyinstitute.org/pdf/deportation.pdf
C3-19 http://www.rense.com/general75/niht.htm
C3-20 http://www.drdsk.com/articleshtml
C3-21 http://www.numbersusa.com/content/resources/video/educational/environmental-voice.html
C3-22 http://www.youtube.com/watch?v=Awa15-QMutI
C3-23 http://www.apfn.org/APFN/camps.htm
C3-24 http://www.youtube.com/watch?v=Io-Tb7vTamY&feature=related
C3-25 http://mediamatters.org/mmtv/200909240014
C4-1 http://www.verumserum.com/?p=14164
C4-2 http://www.youtube.com/watch?v=0jffk2Dxv-A&feature=related
C4-3 http://www.youtube.com/watch?v=aoRz-VmtjRg
C4-4 http://rottenacorn.com/activityMap.html
C4-5 http://www.youtube.com/watch?v=2WJBmrvJyJc
C4-6 http://www.youtube.com/watch?v=7NmaZIdz6Vo&feature=fvw
C4-7 http://www.youtube.com/watch?v=Vg06CC1vkX8&feature=player_embedded
C4-8 http://www.youtube.com/watch?v=iKzyw997WJ0&NR=1
C4-9 http://commieblaster.com/articles/ACORN_REPORT.pdf
C4-10 http://www.time.com/time/politics/article/0,8599,1849867,00.html
C4-11 http://www.washingtonexaminer.com/opinion/blogs/Examiner-Opinion-Zone/Rep-Conyers-Reverses-Stance-on-ACORN-Investigation—44485482.html
C4-12 http://www.youtube.com/watch?v=2WJBmrvJyJc

C4-13 http://www.youtube.com/watch?v=RoAg6h4KQnM
C4-14 http://www.youtube.com/watch?v=XITsKScYMvI&feature=related
C4-15 http://www.youtube.com/watch?v=cy1IlAXeV30
C4-16 http://www.youtube.com/watch?v=NF5Kdm4Eu6w&NR=1&feature=fvwp
C4-17 http://video.google.com/videoplay?docid=-6078900495545253198#
C4-18 http://www.youtube.com/watch?v=7NmaZIdz6Vo
C4-19 http://www.youtube.com/watch?v=xS1NwmYLXIo&feature=related
C4-20 http://www.youtube.com/watch?v=iM708EjH0bs&feature=related
C4-21 http://video.google.com/videoplay?docid=7378422323049062152#
C4-22 http://www.youtube.com/watch?v=Ohp5IX3y098&feature=related
C4-23 http://pajamasmedia.com/blog/the-complete-guide-to-acorn-voter-fraud
C4-24 http://www.youtube.com/watch?v=r9xjNtHo35g
C5-1 http://www.youtube.com/watch?v=xBf5N5Mv_QA
C5-2 http://www.youtube.com/watch?v=Tt2yGzHfy7s
C5-3 http://www.youtube.com/watch?v=c5swzxOYQ0k
C5-4 http://www.youtube.com/watch?v=kFsB1Jk1OQ0
C5-5 http://www.youtube.com/watch?v=AY9F0fwDx2E
C5-6 http://www.youtube.com/watch?v=yTp_atr2G9E&feature=related
C5-7 http://www.youtube.com/watch?v=4TEbIPOHNBQ&feature=related
C5-8 http://www.youtube.com/watch?v=tCAffMSWSzY
C5-9 http://www.youtube.com/watch?v=yTp_atr2G9E&feature=related
C5-10 http://www.youtube.com/watch?v=y6gWsy4ZGAk&NR=1
C5-11 http://www.youtube.com/watch?v=kSqMLrXQ_bA&feature=related
C5-12 http://www.youtube.com/watch?v=1zPdkKuEXFM&feature=related
C5-13 http://www.youtube.com/watch?v=hAYe7MT5BxM
C5-14 http://www.youtube.com/watch?v=jc2FCJ7zWEQ&feature=related
C5-15 http://www.youtube.com/watch?v=UScQ1lqCSmQ&NR=1
C6-1 http://www.youtube.com/watch?v=gG6E-sV1kJg&NR=1
C6-2 http://www.nationalaglawcenter.org/assets/crs/RS20430.pdf
C6-3 http://en.wikipedia.org/wiki/Pigford_v._Glickman
C6-4 http://www.youtube.com/watch?v=E6pU3vNaZQA&NR=1
C6-5 http://www.youtube.com/watch?v=Z7YrkpKNB7M&feature=related
C6-6 http://www.youtube.com/watch?v=urpJ7iP-kFg&NR=1&feature=fvwp
C6-7 http://www.youtube.com/watch?v=qlisSrWOhfM&feature=BF&list=QL&index=1
C7-1 http://mediamatters.org/mmtv/200909240014

C7-2 http://video.google.com/videoplay?docid=-3928169851397891989#
C7-3 http://www.youtube.com/watch?v=lWLdxk3pIR8
C7-4 http://www.targetofopportunity.com/islam.htm
C7-5 http://www.usvetdsp.com/jan07/jeff_quran.htm
C7-6 http://thevailspot.blogspot.com/2010/08/brigette-gabriels-duke-university.html
C7-7 http://video.google.com/videoplay?docid=-3928169851397891989 - docid=7512121877508527087
C7-8 http://www.youtube.com/watch?v=lWtFoRe6a8Y
C7-9 http://education.change.org/blog/view/criticizing_capitalism_in_classrooms_taboo_or_good_citizenship
C7-10 http://www.youtube.com/watch?v=uIV4vmCmx1U&feature=related
C7-11 http://www.youtube.com/watch?v=o27fpnBvxZc&feature=related
C9-1 http://www.youtube.com/watch?v=cAkW56F0bHU&NR=1
C9-2 http://www.youtube.com/watch?v=QEqFtVrAgSo
C9-3 http://en.wikipedia.org/wiki/Bilderberg_Group
C9-4 http://www.youtube.com/watch?v=Rc7i0wCFf8g
C9-5 http://www.youtube.com/watch?v=QOAaUKcFtkc&feature=related
C9-6 http://www.youtube.com/watch?v=IGTScCy-do0
C9-7 http://www.youtube.com/watch?v=Uv5cqh26CC0
C9-8 http://www.youtube.com/watch?v=4bKwH3kJew4&feature=related
C9-9 http://www.youtube.com/watch?v=hZsY5XbLinw&feature=related
C9-10 http://www.youtube.com/watch?v=xSllsTLkBsw&feature=related
C9-11 http://www.youtube.com/watch?v=0CV8Xt2VWvc&feature=related
C9-12 http://www.youtube.com/watch?v=Io-Tb7vTamY&feature=related
C9-13 http://www.youtube.com/watch?v=gG6E-sV1kJg&NR=1
C9-14 http://www.prophecyhouse.com/
C9-15 http://www.youtube.com/watch?v=NmTBnhOXufg&NR=1&feature=fvwp
C9-16 http://www.youtube.com/watch?v=FPgfOShs_Mk&feature=related
C9-17 http://www.sasos.org/ver_video_reproducir.php?id_video=151
C9-18 http://www.sasos.org/ver_video_reproducir.php?id_video=132
C9-19 http://www.youtube.com/watch?v=LcDSep3jzjg
C9-20 http://www.youtube.com/watch?v=oq1Zi_V4KyE
C9-21 http://www.bc.edu/centers/cwf/global.html
C9-22 http://www.youtube.com/watch?v=ty0WyU4fpyk
C9-23 http://il.youtube.com/watch?v=qBqte1FI1X0&feature=related
C9-24 http://www.youtube.com/watch?v=P-GmUA9bVHE
C9-25 http://www.youtube.com/watch?v=Bu_1vV3gJhA
C9-26 http://il.youtube.com/watch?v=5DyHHV59CD4
C9-27 http://ww.youtube.com/watch?v=ncjjY7CTklM&NR=1&feature=fvwp

C9-28 http://www.youtube.com/watch?v=Bk1xao6mvjc&feature=related
C9-29 http://www.youtube.com/watch?v=5GPJretxSsY&feature=related
C9-30 http://www.youtube.com/watch?v=E75AxmKPdec&feature=related
C9-31 http://www.youtube.com/watch?v=Ib7wmzmd6A4&feature=related
C9-32 http://www.youtube.com/watch?v=kSC92m2WEhc&feature=related
C9-33 http://www.youtube.com/watch?v=w7vEZJqqr-U&feature=related
C9-34 http://www.youtube.com/watch?v=QqfXiZ26Thw&feature=related
C9-35 http://www.youtube.com/watch?v=zKe5aiQdiFY&feature=related
C9-36 http://www.youtube.com/watch?v=dFq7NBfXe9o&feature=related
C9-37 http://www.youtube.com/watch?v=eAaQNACwaLw&feature=fvw

BIBLIOGRAPY

Karl Marx, *The Communist Manifesto*, (1848).

Friedrich Engels, *Das Kapital,* (1867).

John Fund, *Stealing Elections* (2004).

Michael Medved, *Hollywood vs America*, (1993)

Nonie Darwish, *Cruel and Usual Punishment*, (2009)

Brigitte Gabriel, *They Must Be Stopped*, (2008)

Tin Cohen, *The Antichrist and a Cup of Tea*, (2009)

Fatih Kocaman, *The Bloody History of Communism* (videos)

Enrique Encinosa, *Unvanquished*, (2004).

William F. Jasper, *Global Tyranny Step by Step*, (1992)

Michael Prell, *Underdogma*, (2011)

Karl Marx, *The Communist Manifesto*, (1848)

Friedrich Engels, *Das Kapital*, (1867)

Stéphane Courtois, *The Black Book of Communism*, (1997)

Michael Medved, *Hollywood vs America*, (1993)

Nonie Darwish, *Cruel and Usual Punishment*, (2009)

Brigitte Gabriel, *They Must Be Stopped*, (2008)

Tin Cohen, *The Antichrist and a Cup of Tea*, (2009)

Fatih Kocaman, *The Bloody History of Communism* (videos)

Étienne Davignon, *The Bilderberg Group*

Roy Beck, *The Dark Side of Illegal Immigration* (1996)

Website, *Numbersusa,com*

Andrew J, Breitbart, *Breitbart.com*

Claire Suddath, *A Brief History of ACORN*

Prince Charles, *Agenda 21*, (The sustainable concept)

John Fund, *Stealing Elections*

RECOMMENDED READING

Stéphane Courtois, *The Black Book of Communism*, (1997). Crimes, terror, repression.

Michael Medved, *Hollywood vs. America*, (1993), How-and why-the entertainment industry has broken faith with its audience.

Mark R. Levin, *Liberty and Tyranny*, (2009). A conservative manifesto.

Michael Prell, *Underdogma*, (2011). How the Left masks anti-Americanism and anti-Western sentiment behind the American tradition of rooting for the underdog.

William F. Jasper, *Global Tyranny—Step By Step* (1992). The United Nations and the emerging new world order agenda.

Ken Ham, *The Lie*, (1999). Evolution and Bible predictions.

Friedrich Hayek, *The Road to Serfdom* (2007). Twentieth century conservative economic and political discussions about The Communist Manifesto.

Nonie Darwish, *Cruel and Usual Punishment,*. (2009). Terrifying global implications of Islamic law.

Brigitte Gabriel, *They Must Be* Stopped, (2008). Why we must defeat radical Islam and how we can do it.

Ayn Rand, Atlas Shrugged, (1957).

Tin Cohen, *The Antichrist and a Cup of Tea*, (2009). The fascinating saga of the British Monarchy's centuries-long endeavor to establish a "New World Order."

Michelle Malkin, *Culture of Corruption* (2009). Obama and his team of tax cheats, crooks, and cronies.

Fatih Kocaman, You tube.com. *The Bloody History of Communism* videos.

Billy Graham, *Storm Warning*, (1995). Examines problems facing America today compared with what is to come as revealed in the Bible.

CPSIA information can be obtained at www.ICGtesting.com
Printed in the USA
240507LV00003B/2/P